Reading the Water

"The best of this year's fishing offerings is far and away *Reading the Water* by Robert Post."
—*Boston Herald*

"With a compelling blend of conversational recollections and his own vivid transitional observations, Bob Post has made us Dopplegangers to the die-hard demigods who blaze new trails in this most intimate and exciting of angling experiences."
—*SaltWater Sportsman*

"A collection of fish stories that delight ... It is [their] ability to describe so well their special passion that is the bonus ingredient."
—*Outdoor Life*

"Post has creatively captured the mystique that surrounds those who haunt the sea rim. The fishermen's own words coupled with Post's humor and insight make these stories a celebration of the sport itself."
—*The Fisherman,* Long Island–Metropolitan New York Editions

"Occasionally a book comes along that is so exceptional it just can't be tossed on a pile after a glance and forgotten. *Reading the Water,* by Robert Post, is such a book ... At the top of fishing literature."
—*The Boston Globe*

"Dr. Post, a mean rod man himself, lets the fishermen speak for themselves in this hilarious, insightful, instructive, and altogether impressive book. ... The hottest selling Island book."
—*The Martha's Vineyard Times*

Reading the Water

*Adventures in Surf Fishing
on Martha's Vineyard*

by Robert Post

Chester, Connecticut

© 1988 by Robert Post

All rights reserved. No part of this book may be reproduced or transmitted in any form by any means, electronic or mechanical, including photocopying and recording, or by any information storage and retrieval system, except as may be expressly permitted by the 1976 Copyright Act or in writing from the publisher. Requests for permission should be made in writing to The Globe Pequot Press, 138 West Main Street, Chester, CT 06412.

Excerpts from "Outdoors: The Bug Bites, But the Fish Don't," by Nelson Bryant, copyright © 1987 by the New York Times Company. Reprinted by permission. Excerpts from the *Providence Journal-Bulletin* reprinted by permission. Excerpts from the *Standard-Times* reprinted by permission. Copyright © Vineyard Gazette, Inc., excerpts reprinted by permission. "Memories of Striped Bass," by Nelson Bryant, from which an excerpt is reprinted here, first appeared in the 1980 *East Coast Fishing Guide (Outdoor Life)*. "Farewell Sunday on Martha's Vineyard," by Al Reinfelder, printed by permission. Excerpt from untitled poem by Nelson Bryant, p. 241, reprinted by permission.

Library of Congress Cataloging-in-Publication Data

Post, Robert.
    Reading the water/by Robert Post.—1st ed.
    p.   cm.

    1. Surf fishing—Massachusetts—Martha's Vineyard. I. Title.
SH457.2.P67 1988   88-14071
799.1'6616–dc19   CIP

Manufactured in the United States of America
First Edition / Second Printing

This book is dedicated to my wife, Pia, who shared with me the sight of bluefish suspended in the curl of a wave at Gay Head, and to my son, Zachary, who often fishes with me on the North Shore, where many evenings we huddled together in a stinging rain waiting for a fish to hit.

PHOTO CREDITS

Page	Credit
2	Robert Post photo by Mark Lovewell. Copyright © Vineyard Gazette, Inc. Reprinted by permission.
8	Steve Bryant photo by Mark Lovewell.
22	Whit Manter photo copyright © Alison Shaw.
38	Kevin Hearn photo by Mark Lovewell.
52	Roberto Germani photo by Mark Lovewell.
66	Kib Bramhall photo by Mark Lovewell. Copyright © Vineyard Gazette, Inc. Reprinted by permission.
76	Sergei de Somov and Kib Bramhall photo by Louise de Somov. Courtesy Kib Bramhall.
86	Dick Landon photo by Bill Mahon.
102	Hank Schauer photo by "Buzz" Palmeri.
118	Ray Metcalf photo by M. C. Wallo. Copyright © Vineyard Gazette, Inc. Reprinted by permission.
118	Bernadette Metcalf photo by Karen Emmett.
132	Ralph Grant photo by Mark Lovewell.
146	Jerry Jansen photo by Robert Post.
162	Francis Bernard photo by Mark Lovewell.
169	Eel-skin plugs photo by William A. Muller.
176	Cooper Gilkes III photo by Mark Lovewell. Copyright © Vineyard Gazette, Inc. Reprinted by permission.
190	Paul Schultz photo copyright © Alison Shaw. Courtesy Vineyard Gazette, Inc. Reprinted by permission.
197	Paul Schultz and Ralph Case photo copyright © Alison Shaw. Courtesy Vineyard Gazette, Inc. Reprinted by permission.
202	Arnold Spofford photo by Mark Lovewell.
216	Janet Messineo photo by Mark Lovewell.
230	Nelson Bryant photo by Mark Lovewell.
236	Joe Brooks photo courtesy *Salt Water Sportsman*.
248	Al Reinfelder photo courtesy E. F. "Spider" Andresen.

PHOTO WELL

Frank Woolner photo by Frank Woolner.
Nelson Bryant's old fishing tackle photo by Mark Lovewell.
Surf-fishing reel photo by Frank Woolner.
Squids photo by Kib Bramhall. Courtesy *Salt Water Sportsman*.
Hal Lyman photo by Frank Woolner. Courtesy *Salt Water Sportsman*.
Dick Hathaway photo by Kib Bramhall.
Oscar Flanders and Buddy Oliver photo by Kib Bramhall. Courtesy Frank Woolner.
Ray Metcalf photo by Everett Howell.
Percy West and Ralph Grant photo by Fred Vytal, *Boston Traveler*.
Bass stand photo by Frank Woolner.
Tisbury Great Pond opening photo by Kib Bramhall.
Cooper Gilkes photo by Mark Lovewell. Copyright © Vineyard Gazette, Inc. Reprinted by permission.

Contents

Foreword		ix
Acknowledgments		viii
Preface		3
1	Steve Bryant	9
2	Whit Manter	23
3	Kevin Hearn	39
4	Roberto Germani	53
5	Kib Bramhall	67
6	Richard Landon	87
7	Hank Schauer	103
8	Ray and Bernadette Metcalf	119
9	Ralph Grant	133
10	Jerry Jansen	147
11	Francis Bernard	163
12	Cooper Gilkes III	177
13	Paul Schultz	191
14	Arnold Spofford	203
15	Janet Messineo	217
16	Nelson Bryant	231
Epilogue		247

Acknowledgments

I would like to thank the surf fishermen who shared with me their stories and expertise. In addition to those fishermen interviewed in each chapter, I spoke with Arthur P. Silvia, Dan Burgo, Bernie Arruda, Dick Hathaway, Fred Kiener, Gus Amaral, Tom Norton, and the late Percy West. I would also like to thank my surf-fishing companions and good friends Michael Dietz, David Finkelstein, Sherm Goldstein, and Ray Houle for providing additional anecdotes. Collecting photographs for the book was a task made easier by Mark Lovewell, Alison Shaw, Spider Andresen, Frank Woolner, Jesse Oliver III, and Bill Muller. Mark Lovewell's work in the field, taking photos of the fishermen, is especially appreciated. The staff of the Dukes County Historical Society was helpful with my research on old striped-bass clubs. Eulalie Regan, librarian at the *Vineyard Gazette*, was always willing to pull pertinent news clippings and microfilm from the files. I would like to thank Patty Kendall for her patience and the quality of her work on the transcripts, manuscript chapters, and correspondence. Her professionalism made my work easier. Stan Hart was always available when I needed him. His advice and guidance from the start of this project were invaluable. He was unselfish and a true friend. I was fortunate to have Stephanie Boyle as my editor. She is bright and friendly—a total pleasure to work with. My wife, Pia, was loving and helpful. She believed in the book and provided inspiration and made suggestions along the way. I always looked forward to being with her after a night on the beach. And to all those other people who gave their time—including Ruth Meyer, Ann Nelson, and Jack Koontz—thank you.

Foreword

Dedicated, even fanatical, the characters in this book are among those who form a subculture in the angling world. Characters they are, too, for they are surf fishermen, not shaped to the gentle mold of the inland-fishing followers of Izaak Walton but by a sterner discipline in which sleep, family, food, and, at times, the risk of life itself are less important than the whisper of beach sand as a wave recedes and the clamor of diving sea birds over a school of harried baitfish.

The anglers interviewed come from all walks of life: artist, construction worker, administrator-turned-lure-maker, pier-builder-turned-journalist. Some have traveled widely throughout the world, fishing as they went, while others have spent most of their lives on the island of Martha's Vineyard off the Massachusetts coast. All have a love for that island and know its fishing grounds intimately, from Tashmoo to Menemsha, from Devil's Bridge to Cape Poge.

Bob Post, an eager surf fisherman himself, has captured here the mystique that surrounds those who haunt the sea rim to cast under a burning midday sun or through the shroud of an inky fog in the dead of night. Surf fishermen are not simply anglers; they are hunters as well and have the instincts of the true hunter. Memory for tides and currents; moon phases and wind directions; baits on which the quarry feeds; and lure variations in size, color, and action —all contribute to a mental storehouse that is used to take striped

FOREWORD

bass, bluefish, weakfish, and other species that at times feed at the surf line. As a hunter follows the tracks of game, so do these experts, based on years of experience, follow the invisible, watery spoor of the fish they seek.

Throughout this book runs a common thread—the angling contest that started back in 1946 and that has become one of the best known events of its kind along the eastern seaboard. Secrecy surrounds the anglers participating in the Derby, and their covert activities have reached phenomenal proportions. Accounts of how fishermen try to outwit their rivals are not only entertaining, but also might serve as models for activities in the Central Intelligence Agency.

No one can directly accuse the group of lying; however, they may well be accused of avoiding the truth. Burying stripers in beach sand so angling success cannot be detected, speeding with a load of fish in their beach buggy from one end of the Vineyard to the other to deceive those who might be trailing them, and swerving off roads in the dead of night to hide in the underbrush until spies pass by are just a few of the ploys involved. One angler discovered another under his car taking note of tire treads to ensure accurate tracking. The sport of angling during the Derby has thereby developed into a sophisticated game of cops and robbers.

These profiles of an unusual group of surf fishermen, however, are not just an account of the Derby and Martha's Vineyard. Woven into the text is a vast amount of detailed information, applicable along all coasts, on how to catch fish. Rigging eels; choosing natural baits such as herring and butterfish; and selecting plugs or metal by color, size, and action—all are among facts that will make an average angler better than average. These talented fishermen have learned through years of experience about tackle and methods that get results. The reader can profit from that experience.

Over and above the mechanics of angling is something more important: the love, perhaps even worship, these individuals hold for their sport. They can be poetic when describing their reactions to their surroundings at the ocean's edge. The solitude, the sense of being one with the mystery of a star-studded sky and murmuring waves, and the challenge of a howling wind and crashing surf are in their life's blood. Bob Post, like all of us who are happy captives of

FOREWORD

this cult, has clearly shown the depth of emotion felt by those who haunt the shoreline.

Finally, there is more than a smattering of history throughout this volume, not just on the development of the art of surf fishing, but also about the evolution in attitude toward the species that is most often sought: the striped bass. Even when these fish were plentiful, the major appeal in seeking them was their elusiveness. When the catastrophic decline in stocks started more than a decade ago, scarcity made the angler's goal even more difficult to achieve. The experts profiled in these pages regret that, in the past, they thought the bounty was almost limitless. Realizing that their efforts should be concentrated on conserving, they now release most of the stripers they are able to beach.

Living legends provide a key to the past as well as the future. By reading the profiles that follow, the reader will have a better grasp of the lore and lure of surf fishing. Perhaps even an anthropologist might benefit by noting the special behavioral niche that sets this group apart from lesser humans.

HENRY LYMAN
publisher emeritus,
Salt Water Sportsman

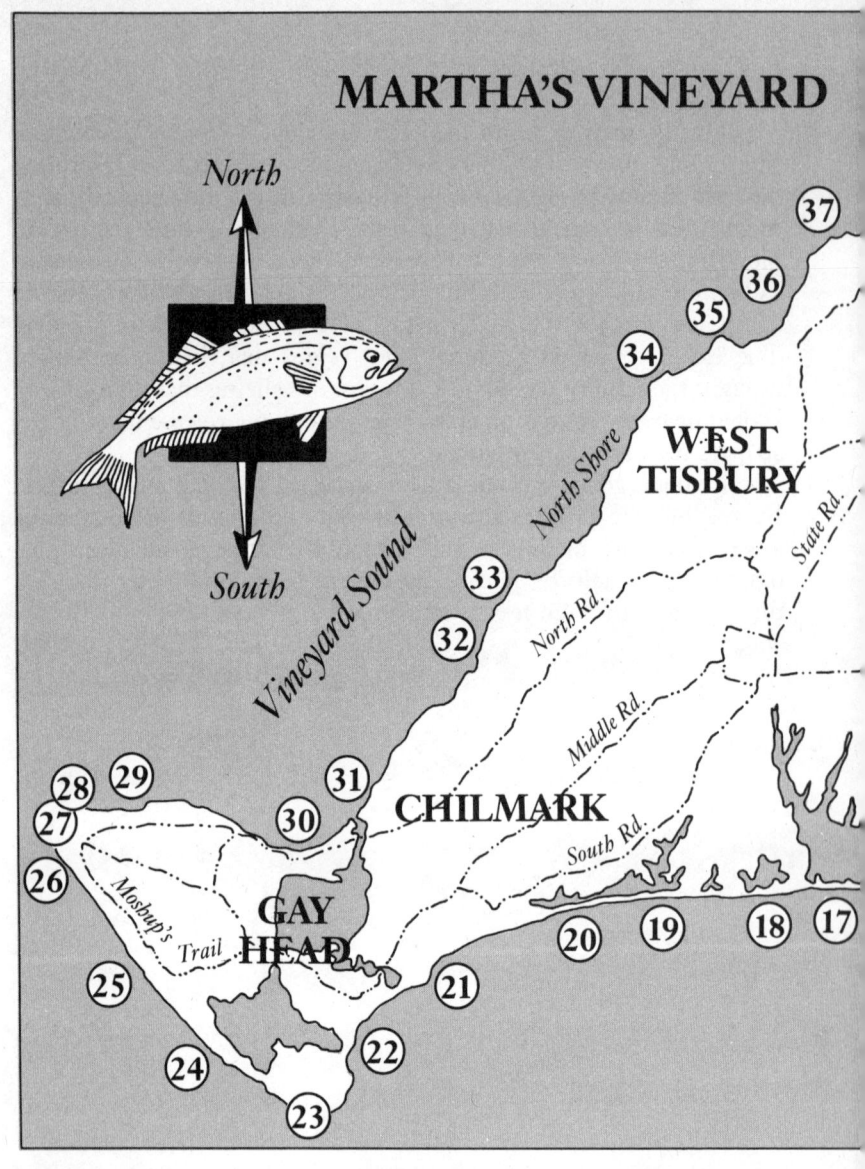

1. East Chop
2. Little Bridge
3. Sengekontacket Pond
4. Big Bridge
5. Cape Poge Gut
6. Cape Poge
7. Arruda Point
8. East Beach
9. Wasque Point
10. Metcalf's Hole
11. Katama
12. Herring Run
13. Navy Bunker
14. Edgartown Great Pond
15. Oyster Pond
16. Homer's Pond
17. Tisbury Great Pond
18. Black Point Pond
19. Chilmark Pond
20. Rum Runners Rock
21. Stonewall Point

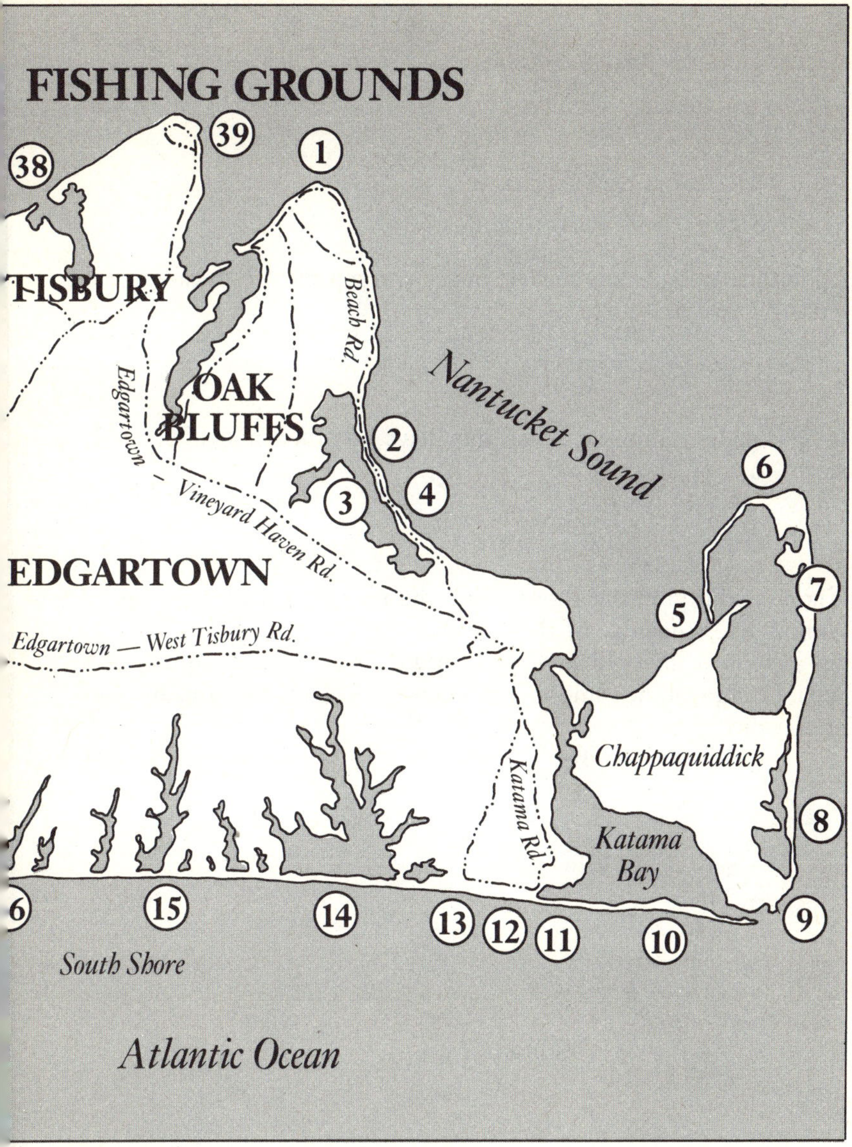

FISHING GROUNDS

22. Squibnocket Beach
23. Squibnocket Point
24. Long Beach
25. Zacks Cliffs
26. Gay Head Cliffs
27. Devils Bridge
28. Pilot's Landing
29. Dogfish Bar
30. Lobsterville
31. Menemsha
32. Brick Yard
33. Cape Higgon
34. Cedar Tree Neck
35. Paul's Point
36. Makonikey
37. Norton Point
38. Tashmoo Outlet
39. West Chop

All wish to possess knowledge, but few, comparatively speaking, are willing to pay the price.
—Juvenal

People seldom improve, when they have no other model but themselves to copy after.
—Oliver Goldsmith

The graceful gull, the shore birds, the pink sea shells, the sunrise coming over the edge of the world, the placid days of summer and the long, soft, moonlit nights of autumn are yours. So, too, are the wild, black, wet, howling nights when dunes shift, and bars and cuts are levelled.
—Van Campen Heilner and Frank Stick, *The Call of the Surf*

Reading the Water

Preface

This is a book about a dedicated group of surf fishermen who share a grand passion for their sport. Their homes and their stories are scattered along the Northeast Coast although they all have a common, almost hypnotic, draw to the beaches of Martha's Vineyard. The fishing stories they tell reveal much about the sport's history and techniques and how lives are lived in small coastal communities.

Their love and obsession for the sport is equal to mine, and that is why I wrote this book. We have shared the invigorating feeling of fishing in the surf. We have been lured from a comfortable home and warm bed at totally unreasonable hours in often miserable weather to seek gamefish from the beach. My interest in surf fishing, which can border the fanatical, enabled me to meet the fishermen in this book. Their unique stories are told in their own words and introduced by my observations. To distinguish the two, my narration is set in *oblique typeface.*

Some of the stories don't involve catching fish but pursuing the fish instead. Sometimes nature provides rare glimpses of beauty that have a lasting impact. Whether I'm thinking of a seal breaching through the Menemsha Channel chasing bunker or a striped bass silhouetted in the curl of a wave at the Edgartown Pond opening, I remember them with awe. I remember, particularly, an evening at Gay Head several years ago.

On the Sunday after Thanksgiving in 1979, I decided to fish for striped bass. The fall was warm, and water temperatures around the

PREFACE

Vineyard were still comfortable for baitfish and bass. When I arrived at Zacks Cliffs, the first thing I noticed were thousands of screeching, diving gulls working the water. They were fifty yards out from the faint tide line etched in the sand, feeding on sand eels.

I walked a few miles around the first point. After an hour, stars provided the only light. I cast my large Atom swimming plug into the calm ocean darkness. I was expecting a bass to take the plug with every cast, but I left Gay Head without catching a fish. In fact, I never had a hit, but it hardly mattered. I knew within myself that by late November the bass would be gone. What did matter was my solitary invasion of raw nature, the beauty of the surf and its roar in the night, the screaming gulls, and the sand eels gasping in panic.

Several fishermen tell unusual tales about lost fish. Many of the fish that are most memorable are those lost after a dramatic heart-pounding fight. Like most surf fishermen, however, I can remember the first bass I was able to land. It was caught at the foot of the East Chop cliffs in 1973. I was just starting to fish from the beach. I was hardly a die-hard fanatic or a knowledgeable beginner. My Grandpa Louie left me his bamboo boat rod with an Ocean City conventional reel. The reel was still loaded with braided nylon about twenty years old.

The gear's condition was quite poor. The drag wasn't working. To strip off line, I had to throw the lever arm, putting the reel in free spool. I half slid and half stumbled down the cliff, finding a comfortable rock to stand on. The surf was gentle, splashing off the rocks in a fine spray.

I used a one-inch square of frozen squid for bait, placing it on a rusty hook. Unable to cast because I was using a boat rod with a jammed reel, I just lowered the bait into the water, where it bounced pathetically off the rocks. I was suddenly jolted by a hard tug on the line, almost losing my balance.

A rod can only do so much. Acting like a lever with the fisherman on one end and the fish on the other, it needs the help of line running out over a smooth drag. Fortunately, this fish was hooked well, so after several tugs back and forth it flopped up on the rocks. It was an eighteen-pound striper. Catching that fish taught me that good luck can overcome ineptitude and a lack of experience.

For many of the fishermen in the book, myself included, partic-

PREFACE

ipation in the annual Martha's Vineyard Striped Bass and Bluefish Derby is eagerly anticipated. The competition and camaraderie are the source of many stories. We often forget family and work, pushing ourselves through the night, searching for the "big" fish.

According to Al Brickman, a member of the original Striped Bass Derby Committee in the late 1940s, it was Nat Sperber, a public relations expert with the advertising agency of Chambers and Wiswell, who thought of the concept of the Derby. In 1945, when Vineyard residents Ralph Hornblower and Russell Stern bought the Martha's Vineyard route from the New England Steamship Company, they were interested in increasing their profits. They wanted Sperber to devise a plan for extending the tourist season in the fall.

The first Derby was in 1946 and did not include bluefish because few were around. It was simply called the Martha's Vineyard Striped Bass Derby. In 1948, bluefish made a small comeback in Vineyard waters, so they were added as a Derby fish. The grand-prize bluefish winner in 1948 was Henry Hartley of Boston with a four-pound, six-ounce fish. Blues were removed from the Derby again in 1952 and 1953. Since their permanent return to the Derby in 1954, they have been abundant and large. Striped bass were removed in 1985 as a symbolic gesture for a troubled fish. Bonito, false albacore, and weakfish were substituted. Various prizes are awarded in categories for residents and nonresidents. How the fish is caught, such as from a boat or the shore or with a fly rod, is a determining factor, as is the age and sex of the participant, because special prizes are awarded to juniors, seniors, and women.

Prizes awarded to Derby winners over the years included such generous items as boats, cars, and trips. One of the most memorable prizes was a redwood hunting lodge from the E. C. Young Company, erected on Island land donated by Cronig's Real Estate. This was won by Louise de Somov in 1955.

Although not as grand, some of the other prizes were unusual. These included cooked hams, a case of canned peas, three hundred chopsticks, Nettleton shoes for men, and I. Miller shoes for women.

The greatest prize, however, is the gain in stature and reputation in the tight-knit Vineyard fishing community. Having your name in the local papers or on the Derby chalkboard for all to see is a satisfying testimonial to the abilities of a surf fisherman.

PREFACE

Early Derby stories were both tragic and humorous. In 1947, John Beal of Boston was killed when his plane crashed as he was trying to land on the beach after spotting a school of striped bass. His passenger, Alan Hall of West Harwich, was injured.

In 1948 a fisherman reported catching a fish that lunged at his pocket, as he stood in deep water casting. The pocket contained both a spare Atom plug and a ham sandwich. The fisherman claimed the ham sandwich created a slick which attracted the bass.

The Martha's Vineyard Rod and Gun Club sponsored the Derby until 1950, when the chamber of commerce took over. In 1986, the chamber withdrew as a sponsor. The 1987 Derby was the first Derby run entirely by the Derby Committee, which is composed of Vineyard fishermen.

Although the Derby temporarily increases the pace of surf fishing, dedicated surf fishermen continue to fish through the fall until the bass and bluefish leave Vineyard waters. The surf-fishing fanatics included in this book are driven more by the challenge of their goal rather than its attainment. Discovering where fish are feeding and catching them can be very satisfying, but also satisfying is learning wind and tide patterns, reading the water, spotting cuts in offshore bars, and finding deep holes filled with bait. We enjoy being outdoors surrounded by nature's elements, experiencing all she has to offer.

If fish were caught every time out, fishing would lose some of its mystery. It's that mystery that appeals to the surf-fishing fanatic. The unpredictable nature of surf fishing creates a challenge, and for many the challenge has become an addiction.

1

Steve Bryant

During a driving southeaster on a warm June day, I decided to fish Wasque Point. Although an east wind flattens the rip at this unusually consistent fishing spot, I still wanted to be out on the beach. The water is fairly clean during the first day of a storm, and at Wasque anything is possible.

Four-wheel-drive vehicles normally enter the beach at Katama, pass the Mattakeset area, and continue past Metcalf's Hole to Wasque. On this day, the vehicles were packed together at Katama, looking like a wagon-train circle that unraveled. Fishermen were running frantically on the wet sand, arming themselves with rods and plugs against some imaginary foe.

I was curious about why so many fishermen were gathered at such an unlikely spot. Approaching from the east, I could see gulls working, snatching shredded baitfish from the turbulent water. Large bluefish and striped bass were already scattered on the beach, many sticking halfway under vehicles as if they were trying to hide.

In the crowd of active fishermen, I look for a friendly face. I want to fish next to someone who knows what to do and is "even-

tempered," so I fished next to Steve Bryant. One time Steve was angry at some town official on the Island. He told him, "May the hairs on your ass turn to fish hooks!" I respected Steve's way with words, along with his fishing ability.

I remember as a youngster taking trips—but not fishing trips —with my father, Nelson, and my Uncle Danny. I caught my first fish from the surf when I was eight years old. I was with Bob Morgan and my father at Metcalf's Hole, right at the end of Katama. It was on a Sunday, middle of the summer—kind of very quiet, doldrum sort of day. We used sea clams as bait and fished them on the bottom. I just fished as a matter of routine. I wasn't particularly interested in it at the time, and I remember I was the first one to get a hit, to set the hook.

It was high noon. I remember eating lunch on the beach at that time. And we caught fish. They weren't big fish; I think they were about eight-to-twelve-pound bass. They weren't large by the big standards of bass, but they were big for a little eight year old. We caught four total. I caught one, my uncle caught one, and my father caught two. It was quite a thrill to catch a bass. I remember that was a big deal.

Now people mostly fish at night, evenings, and dawn. In those days, though, we seemed to fish a lot more during the day, and we were quite successful.

It wasn't until the late sixties that I became a real die-hard. At that time I had no responsibilities. That's when I really got into it, especially fishing Chappy and the South Shore area—Tisbury Great Pond. I went morning and night. I worked in between fishing trips. It was when I was eighteen or nineteen, before I went into the service, that I really started fishing heavily.

I got married shortly after I got out of the service and back from Vietnam. There was the new responsibility of being married, and my gear had long since disappeared. I can't remember what happened to the rod, and my plugs were gone. I started off again though. This is a good story because I hadn't been fishing for two-and-a-half years when I decided to go again.

I heard that they were catching small bluefish at Lobsterville.

STEVE BRYANT

This was the first fall I was married, and I said to my wife, Lissa, "Well, let's go up there and get them." My father had given me a telescoping surf rod, about a nine-footer that somebody had given him, so I had that and an old Mitchell reel. I had one Atom popper. That's all I had to my name at the time. So we drove up there, and there were all these fathers, sons, daughters, and mothers lined up along the beach; and everybody was catching little bluefish as fast as they could throw their lines into the water. I could see that they were using small Rebels or Rapalas or light gear. And I didn't have it, so I was frustrated by that. The fish were breaking everywhere. Finally, using my large popping plug, I felt a tug on the line, so I set the hook, and I said to Lissa, "I've got one, I've got one!" I reeled it in, and it was a sea robin. In disgust, I took it off and left, but I knew I had to get back into it again by sacrificing a little money from the rent, or the fuel bill or gas, or whatever. I didn't have the gear and I didn't have the wherewithal. I had to relearn a little bit. That was an embarrassing time for me. It was frustrating more than anything else.

After that, we lived in Amherst for about six years. We came back to the Vineyard every summer, before returning permanently. I fished hard during the summers. My wife has always been very good about giving me a lot of freedom to do the things I wanted—as long as I took care of business and brought money home. So, I did fish hard, usually in the mornings and the evenings. Actually, I fished harder than I had before, especially when the pond was open or things were looking good. There was good fishing around here in the early and mid-seventies. You'd go anywhere, anytime, and catch fish if you caught the tides right.

The time that really stands out in my mind was back when we were living here again, around 1976. Tisbury Great Pond was opened during midsummer then. People were catching fish there during all tides.

I've caught just as many fish at the pond's opening on the incoming tide as at any other time. I learned that from two guys from Vermont who came down every year to fish. We'd see the drag marks coming off the beach where they walked all the way back to the Quansoo Crab Creek Bridge with bass. And that's the only time they ever fished—the incoming tide in the middle of the day. So I learned a lesson from some off Islanders.

I recall reading an article by Steve Bryant's father, Nelson Bryant, in an old Outdoor Life. *He saw the striper as a symbol of the world he loved. "An incredibly diverse world of sand and surf, of wild water breaking over black rocks, of tidal ponds and rivers where in the spring school bass feed on hatching marine worms or small baitfish." In the same article he also wrote about his favorite fishing spot off the North Shore. What fascinated me when he talked about the spot was that he often got spooked. He thought the rocks were "strange sea people" observing him. "It is an eerie place," he wrote, "and when I fish it at night I am half afraid. Over and over I have the feeling of being watched by ancient eyes, and sometimes the sensation is so overwhelming that I seize my rod and leave, slipping and sliding over the cobble and glancing behind as Robinson Crusoe did when he found the footprint in the sand. But unlike him, it is no mortal I fear."*

I get spooked sometimes when I'm out by myself at night. It depends where I am. Night fishing can be strange, especially on deep black foggy nights, when you can't even see the tip of your rod. I was wondering if Steve inherited this fishing trait from his father.

Oh, I definitely have, especially on the dark nights with fog or mist. They're very eerie—not so much on the south side of the Island because there's a great expanse of beach. The North Shore or up around Gay Head or Squibnocket are kind of eerie, though. The water dashes to the side of you, you hear a gurgle, so you turn and look. Or you'll get spooked by another fisherman, who appears out of nowhere and says, "Hi, did you catch anything?" That always sets my heart in my throat!

I've never gotten over my fear of darkness. I think part of it is that you're on edge. You're keyed up, fishing. And at night, because I can't see, I turn my hearing on as best I can, so I'm kind of keyed up. Certain noises or certain atmospheres just make you nervous, make you jump.

STEVE BRYANT

I have a morning-night story. While fishing an eel at Makonikey on the north shore of the Vineyard, I managed to lose two beautiful stripers—one at dawn and one at dusk. The water was flat calm, looking more like a trout pond than an ocean. Both stripers hit with tremendous force, spraying water high into the air, actually startling me. I was so surprised by the force of the hits that I set the hook too soon. I popped the eels right from the stripers' mouths, as if I was removing a cork from a bottle of champagne.

I remember one morning; it was absolutely flat—kind of a hot, muggy morning in August. I'd gotten up late. It was light out already. I drove down to McAlpin's where I had my boat. I call this my morning-night story.

The boat was the quickest way to get across the pond. I didn't have a four-wheel-drive vehicle. The sun was just above the horizon, so I imagine, at that time of year, it must have been five forty-five, six o'clock. Very heavy fog was just lifting, so I could see easily across the pond. It was absolutely flat calm. You could see there wasn't going to be a breath of air that day. When I got to the other side, another fisherman was in his Jeep and just leaving. So I said, "Oh God, he's leaving. That doesn't bode well for the fishing here." It's now six-thirty or so. It was really hot. The sun was just breaking out. There was hardly any opening left. The water was just about dead low, hardly any rip going. I said, "Well, I came at the wrong time. I should have been here two hours ago." So, I was using a big, light blue Danny swimmer, made one cast, started to reel it in, when I saw this bronze flash underneath the plug. It was a silhouette of a bass. It got me pretty excited, so I reeled more and saw another boil behind the plug, another flash and a boil. The third time it happened, I was on to a fish. I played the fish and got it onto the beach. It was a good fish, weighing in the high thirties.

Usually, fishing from the surf, you've got a good surf running or, if the tide is running hard out of the pond opening, you end up walking down the beach a way to get the fish in. I was fishing with seventeen-pound-test line and an eleven-and-a-half-foot rod. The fish made one good hard run, straight out. Then I just steadily pumped the reel all the way back in. There were a couple of little feints at the end, but it was a fairly quick job of getting the fish in.

So, I got him in and made another cast. Reeling in I saw lots of boil behind the plug. I could even see the caudal and dorsal fins of several fish behind the plug, nosing at it. When the plug would hit the water there'd be flashes and boils, then fins behind it. The fish would just kind of slurp behind it. Every now and then I'd feel a whack on the plug. Now my heart is in my throat. This happened on two or three casts, though there were no solid hits. The fish would come out, there'd be a geyser of water and a whack at the plug. Now I'm getting frustrated.

I once listened to an old-timer say, "Well, if you can't catch them with what you got, go to something 100 percent different." I was fishing on the top of the water with a big plug, so to get down deeper, I put on a large white Stan Gibbs swimmer. I made about three cranks of the reel, got a good solid hit, and was onto another fish. I played that bass to the beach—same weight as the first one, about thirty-seven or thirty-eight pounds, which is what most of them weighed in the end.

I cast again. I couldn't see fish playing because it wasn't a surface plug. When I got the plug close to the beach in the last wave, though, I could see fish silhouetted in the wave, just following the plug.

So, I knew there were a lot of fish there. They weren't hitting well; they were finicky. It was clear water and very calm. After three or four more casts with that plug, I went to a Stan Gibbs trolling plug. It swam sub-surface for maybe a couple of feet, I cranked the reel three times, and, bang, I was on again. So I just kept rotating these three plugs until about nine-thirty in the morning. I never went to metal, and I never went to anything really out of class. There were bunker around. I was frustrated because I couldn't catch the stripers on the same plug. Once I got into the routine of switching, I would get a fish immediately. It was almost as if the change of a plug was enough to tantalize a fish to hit. Maybe once or twice since then I've used that technique when fish were fussy. I ended up with eleven fish. The biggest weighed forty-seven pounds, and the smallest was thirty-six pounds. That's an incredible morning, but that's not the end of the story.

It's nine-thirty, so I went to work. Well, I was all excited about going back that evening, and my brother-in-law, John Beecher, was coming down to visit for the weekend. So I said, "Well, hell, if he comes down, I'll take him there and maybe he can catch a fish." I was excited about that. I said, "Once we get everybody to bed (we had some of the nephews here) and everybody is quieted down, we'll go down to the beach." I didn't feel it was important to get there by sunset. I wanted to get there later. I wanted to get the nephews in bed, get through supper, spend some time with the family, then head down.

John and I took the boat across again. It was a nice flat, calm night. I could see that there was fog hanging offshore. I said, "Well, damn, we might get caught in that. I don't know." I didn't bring a compass. So, I have to make a couple of points to get across the pond and into the channel. We got across to the opening and the tide was running in. I said, "We'll fish the bottom with eels." I brought two rods and I had my plugs, but I also brought some live eels.

We were the only ones on the east side of the opening. This is also called the Scrubby Neck, or down-Island side of the opening. That's where I caught the fish in the morning. So we're on the east side, and I could see Whit Manter and Alan Cordts on the west side.

I found it interesting that Whit and Alan were there. I always think of Whit as a guy who just sniffs out these fishing experiences. There really was no reason for anyone to be there in August, certainly not a prime bass fishing month on the Island. Alan, a cardiovascular surgeon from Falmouth, often seems to appear out of nowhere. You'd be walking down a beach, at some ungodly hour, and there would be Alan Cordts walking along, steely gray eyes piercing the night, as if he had risen from the dead.

So there we were. I cast a few times. I threw an eel out for John, and I cast with plugs, but nothing happened. So I decided I'd put an eel on, too, and I put it on my big rig. It's called a Hatteras Heaver. It's a great big meat stick, with fifty-pound-test mono. We both sat down on the beach. Then fog started coming in. I was getting a little nervous about getting back, so I was thinking, "Well, maybe we'll fish for another fifteen or twenty minutes, then head back." The pond isn't very long but it's somewhat treacherous in spots.

Well, the fog bank was holding offshore, and you could just see it. It was nighttime now, but it was a fairly light night because of stars and everything else, and the fog hadn't reached us. You could hear the fishermen talking on the other side of the opening and a car door slam. What breeze there was was somewhat from the south-southwest. Then this wet muggy mist came over us and the sound deadened, and everything was scary. Of course, it's very eerie because you can't see far. Any lights that show are refracted and reflected from the fog above. Even a flashlight looks like it's coming from above instead of from across.

If Beecher wasn't with me I would have been spooked—guaranteed—because it was very, very still. There was hardly any surf at all.

I had the line in the water, and I was using a conventional reel; the clicker was on. Then I heard *uurrag*, probably the line running out with the surf, or the eel pulling on it. Then it just picked up and the clicker started screaming. I had a fish on, so I took the clicker off and let it run. The line just started screaming out, and I knew then it was probably a good fish or, at least, a reasonable fish. I thumbed the line, and the fish ran for about ten seconds and stopped. I could feel this gentle tugging on the line, and I said, "Well, if it runs again, I'm going to set the hook." And it did run again. I threw the reel in gear, pointed the rod at the water, waited for the line to straighten out, and set the hook. This is big gear I'm fishing with, and the drag is set very tight. But this fish, with no hesitation at all, was immediately into the drag and stripping line off, heading at an angle down the beach to the southeast. I said, "My God, a good one." I've caught sharks there quite frequently on quiet August nights, so I thought maybe it was a shark—a good shark. Sharks down there sometimes weigh more than a hundred pounds and they'll give you a hell of a fight.

This fish, though, made one good long run. A shark will run and it'll fight you all the way into the beach, get into the wash, and go back and forth; this fish didn't.

We had one very weak flashlight—one of those little disposable types. I'm just pumping the fish in. It made one long steady run and a couple of short shots when it got close to the beach in the wash, then it came in. I turned the flashlight on and pointed it about twenty yards in front of me. I saw this great big white body facing me—great big full shape. I said, "That fish is over fifty pounds!" I went down there and pulled it up. We were extremely excited because of its size. At night, it seemed to loom even larger. I had no scales with me, but I held it up and guessed its length.

So I rigged up again very quickly. I remember John Beecher saying, "God, I'd sure like to catch one like that!" He kept saying it about ten times—"I'd sure like to catch one like that!" But that was it. We fished hard. We waited another hour and said, "That's it. Let's go back." The fog, meanwhile, had become very, very thick. We saw a commotion on the other side of the opening—light shining at regular intervals. Come to find out that those fishermen caught, I think, four or five very large fish in about the same period of time I caught this one.

The story doesn't end yet, though, because now I wanted to weigh the fish. I was sure that it was my first fifty-pound fish. The length was about right; it was forty-nine or fifty inches long—about a pound per inch when it gets to that length. So I said, "Let's take it home. I've got a fish scale at home."

So we dragged the fish and the gear over the beach and threw it in the boat. Now it's absolutely pea-soup fog. You couldn't see ten feet. We just had to go by dead reckoning, so I threw the outboard in gear and kind of puttered along the beach. I ran aground a couple of times. Then I said, "I'll steer by the wake." An old-timer told me you can steer by the wake if you get in tough stuff. I was steering by the wake and ran it for about four minutes, which is about the time it takes me to get across. The next thing I know water's rushing by. I shined a light out, and it was only about a foot and a half deep. We're right back in the middle of the opening again. I made this great big long loop for four minutes and came right back to the opening, so steering by the wake doesn't necessarily work.

Finally the way we got home—and it took us almost *two hours* to get there—was to just roll and bounce along the whole western pond shore, cross the opening to Deep Bottom and finally to McAlpin's. I got home and weighed the fish. On my scale it was fifty-four pounds. The next morning when I weighed it on the official scales, it was fifty pounds, twelve ounces. I got my fifty-pounder.

It takes great talent and experience to fish eels properly. Kevin Hearn, possibly the most respected eel fisherman on the Vineyard, likes to cast and reel them in like a lure. Hank Schauer, a frequent visitor to the Island from New Jersey, prefers to rig them with wire, double hooked with a leadhead up front. Steve happened to be fishing his eel on the bottom. This is an especially difficult technique. It takes great timing and patience to let the fish run with the eel and then set the hook just at the right moment.

On nights when there is a lot of surf and a chance of the line getting ripped around, I use weights. I use a four-ounce sinker and rig the eel to a sharp, fairly short-shank hook. I like the Mustad hook—a No. 8. I usually hook the eel through the bottom lip. If there are bluefish around, I hook the eels in the middle because bluefish have a tendency to chop the middle of the eel first. When I'm fishing for bass, I take the eel and beat it against a sand spike to slow it down a little bit. Otherwise, it could easily tangle the line. It tangles more if you use a weight because the weight is stationary, and the eel just pivots on that point and tangles the line.

On the fifty-pounder night, it was particularly weird because there was hardly any surf and no tide running so I didn't use a weight. I just threw the eels out there, let them sit and swim around. I wasn't casting and reeling in. I used a three-foot wire leader covered with black plastic. If the opening is running strong, though, you can just let the eel out and hold it into the tide. That's a fine way to fish.

On a perfect late October night for surf fishing, I was attending a going-away party for Hank Schauer. He had completed his annual fishing trip to the Vineyard and was returning to New Jersey the next morning. During many of the preceding nights we had fished together at our favorite up-Island spots, including Long Beach. Unfortunately, the night of the party I was being socially responsible, a damaging trait in a die-hard surf fisherman, which can lead to many missed opportunities and frustration. The evening of Hank's going-away party was also what I call, "The Night of the Weakfish." Steve Bryant was at Long Beach that night.

I was sitting around the house one night when I got a call from two surf fishermen, Rob Fair and Rick Newman, who sounded very enthusiastic and wanted to go fish along the beach. I hemmed and hawed, but they finally talked me into it. It was a good thing they did, too.

We were fishing the tide. I remember it was halfway up, so we had a fair amount of time to fish. It was very clear, very cool—almost frosty. I think it was very close to freezing that night. I would say the water temperature was in the low fifties. So we rigged up and went down to Long Beach. We planned to walk way down to the point of Squibnocket. We were all rigged with any manner of swimmers. I had a big Rapala with a fly teaser. Robbie had a Stan Gibbs swimmer with a Red Gill teaser. Rick was using a Danny plug with a fly teaser. Most of the bait available at that time of year is sand eels, so teasers seemed like a good idea.

As we were walking along the beach, I was shining my flashlight into every little cusp and bowl to see if any baitfish were up on the beach. We came upon one cusp where there were sand eels at the tide line and scattered up on the beach—all flipping and flopping. The water was just shimmering with sand eels. So I told the guys, "We ought to stop here. I don't think we have to walk to the point. We should fish this spot."

From the time we started, we caught a fish on virtually every cast. There were a lot of three-to-five-pound bluefish. During the first ten minutes Rob caught a bass on his Red Gill teaser. He caught two more stripers right after that. All of them were thirty-to-thirty-five-pound fish. Rick and I were using streamer fly teasers, but the bass would only hit the Red Gill. We were catching big weakfish. My first weakfish was eight or nine pounds. Rick caught one even larger, pushing past ten toward twelve. Then, the rest of the night, within two hundred yards of that one cusp, we'd catch a weakfish or a blue on almost every cast.

The thing about weakfish is that they're good fighters—kind of between bluefish and bass. A bass gives you that one good hard run. It's like a sack of potatoes. The bluefish is head jerking and thrashing all the way in. A weakfish reminds me of a big trout. I've caught trout up to four, five, and six pounds up in Canada. And it's that hard driving run—never giving up.

The weakfish seemed to get bigger as the night got longer. This was for a period of about four hours. I was exhausted by it. I would bury the fish on the beach so the skunks and raccoons wouldn't get them. During the last couple of hours, all the fish were in the twelve-to-fourteen-pound class. *Very large* weakfish! I've never caught them that big before or since.

These were wonderful fighting fish, and they're great eating fish as far as I'm concerned. I kept about ten weakfish before I started releasing them. I returned about twenty or twenty-five fish. We figure we released fifty fish total. We kept the three bass and a couple dozen weakfish and released all the bluefish.

It was a perfect night; no wind at all. We didn't have to walk the long distance to the point. The fish were right there, within a couple hundred yards to the end of the rock pile. All I can remember is being insatiable about it. I couldn't stop fishing because it was incredible. Every time you'd throw the plug out and take three or four cranks, you'd be on—either a bluefish or a weakfish.

From the number of weakfish that I've caught, and what I've heard other people say, you get a weakfish over fourteen pounds, it's like reeling in a fifty-pound bass.

It was an amazing night. And what was even nicer is that we got so many that we could release some of them. It was amazing to catch upward of thirty or forty weakfish and have every one weigh ten pounds or better. It was a wonderful way to end the season. And the only impetus I had was those two fellows who called. They got me out there, and we had a ball. It was one of the most amazing nights of fishing I've ever had, just because of the numbers and size of the weakfish. There was no moon that night, but there were stars out so you could really see quite well.

I don't think I'll have an experience like that again for many reasons—the cyclical nature of the fish, plus I don't fish as much as I used to. I've got a child now, so I'm home even more than I was. My job responsibilities have gotten far more strenuous, too. So, that's probably the last time I'll see weakfish that way.

STEVE BRYANT

O.H.P. Rodman, in his 1948 fishing book, The Saltwater Fisherman's Favorite Four, *describes weakfish this way: "To describe the colors of this fish is beyond our feeble verbal or written powers. Suffice it to say that this is a handsome fish, both in shape and color. And when he hits your lure, watch out! He may have the name of weakfish; but that does not apply to his fighting or striking powers, which are surprising for its size."*

Since the "night of the weakfish," weakfish, known for cyclic periods of abundance and scarcity, have been scarce in Vineyard waters. Steve, Rob, and Rick seem to have caught their fish at the top of the cycle. The weakfish used to arrive regularly at Lobsterville Beach in July. Large schools would be herding bait toward the gently sloping beach, croaking sounds filling the air. Small brokenback Rebels were used most often to fool them. Commenting on the cyclic nature of the fish in The Complete Book of Weakfishing, *Henry Lyman and Frank Woolner wrote: "There is—and mark this well—no definite pattern in these cycles; the fundamental causes of them have not been determined. Some claim that weaks are plentiful when bluefish are scarce, and vice versa; others say that the controlling factor is the supply of menhaden or other bait fish. The only definite conclusion is—that nobody knows."*

I get palpitations when I fish. I love fishing with surface plugs at night when it's absolutely quiet and still. You can hear the fish splash behind the plug before you even feel the tap. But that's when I hear that *spaloosh* out there, and I know that there's going to be a *wang* on the end of the line and the rod's going to dip from its weight. And that's when my heart is always in my throat! I can make twenty or thirty casts with nothing happening and all of a sudden a hard strike just jerks me right up—I still get excited.

2

Whit Manter

Several years ago, just after sunrise on the last morning of the Derby, I noticed Whit Manter at the Tisbury Great Pond opening. I had just finished fishing with chunks of fresh mackerel at the opening to Chilmark Pond. Curious about the other fisherman's success, I drove my Jeep down the beach to gossip and do some more fishing. Whit complained a little bit about how slow fishing had been. "Certainly not much going on this morning," he said. I didn't know, as I stood next to his truck, that he had already landed a nice striper, one weighing about thirty pounds, on an eel. Whit always had a sense of humor to go along with his great fishing talents. No other fish were caught at the openings that morning. With only minutes left before the weigh-in station closed, Whit appeared with the fish that took the daily Derby prize.

The Derby was always big for my Dad. Before he had so many family responsibilities, he used to fish every night during the Derby. I used to watch him prepare his gear and listen to his stories. I was always excited about surf fishing. I was nine years old when I first went fishing; I didn't catch anything. And, then, when I was ten years old, it all took off. I caught my first bass that fall during the Derby, just bottom fishing. Dad helped me cast the bait out. It was my first bass. I took it down to the weigh-in station, and most everybody said, "Oh, what a cute kid and cute little fish." I didn't win anything with that striper, but it was kind of fun to go through the process of weighing in my first bass.

Then about a week later, during the second week of the Derby —it was September 26, 1965—I was sitting between my father and his good friend, Mert Snowden. They used to fish together all the time. It was just after dark. I had my eel on the bottom, with a sinker. That was just the way we used to fish. There were rocks there, so you'd stun the eel and throw it on the bottom; then it couldn't swim in the rocks and tie everything up.

Anyway, we're fishing, and I got a tremendous fish on. Of course, Dad helped me with the reel. He'd left the drag too tight. So I've got a death grip on the rod and there's no line going out, so the fish is starting to pull me into the surf. So Dad had to grab hold of me. Once the drag freed up, the fish started peeling out some line. Then I was all excited. I was only ten, and it was twenty years ago, but I'll never forget the adrenalin pumping through me. Once Dad got me back on my feet and got the drag out, I was able to play the fish. Dad told me how to pull it up with the wave; it came up, and he jumped on it. It was a nice fish—thirty-one pounds. It was a whole different story down at the weigh-in station that night. I was in the week before with a six pounder; this time, I walked in with a thirty-one pounder. I could barely carry it. While I was dragging it across the floor to the scales, I had everybody clapping and yelling. So, I won first daily, and I won the Junior Division of the Derby that year. I had fishing in my blood, and on that night it turned into a fever. It was a few more years before I caught one weighing more than that thirty-one pounder. I had the fever, though, and it's just never let up.

It was a real status symbol to be a successful bass fisherman. Still is, but it really has changed some in the past few years because the bass have declined and are considered in trouble. But at that time, there were still familiar people around, like Dick Hathaway, Sergei de Somov, and Francis Bernard. The guys who were successful bass fishermen and the guys who won the Derby were considered folk heroes.

So anyway, my fishing career really took off. I went when I could. Until you get a driver's license, though, you're severely handicapped. I was very dependent on friends for rides, and Dad would give me a ride when he could. He'd sometimes get up at four in the morning and drive me down to Quansoo or drop me off at Crab Creek and then pick me up three or four hours later. He knew it was important to me.

I bought a Jeep the year before I could get my driver's license —a 1948 Universal Jeep. I fixed it all up. So, it was my first fishing Jeep. I didn't set the world on fire with my fishing, but I got the wheels and got some experience fishing different places around the Vineyard.

Most successful surf fishermen, those who have become folk heroes, put in long hours on the beach, often becoming strangers to their families for weeks on end. You can see them stumbling around the Island at Derby time. They are usually unshaven, unkempt and exhausted. Looking like a group of escaped convicts in need of room and board, these are the fishermen who are catching the big ones. While some basic techniques can be learned from books and other fishermen, there is no substitute for experience.

There's no one who's successful who'll tell you fishing isn't self-taught. You pick up a tremendous amount from the older fishermen, but you still have to go fish. None of them'll tell you any different. You just get out there and go, go, go. Usually when I say fishing, I mean bass fishing. I don't mean to put anything else down, but it's the fish I like to go after most. It's tough, though. It's tiresome. You go out for a couple of weeks, you fish hard every night, and you haven't even had a hit. Everyone thinks it's so easy because I come in with a big fish. They only see me when I've got them hanging over the tailgate. They don't see me during the twenty nights when I didn't get anything and froze to death. It can be hard, but that's all part of the mystique and the whole aura of being a successful surf fisherman. Actually, though, I love it at night. It just doesn't matter that it's dark. Sometime you get a really eerie feeling when you get a dark and thick fog, especially if it's one of those nights when it's pitch black. You just have no depth perception at all. Those nights don't scare me but they're very, very eerie.

On the morning of the second day of the 1972 Martha's Vineyard Bass Derby, when Whit was seventeen and a senior in high school, he landed a forty-one-pound striped bass. Just days later he caught a seventeen-pound, nine-ounce bluefish that won second place for a shore blue taken by an Islander. During the other days, the fish he weighed were large enough to win all the daily prizes available for shore stripers and shore bluefish. The consensus in the fishing community was, "This guy's here to stay." Several years later, Whit landed a forty-five-pound striper within minutes of the start of another Derby.

    It was high water around midnight. I had headed up to the bass stand at Squibnocket around ten, ten-thirty. I thought, "Well, I'm going to fish the tide and just see what happens." I like to fish the end of the coming tide. Because it was the first day of the Derby, I had to go and fish. I fished for a while and nothing. It was a pretty night. I don't remember there being moonlight. There was a light surf. So I sat, took a break, then got up and started fishing again. And, damn, I had a tremendous hit! Just *blam, smash;* water went everywhere. The fish made a great run. Later, after I landed the fish, I looked at my watch and it was ten past twelve. I could've hooked the fish before midnight, but I landed it after midnight. Right around midnight at the beginning of the Derby, I landed this forty-five-pounder.

    So anyway, the fish stays in the lead for three weeks. Another fisherman weighed in a forty-eight-pounder and knocked me into second place. He did it during the last week or the end of the third week. I'm sort of relieved. I don't have to worry about whether I'm going to be first or not. I've only got to worry about if I finish in the top three. So on the *very* last morning of the Derby, Francis Bernard came in with a forty-nine pounder and won it all. It wasn't until just before the awards ceremony that I found out that the fisherman who caught the forty-eight-pounder had come in and taken his fish out of the running. Apparently when he'd caught it, he didn't have a Derby pin. So even though I didn't know it, I really led the Derby from the first moments until the last hour.

I have missed many good fishing events over the years. I once arrived at Stonewall Beach only to see Kevin Hearn walk off the beach with a stringer of six large stripers glistening in the moonlight. I left Pilots Landing an hour before high tide during a driving southeaster, even though the water was alive with mullet. The mullet attracted the bass. Ed Jerome and Ed Medeiros stayed and caught bass. I left Long Beach in Gay Head a Sunday after Thanksgiving well before the top of the tide, even though the water was thick with sand eels. Bernie Arruda, Tom Taylor, and Jack Coutinho caught more than thirty bass that night. Even more memorable was Columbus Day, 1981. I was flying to the Vineyard from New York City in a nine-seat Cessna. As we approached the Vineyard airport, heading over South Beach, in the area of the Tisbury Great Pond, I saw about twenty-four cars on the beach. I thought this was very unusual because it was three in the afternoon on a bright, sunny calm day. I remember commenting to Dr. Michael Jacobs, a local internist who was sitting next to me, "I wonder what all those cars are doing on the beach in the middle of the day." Whit Manter was on the beach that day, and that day is now called the "Columbus Day Blitz."

The area between Homer's Pond and Tisbury Great Pond is a good area for catching fish. Many fish that won the Derby have come from that area. It's a place I often move to toward the end of the Derby, even if the ponds aren't open, which they weren't during the Columbus Day Blitz. On the day before Columbus Day, I took a ride late in the afternoon just to scout the area and look for possible holes to fish in and signs of activity and to see where the birds were working. When I got there, there'd just been a small blitz. I know Jackie and Dick Coutinho were there. And I think my cousin Chris Keniston was there, too. It was all over when I arrived, but they had just had some bass chasing bunker along the beach, and they'd each caught some fish weighing up to forty pounds. They're all trying to hide the fish and keep it real quiet. Of course, I know the area pretty well, and it didn't take me long to figure out what was going on. I said to myself, "I think I'll come back here in the morning." I called my friend Roger Silva and the two of us got down there before daylight the next day. We fished bait on the bottom for a little while. We're off the Old Tisbury Pond Club, and nothing happened. As soon as it got daylight, I looked down the beach and could see that my cousin Chris and Jack Coutinho were fishing down by the Great Pond where the opening would be if it were open. It looked like they might be doing something. So we go scooting down there, and sure enough, my cousin has two big fish—a couple of forty-pounders. Even though he had two nice fish, he had to leave and go to work.

Then it just—I can't really describe it—it just started. All of a sudden there was a school of bunker flapping up on top, maybe thirty or forty yards out. I had brought some weighted snag hooks with me. I took my rod, cranked it out there, and snagged bunker. I just let the bunker sink or run; and it wasn't long before I had a fish.

It became obvious that there was a school of large baitfish. Something was chasing them; they were up near the surface quivering, jumping, and flipping around. It was a good-size school, but it wasn't huge. Actually, there's a special treble hook for these situations. It's a big treble hook and it has lead on the center shank—just to make it heavier. So you can cast it right out there like a bullet and just let it sink for a second into the baitfish. Then you give a sharp set on the rod and, you hope, snag one. It seemed to work. You really didn't have to do anything fancy. I was real lucky in the beginning. I nailed four or five bass during the first hour.

You really couldn't see the school of fish or how big it was. It started out as a pod and an occasional bass boil. Then you'd see five or six boils at once. They were out a little way.

I was having a little more success than the other people there. Besides Roger Silva and Jackie Coutinho, there were two or three people who were down for the weekend. They had tiny rods and reels and were just sort of staring in awe at what was going on.

The baitfish finally moved a little closer to shore. I was using my big thirteen-foot-long rod, so I could snag the bunker. What I started to do was reel it in and rehook it. Then I'd throw the bunker on the outside of the school. That seemed to be where the bass were—on the outside of the bunker. I'd usually be on to a fish within seconds.

Live baitfishing can be tricky. I'd throw out the bunker and open the bail and just hold my finger lightly on the line and wait for a bass to pick it up. These were big stripers. There was no question when one was picking this baitfish up. Then I'd let the bass run a little bit until they had a chance to get it down. These fish were feeding hard; they were hungry. You didn't have to let them mouth it much because they were sucking them right down. When it's daylight, you can sometimes watch the bunker. The one you have on the hook will be flipping around right on the surface, and you can see the bass come after it.

Now it's the middle of the morning, and we've caught eight or nine nice fish. This whole day was one experience, so it's really hard to describe it in individual pieces. After catching a few more bass, the bait moved farther out and the fishing was more sporadic. You'd maybe get a couple, then nothing; then the bunker would come back.

More people are showing up all the time; at the same time, it became obvious there was another group of bass and bunker about a mile to the east of us, down off Hadley's—off Homer's Pond. That's down where Bernie Arruda, Eddie Medeiros, Cooper Gilkes, and Ed Jerome started. The two groups of surf fishermen worked all day. The two schools of bunker worked toward each other and finally met off the Old Pond Club. The groups of people were working toward each other, too. Roy Hope showed up. He and his wife did very well. Bernie Arruda told me later that he caught quite a few fish on plugs. But he was fishing that other school, and he was probably the first one on those bunker. Then Cooper and Eddie Jerome and Eddie Medeiros showed up.

From noon to two there was a slack period. People were still catching bass, but there was a definite pause. We had about twenty-four bass at that point. The only question in our minds was whether we had anything big enough to win a grand prize in the Derby.

Around two it started to pick up, and we caught eight more stripers. By the end of the blitz, fifteen or twenty of us are fishing —we're spread out but trying to fish one spot. It was real good because everyone already had just the dream day of fishing. Everything else was gravy. All I think people wanted was the biggest bass.

We had nothing else to prove. We just wanted the one big one. Roger and I had thirty-two bass between us. I think I caught seventeen and he caught fifteen.

As it turned out, Eddie Medeiros had caught the winner, a fifty-five pounder. Henry Burt was there and he caught a fifty-two pounder. What's interesting is that three of the bass that won in the shore-bass category were caught by residents on that day. Eddie Medeiros finished first, Henry Burt finished second, and Eric Pachico finished third with a fifty-one pounder. Bernie Arruda had one fifty pounds, but he didn't even get a daily prize with it.

There were four fifty-pounders; who knows how many forty-pounders. People will tell you 300 to 400 fish were caught. The number's probably closer to 150 to 200.

One other highlight concerns Eric Pachico. He caught the third-place bass and the first-place bluefish that afternoon. He caught a fifty-one-pound bass and a twenty-pound bluefish during that blitz. As many fish as I've caught, I don't think I'll ever live to see the day when I catch a fifty-pound bass and a twenty-pound bluefish in the same day.

I'm thankful I was there. Anything to do with Tisbury Great Pond is important to me. A lot of people fish there, but it's my home turf. I grew up fishing there. If I had missed that blitz, I would've felt just *horrible*. I am just very thankful that I was one of the fishermen who was a part of it, not one of those who had to listen to the endless stories about the big stripers caught that day.

I've got one serious parting thought on this whole thing. This all took place in 1981. The striped bass fishing has really slacked off since then. The publicity about the bad position striped bass are in, of course, affects all of us. At the time of the Columbus Day Blitz, those of us who'd been through it and had the big piles of bass were all feeling pretty good about ourselves. We're walking around with our chests puffed out; everybody had to listen to our stories, and everybody had to ask us about them. We were sort of heroes. Just at that time, though, an awareness about striped bass possibly declining was beginning. So I feel kind of funny about this whole thing in retrospect. The experience was great, but I'm certainly not proud today. I certainly don't go around bragging. We killed a tremendous number of reproducing female bass. We really did some serious damage. So I'm more proud of my other fish stories. Ten or fifteen years ago, if you had a pile of bass, people said, "Wow!" They worshiped you. You were someone great. You show up with a pile of bass now, and they'll stone you. That Columbus Day would be like a hundred years ago when the frontiersmen out on the plains shot a herd of buffalo.

A similar blitz took place on Cape Cod's Nauset Beach near Pochet Hole ten days later. It was estimated that sixty stripers weighing more than fifty pounds were landed. A New England taxidermist was commissioned to mount four bass that weighed more than sixty pounds each. Hundreds of trophy-size fish were taken. When you consider the number of fish killed during the two blitzes, it probably was very damaging overall. Hindsight is always wiser, though. I know a lot of men who would have fished differently if they had known what was going to happen to the stripers.

The "Columbus Day Blitz" was a once-in-a-lifetime experience for many fishermen. What happened to Whit, however, at one of his favorite up-Island spots, is so unique that if I didn't know it to be true, I would think Whit had fallen out of character and was spinning a tall tale.

I was fishing in one of my favorite spots—the bass stand at Squibnocket. I'm pretty sure it was 1983, the year that Stevie Morris won the Derby.

I love it there. I don't lose many fish, but I lose them there, because there are so many mussel-encrusted rocks. It was the middle of the Derby. I headed up there to fish the end of the coming tide. It was a beautiful night. The surf was moderate. Just nice fishy-looking water. There was moonlight, but it wasn't a full moon—maybe a half moon. I just really enjoyed it. I was thinking, "I'm going to enjoy it whether I catch anything or not." But I want to catch something, of course. I get there and Tom Norton, who also likes to fish, is there. There wasn't much going on. We'd cast for awhile, take a break, and yack a little bit. Then we fished again for an hour. Anyway, I see Tom set back—he's fishing on my right. Of course, the first thing you think when the guy next to you gets a fish on is like, "Oh no! I hope it's not a big one!" I don't care what people say.

Deep down inside you always hope the guy next to you doesn't get one bigger than you do. He had a small bluefish, maybe a four-pounder. But that's fine. Something happened, so I'm a lot more alert. It wasn't long after that, I had a hit all right.

I was using a large white surface swimmer, called a Danny plug. I'm using a good bass lure in a good bass fishing spot. I got a good fish on. It was a solid hit, but nothing other than I would expect a medium or large bass to do. It was a good hit, but a *tremendous* run. The run was like a freight train. All of my adrenalin's pumping. And the area's just a field of boulders—one of the hardest places to fish there is. I don't pretend to be a light-tackle fisherman, though, in that area. I've got a thirteen-foot rod and thirty-pound-test line. With the long rod you get the line up in the air and clear a lot of the rocks.

My main thought is that I probably had a good bass. The only thing I could figure, because it ran so far, was that I must have had it foul hooked. So, I want to pull, but I don't want to pull too hard. I want to get this son-of-a-gun. I started working, and it's coming pretty good. Then it takes off again! This is another really good run. We speak in terms of striped bass with a great deal of awe. But, in all honesty, pound-for-pound they're not the greatest fighting fish in the ocean. I've had some big fish come in like logs, but just getting them on is what counts. So, you're always nervous with fish, and I'm getting really nervous now. My mind is really starting to think—two long screaming runs. I've caught bass weighing up to fifty-two pounds and even that one didn't run quite this far. A striper will make a good initial run, but the runs always get shorter. For it to make two long runs, it obviously has to be foul hooked.

So, I work it in again. Time's starting to slide by a little bit. Bass just don't last long. I mean, ten or fifteen minutes, you've got them, unless you're using light gear or something.

I still haven't seen the fish. It's dark—moonlight. I'm working it, and it smokes off again. A little shorter run this time. I still just can't believe how much strength this fish has left. It'd come in pretty good, but it'd be able to swim away again. At the time, I didn't know what it was. I was using a big wooden surface swimmer fishing off the point. I had no reason to believe that you would catch anything there except bass.

WHIT MANTER

I'm finally starting to believe that this is a good fish. I don't know how many prayers I said 'cause the area is just strewn with boulders. It's just one big boulder field.

Finally, I'm a little tired. My arms are starting to hurt a bit. But I got this fish coming, and finally it comes up and boils in the surf. It's only about ten yards in front of me. For the first time I can see it, and I can see how *big* it is. I was euphoric; this thing is bigger than any striped bass that's ever been caught before. It looked six or seven feet long. The only thing that matters is if it was a bass, it's the biggest one that's ever been caught. No question! And the fish is beat. It's coming real, real hard but steady. It's not jerking or doing anything that's going to cut the line on a rock.

My euphoria only lasted a second or two. It came up and boiled, then it disappeared. Then it was back up and I could clearly see the outline of fins in the moonlight. When it boiled once, all I could see was how long it was. I couldn't see the fins. Then it cut in the moonlight just right and I could see the outline perfectly: It was a shark!

I felt both letdown and relieved. At least I knew what it was. Anytime you hook something, you want to know what the hell it is. Say I'd lost it between the two times I saw it, what a story I'd be telling: "It was the biggest bass that ever lived." Anyway, this shark has one of my favorite plugs. He sure wasn't going to get my plug if I could help it!

I brought the shark in the last ten yards. Then Tom and I pulled it up on the edge of the surf and looked at it. Landing a fish that size under those conditions takes a lot of luck. This was my greatest angling feat of catching something on rod and reel. It weighed two hundred twelve pounds and was seven feet nine inches long.

Whit's shark was a true sand shark. Not the sand shark often called a dogfish by surf fishermen. The sand shark, Carcharias littoralis, *is usually a warm brown color sometimes blotched. Common from Cape Cod to Hatteras, they feed on small fish and, to a lesser extent, on squid and crustacea.*

This is my best fish story. You think the shark was good? This is the good one! This is really a story about bird watching; and then it's a story about fishing; and then it's a story about bird watching again.

It's the second week of September, several years ago. Five of us are out bird watching. We're doing what we call a century run or a big day. What we do is go out for the entire day—from daylight 'til after dark—and see how many different bird species we can find on Martha's Vineyard. We all met at Dick Sargent's. He's one of the old men of birding on the Vineyard, and he's been doing this for twenty-odd years. He was doing a bird count during September. Just recently, Vern Laux and I have been helping him out. From Dick's house on Quitsa we head down to the Chilmark town beach parking lot at Squibnocket. There were five of us. We're looking for ducks and any unusual gulls. We're counting off the different birds we see. Three black scoter over here, twenty common eiders over there, a flock of herring gulls, a couple of ringbills, a blackback gull. I take my 'scope and I scan along the shore west to the Mussel Bed. I see a fish fin only ten to fifteen yards off the beach. Now, you know we're bird watching, but I've done quite a bit of fishing in my life. I've spent quite a bit of time offshore chasing swordfish and tuna fish and whatever. So I'm used to seeing fish fins, but not here. I'm yelling at the other guys, "Hey, look at this down here!" It was about a hundred yards down the beach to the west. We're just in the town parking lot looking down that way, and all I could see is this big fish fin. I thought it was a swordfish at first by the way it was acting.

Vern got the idea that we've got to go and try to catch it. I didn't even think twice. We went running down the beach and stripped down to our underwear. We waded in after it to waist-deep water. Fortunately, when I got closer to it, I realized it was a tuna fish and not a swordfish. If it had been a swordfish, I'd probably be permanently injured.

We never thought to get a club, a stick, a piece of rope—anything. We must've looked like a couple of barbarians who hadn't eaten in a month. It was just us and the fish, and the fish looked pretty impressive. Obviously, there was something wrong with it. Its navigational equipment was screwed up. Tuna are usually a few miles offshore. This bluefin was just swimming in lazy circles, not far off the beach. Vern and I hadn't really thought about how we were going to catch this fish. A tuna fish is not too easy to grab. The only place you can grab one is right next to the tail. So we think if we can get outside of it, we can head it toward the beach. The tuna just didn't seem to change its pattern. It would come swimming by and it'd scare you half to death.

We have to do something. So, the two of us jump on it. Both of us are trying to get our hands by the tail. When we grabbed it, it was obvious that this fish, although its navigational equipment might not be working, was still physically sound. It knocked both of us right off. Vern and I are not little people. I weigh a little more than two hundred pounds and I'm more than six feet tall. Vern is larger than I am. We tried to grab it by the tail and it just flipped us. We couldn't do it. The footing was tough and the fish would just thrash and break free. Vern hurt his hand; I hurt my foot—but not badly.

Yet when the fish would break our grip, it wouldn't swim off. It would just go back swimming in a lazy circle again. What we finally did was grab it by the tail and point it toward the beach. In breaking free, it would drive itself closer to the beach. We grabbed it and turned it to the beach two more times. Now it's do or die. We've either got it or we don't. We grab it by the tail again. Neither of us let go. Finally, we got better footing. The fish is just throwing water and sand everywhere. I have sand in my eyes, sand in my ears, just everywhere. But we got it! We've won. We're hauling this son-of-a-gun out of the surf. Here we are jumping up and down in our underwear by this tuna fish. It was quite a sight!

We decide to load the tuna into my truck. We want to keep some of it to eat and, obviously, we had no means of processing the fish. So the other guys are going to continue the bird count, while I take the fish to Poole's Fish Market in Menemsha.

So I head into Menemsha. I put my pants on; that was about it. I had sand caked in my hair and in my ears. I didn't even put my shoes on. I pull into the fish market. I blow the horn. Mr. Poole saunters out. He figures I must have a load of bass in the truck. I said, "Nope. Not this time. I got a *tuna fish!*" He laughed pretty hard. Tuna live out in the ocean.

So I struck a deal with Mr. Poole. He would cut up the fish, keep some for himself, and give the rest to us.

Vern and I were quite proud of ourselves. We don't expect to do it again. This was probably a once-in-a-lifetime opportunity. We made the most of it. We're pretty tough guys—or we thought we were. We figured this fish weighed at least two hundred pounds—maybe two twenty-five to two hundred fifty pounds. Well, I'm embarrassed to say—but I'm not going to lie—that the fish weighed a hundred thirty-seven pounds. Remember the number. We haven't come to the highlight of the story yet.

The village of Menemsha is abuzz with my great story. But I leave. I can't hang around. I left the fish at Poole's and took off. I've got to go find the rest of the bird watchers, so I head for Gay Head. I finally catch up with them and tell them the details.

After a long day, from dawn until dark bird watching and the tuna fish episode, we sit down and have a couple of cocktails, and count the number of bird species. Well, as it turns out, we saw one hundred thirty-seven species on Martha's Vineyard that day. *No lie!* One hundred thirty-seven—the highest number recorded on the Vineyard in one day. And we had a hundred-thirty seven-pound tuna fish.

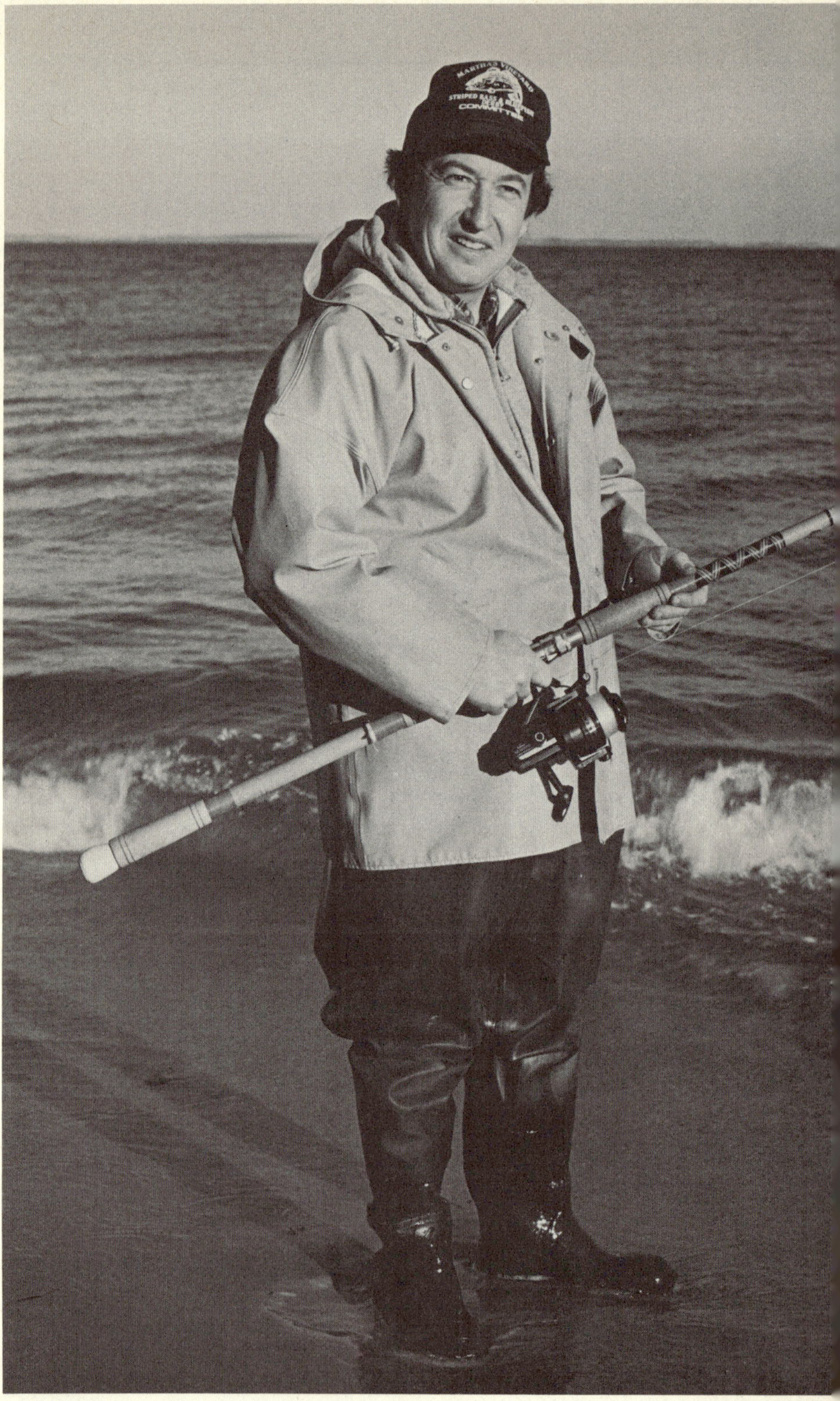
MARTHA'S VINEYARD
STRIPED
COMMITTEE

3

Kevin Hearn

Only one vehicle, a pickup truck belonging to Kevin Hearn, stood in the parking lot at Mink Meadows Beach near the Goff house. Although he primarily fishes along the North Shore, few people have seen him skillfully casting eels along its mysterious rocky shore. His piscatorial accomplishments are rarely witnessed.

Joining me for a fishing expedition were two dedicated surf fishermen, Sherm Goldstein and David Finkelstein. For years we had hoped to catch Kevin fishing on the North Shore. Approaching the jetties, we scanned the beach. Kevin was not visible. Like disappointed children, who just missed shaking hands with Ted Williams, we were almost insulted he would think of leaving without sharing some of the information that makes him excel.

Preserving his need for secrecy, Kevin hid from us in the dunes with two large stripers flattening the beach grass. If there were no dunes at Mink Meadows, it wouldn't have surprised me if Kevin tucked a bass under each arm, took a deep breath, and submerged himself in the chilly salt water. Sitting on the ocean floor with the tiny sand fleas, scavenger crabs, and listless seaweed he would wait until we passed by. Then, unseen by us, he would make a wet dash for his truck.

The first fish I caught from the beach was at Makonikey. I was about ten years old. I was with my father Kenneth, Sr. He had fished for a long time. He was working for the phone company. He often was away in Nantucket because there were some big projects going on there. We were fishing down by Split Rock. I can't remember the conditions at the time. I know it was probably just about dusk. The fish, a striper, weighed around ten pounds.

I didn't get to catch many stripers, even though there were plenty of them around. I just wasn't good enough. I tried hard, but there's just so many little things that you have to know about fishing. Many things you've got to learn by yourself. After I caught a fish from the beach, though, I got much more interested in fishing. From then on it was a slow uphill battle. Success didn't come overnight. There was hard work involved.

Twenty-six years ago there were a couple of outstanding surf fishermen—Buddy Oliver and Owen Rabbitt. I finally got up enough courage to talk to them because they really weren't close friends of mine. I knew about them because of their surf-fishing reputations.

I was about fifteen. I knew if I got a negative response from them I'd feel kind of stupid. So, I had to lead up to talking to them gradually. I went out of my way to say "hi." I never met them on the beach too much because those kind of guys were too secretive. Finally I broke the ice with them.

I didn't necessarily ask them about a style of fishing, like what kind of plugs they used. I wanted to know what to look for. I went after what they had deep down inside that made them successful.

So, they told me some things about the tides and the winds. The tide and wind determine if the bait will school in a certain spot. Sometimes the bait was there and the fish were other places. But, those guys knew where the fish would be, just based on the conditions.

You have to learn for yourself. You've got to find your own spots. I knew they fished certain areas like West Chop, Makonikey, and Gay Head. I knew one of them did really well at West Chop. After a while, he told me where he fished there.

Many people keep fishing logs; I decided to write the stuff down about the tides, the winds and the moon, but then I stopped because it got kind of involved. Once I had the experience of really catching some fish, I didn't have to write it down. I could remember it.

Owen and Buddy both told me that you had to do it yourself. There are certain techniques for keeping bait off the bottom. There's a certain distance to avoid skates. I tried all that stuff. I went to South Beach for a couple of Derbies, and I didn't catch any fish at all. I said, "That's it!" I was going to start my own little routine and it was going to be eels. So back then, when I was about eighteen, I started using eels.

Eel fishing has been described by my wife, Pia, as "earthworms on a grand scale." My early experiences with eel fishing never gave me the self-taught knowledge that would lead to future success. I spent many nights fascinated by the glistening intricate shapes my eel would form as it wrapped itself around my leader and line. The contortions were truly clever. I was often reminded of some triple-jointed, side-show carnival entertainer entangling her arms, legs, and torso into such a knot of flesh that it looked like several people had been glued together. The knotted eel balls of gray–black slime were of such a wondrous variety they could fill a unique sporting-goods store. Softballs, hardballs, tennis balls—all with a little smile and beady eyes. I vowed never to fish with eels again.

Vlad Evanoff, a striped bass aficianado, said about the history of striped bass and eels:

"The lowly eel has been used in one form or another to catch striped bass in salt water for at least 150 years. Anglers fishing during the early and middle 1800s in New England and at Montauk, New York, used eel tails and metal squids covered with eel skins to catch stripers on handlines by the heave-and-haul method. Throughout the 1800s anglers used eel tails and eel-skin lures while casting for striped bass. Then, toward the end of that century, they discovered that live eels were even more effective than dead ones.

KEVIN HEARN

The use of live eels died out or rather never really became popular during the early 1900s. Around the mid-1950s fishing with live eels spread rapidly all along the East Coast, from Maine to Chesapeake Bay."

Kevin has become one of the masters of the eel. Combining the desire to excel at an activity and an uncanny ability to read the water, he has changed a stomach-churning fishing experience into an art.

Few people on the Island were using eels back in the 1960s. Fishermen were casting lures and bottom fishing with cut bait. The people who were using eels fished them on the bottom. So that's what I did. I didn't have very good luck at it, and the other people really didn't have good luck at it, either.

After I got into eels, I got a little disgusted with bottom fishing because I got lazy fishing eels on the bottom. So I figured I'd try something different with the eels: I would cast and retrieve them.

There were many things I had to learn about eels; and I guess it worked out well. I think I developed a good reputation for fishing with eels. I know how to keep them; and I know how to catch fish with them. After a period of trial and error, I finally started to hook into some nice fish with eels.

One technique I learned was to put them asleep before attempting to hook them. Don't kill them and don't try to put them on fully alive. By giving them a little whack on the head or tail on the edge of a bucket or rock, it numbs them up enough to switch them around and hook them. If they're moving around too much you can stick your finger. If fish are around or the signs look good, that's the last thing you want to do.

I grab the eel about two or three inches behind the head to get the leverage to hook it right. I like to hook them from underneath and come right up between their eyes.

I use a small hook. I'm not tuna fishing. I use a No. 5/0 or No. 6/0. If a bass is very finicky when it grabs an eel, even though it hits ferociously, it generally grabs the eel by the head. An eel with a No. 8/0 hook in it is going to feel funny, and the bass is going to drop it. I'm not going to have very good success with a great big hook.

It's more difficult to cast an eel than it is a plug. People can outcast me, especially in the wind when they put on a popping plug to get more distance. I cast hard to get out as far as I can. Most of the time I'm at least halfway in, no matter how far I cast out, before I get a fish.

Many people don't know what to do after they cast the eel out there. They say, "I'll just let it sit there and let it go with the tide." When I first started, that's what I used to do: Let it sit before I started reeling. Then I would really get hung up because the first thing an eel's going to do is head right for the rocks or seaweed and hide. So now when I cast, as soon as it hits the water, I move it—just enough to give the eels some direction toward the beach.

It takes experience to successfully fish an eel. I've had people say, "Oh, I'll take your grass off your line." Then they take the grass off the line and spend five minutes studying my rig. Granted the rig is important, but it's how you use the rig that is more important. I really couldn't ask anybody how to use it. I had to learn by trial and error.

People often ask me when should they set the hook. Should they set it right away or wait a little, letting the fish make a run and swallow the eel? Many times fish run and drop the eel. And usually they drop it because the hook's too big, your leader isn't on the right kind of set-up, or there's too much tension on the line. The bass says to itself, "Something's screwy with this eel. Something's wrong." With a nice sleek rig, though, the bass hits the eel on the head. I let him think that the eel is just going where he wants him to go. I've got to be quick. I don't fool around. I flip the bail quickly. I've got to have the "feel."

My rod tip's always high. When I have a hit, I have a split second to flip the bail. When that fish hits, he's going fast. He's flying. You can see how fast the rod tip goes down if you don't flip the bail. When I feel the initial bump, I lower the rod tip and flip the bail immediately; then grab that line. My fingers are on that line at all times. The fish runs with the eel in its mouth. If you had a picture of it, you'd see the tail would be sticking out of the mouth of the bass. I like to have the fish swallow the eel. If my execution is good, I won't have any problem hooking the fish. Landing him is a whole different ball game. But hooking bass, that's the whole secret of eels.

After that crucial time of having the fish hit and then having it keep the eel in its mouth, the fish stops, swallows the eel and takes off again. His first run can be three to ten seconds long. There's a lot of things I have to consider before I decide how long I want to let him run. If I hook the bass in the belly I've got a good chance of landing the fish. If I hook him in the jaw, my chances are fifty-fifty of landing him without the hook coming out. So , I keep my fingers on the line. When he slows down a little bit, I let him have it. I let that tip go right down. When I set back, the drag is tight enough so it won't break the line. Every three casts, I check my drag. Drags are never perfect. And I've lost a lot of fish by not checking my drag.

Many times fish drop it, and very seldom will they come back. I think the fish says, "There's something really fishy with that. I'm getting out of here."

When I'm fishing, I know the rocks. I know where to stand. I know where to direct my eel when I'm casting. It takes experience to recognize a ripple or a couple of rocks that make up a nice eddy where the bait just hangs. Even though it may be dark, I always know where I am. I swear a fish will head for the rocks. He's not stupid. After you hook him, you still have to bring him in. You learn from experience and from making mistakes.

I also catch bluefish with eels. I've tried two-hooking them. The double hook is terrible. A bluefish seems to hit in the middle. When you bring in the eel, you see a mark four inches from the tail and a mark four inches from the head. You end up with two pieces of eel on two hooks.

I like to fish for bluefish the same way I fish for bass. I think the whole secret is to throw the bail quickly. Let the fish run. A fish won't know what's going on. It thinks it's grabbed an eel. They're just going to swallow it while they're running. But if you're holding it in and there's resistance, it's not like the natural thing, so the blue is going to chomp, chomp, chomp until there's an inch of eel left. Don't be afraid to cast that eel again. When he gets this remaining piece, figure it must have it in his mouth. You've got to set quickly. Don't get frustrated fishing for bluefish with eels because it works.

To the right of the path leading to Stonewall Beach a small sailboat rests on the embankment, tenuously stored for the southeasters that may blow in during the off-season. Even the slightest breeze causes the halyard to bang against the aluminum mast. This marks the spot I bottom fish at Stonewall. While fishing chunks of fresh mackerel on the bottom at the top of a late night tide, I have landed stripers that weighed about thirty pounds each.

To the left of the path is Stonewall Point. Covered with round, slick weed-covered rocks, it forms an ideal home for baitfish in their usually fruitless attempt to avoid hungry bass and marauding bluefish. During periods of the southern migration in the fall, it is a favorite feeding area for different game fish. Blitzes, although not common, have occurred here. Bass had been schooling off the point for several days. If a storm didn't change the conditions by driving the bait into deeper water, the potential for a blitz increased at dusk. Kevin Hearn knew this, so he arrived with his eels shortly before the sun set on a late October day.

Speaking about eels reminds me of several stories. One that particularly sticks in my mind was a blitz at Stonewall Beach.

When I left the house that night, it was an ordinary night after the Derby. When I got to Stonewall, I was surprised; I found a lot of company. So much company that I really couldn't find a spot on the beach. I got to the point and I looked toward Squibnocket and back toward Edgartown, and there wasn't an awful lot of room. I just stayed up on the bank and watched. It was before dark when I got there, and I wasn't excited about having company. Just at dark, I decided to make my move and wiggle in between a couple of guys. I didn't want our lines to cross. Sometimes the fish up there have a tendency to run to the side rather than straight out.

The water wasn't terribly rough that night. I think it was fairly clear, and you could see the people along the beach. They were whipping plugs out there left and right. I knew the fish would be in there soon because they had been during the past two or three nights. So, my eel went out there. It no sooner hit the water than I had a run. I kept my rod down because I didn't want to get the guy next to me saying, "Look, he's already got one." When I'm catching fish like that, there'd be so many people around me, it would just choke me. I can't fish like that.

I set the hook with the rod down and out. I played that fish. It was hard getting him in there. It was about a twenty-five or thirty-pounder. The guys standing six feet away from me never knew I caught a fish. So I nonchalantly reached my hand down and grabbed him by the gills. With an eel, by the time the fish comes in, it's pretty tired out. There's not a lot of flopping around. If you grab him quick and hard, and keep his tail in the water, he really won't make a lot of noise. So I just walked up on the beach, right up the bank, and found a spot away from the path where nobody would trip over it. Then, without a flashlight, I took the hook out. When I got home that night, my hand wasn't bloody, but it was very, very scratchy.

I went back down to my spot. The next cast no sooner hit the water than I had another one! I brought it in again. This time I wasn't sure whether they saw me or not. I said to myself, "If they saw me, I'm going to be in deep trouble." I think the person on my right was getting a little curious because I walked to the bank again.

Then I went back down again and the fish I had stashed started flopping around the beach. I think a couple of people might've heard it or figured out what was going on. By then, I had to change the eel because there wasn't much left. So the next cast—*baam!* I had another one. Then the other fishermen started to realize what was going on.

So, I went up to this other spot and within a couple of casts, I had a couple of hits and lost them. And then *baam!* I caught another one. This is my fourth fish. I wasn't about to hide anything. It was dark then. I just wanted to be left alone. I really wanted to catch fish, but I wasn't that excited about catching fish with everybody there. If you catch a fish, you want to get that fish off and go back to the same spot. The fourth fish was a little bigger, about thirty-five pounds. I put him up with the others. Then, I went down to the right where it was real shallow. And *baam*, I caught another one.

Then I ran into Whit Manter. And he said, "I've been here half an hour, and I haven't caught a thing. How are you doing?" I said, "Well, this is my fifth."

"You're kidding me! You can't have five fish!"

"I've got five fish," I said.

"You're using eels?"

"Yeah. They must be thick out there. They have been during the past few days."

"Well, boy, I got a couple of taps and that's all."

I told Whit to save me a spot while I put the fifth fish up on the beach. So we stayed right there and people kept their distance. I had no sooner made a cast and I had another one. That was my sixth.

I finally said to Whit, "Look, would you like some eels?" He said, "You know, I've got a ton of them, but I haven't got any with me."

"I've got plenty. No problem."

"I haven't got any hooks."

"Don't worry about it. I've got plenty of hooks."

I gave him a hook and an eel. Well, wouldn't you believe that he caught five, and I didn't catch any. And he was right next to me. I don't know what it was.

After he caught five stripers, I started catching them again. We were going back and forth. Well, don't you know he ended up catching more fish than I did that night. I think he caught ten or eleven. I had nine or ten; I was one behind him.

Everybody next to me had been plugging. I think they caught a few. Down at the other end they were catching some fish. There was a gang down there that had a bunch of fish strung up. All their fish weighed between fifteen and twenty pounds. There were about eight guys fishing and they got maybe thirteen fish.

I had told my wife that I'd be home in an hour or two, and I didn't get home until after midnight. She was almost ready to call the Coast Guard. It was great fishing. We worked hard catching the fish, then lugging them to the truck.

The Tisbury Great Pond on the south side of West Tisbury is seldom opened to the ocean by the pounding surf. In 1985, Hurricane Gloria pushed the surf across the sand into the pond and, with it, oysters, herring, and eels. The riparian owners open the pond about four times a year, when the water level in the pond reaches forty-two inches. (In the late 1960s, the owners often delayed the opening until after the Derby to discourage the hordes of surf-fishing fanatics who would camp on the beach.)

Kevin has watched water rushing from the opening bend east, down-Island, or west, up-Island, depending on the formation of the sand bar offshore. I learned how important reading the water could be at dawn in the late fall. As I fished the opening where the water was running from the pond, Bernie Arruda arrived. He looked at the water, saw a rip running parallel to the beach for fifty yards, then took almost a ninety-degree turn straight out. He cast a large swimming plug at the bend in the rip. Within fifteen minutes he landed two stripers topping thirty pounds. Bernie didn't have to say a word. He was my quiet secret teacher; I was the tired perplexed student.

I have been at the opening in some totally miserable weather. Cold drenching rains often tested the waterproofness of my slicker and waders. Damp fogs often rolled in covering my eyeglasses with a fine mist that only windshield wipers would efficiently remove. I don't like to fish when there is lightning, however. That's one reason I wasn't fishing the opening with Kevin during a driving northeaster.

There is another story that really stands out when I planned on fishing alone, which I usually do, but ran into somebody. I went fishing at the West Tisbury opening in a northeaster. It was a brutal night in early November. A night that people really should've been home rather than out fishing. It was another one of those evenings that I told my wife I'd be back in about an hour or two.

The wind was at my back and blowing a gale, but the surf was fairly calm. On the way down I could see a big bunch of gulls working a half mile offshore. There was one other Jeep there; it belonged to Tom Norton.

I knew the fish were going to come in because it looked like there was a tremendous amount of bait out there. Hundreds of gulls were working over the bait. Tom told me he hadn't caught anything. He was plugging with his conventional surf-casting rod and reel. I haven't seen too many people do that in recent times, but Tom was good at it. He likes the style of fishing with conventional gear.

I told him, "Just hold on because they're going to be coming in." We waited maybe twenty minutes. Here I am with my eels, and there's Tom Norton with his plugs. Well, Tom catches the first fish. I said, "Son of a gun, they're coming in; they're coming in!" He takes the fish off; takes him five minutes. It was a striped bass. He comes walking nonchalantly back down; goes out there; casts out again and he's got another one. "What am I doing wrong?" I say to myself "Something's screwy here." But I stayed in my spot. Tom went by me again with a fish, came back down and asked, "Kevin, you want to try my spot?" I said, "Nope. I'm going to stay right here because I'm going to catch a fish."

Well, he no sooner got his plug out there again and he gets his third fish. Now I said, "Something's got to change." So, he came back again; he said, "Would you like to try my spot?" I said, "Sure, I'd love to." So he took over my spot, and I took over his spot. He got his fourth fish. I hadn't had a hit. I said, "Hey, something's really wrong here." It was dark; and I was casting a long way out because the wind was at my back. But he had a Stan Gibbs on, which will really fly when you cast out with a wind at your back. I think he was casting forty to fifty yards farther than I was. He was telling me as soon as his plug hit the water, he'd have a fish. I couldn't get a hit, but I did happen to have some plugs with me that night. And I did switch. That was the only time that I can ever remember switching from eels to plugs because I wasn't catching anything.

That opening can be a funny place to fish. At times the fish are right inside the bowl; this time they were outside.

We ended up catching quite a few fish. Tom ended up with about fifteen fish. I had about thirteen. His biggest was around forty-five pounds; mine was just more than forty. But they all weighed more than thirty—all nice fish.

I was fishing the opening on the south side because it was a northeaster late in the fall when the fish have left the north side. After mid-October, they hang on the south side. I've had good fall fishing early on the North Shore, but then it stops. You don't get the quantity of fish that you do on the south side.

We could hear guys on the other side of the opening; the down-Island side. One guy started to come over. We could see the guy's flashlight. The opening was big and deep. Tom and I were concerned because he had tried to wade over before, especially when we were making a lot of noise. The light got closer and closer. All of a sudden, we see a light go up in the air and disappear. Our hearts were in our throats. He had fallen in the opening, but had managed to pull himself out of the water before drowning. He was very lucky. He didn't come back. He must have been so frustrated to try wading across. They just couldn't reach the fish from the other side.

I think everybody has a goal. I had a goal to do something different about fishing and be successful. But there was one thing I hadn't done. I hadn't caught a fifty-pounder! I'd come so close—forty-nine, forty-nine-and-a-half, forty-eight. I wanted to do it on the North Shore. I concentrated on the North Shore during the Derby, then switched to the south side, even though I was known as a North Shore fisherman.

One time I was fishing Squibnocket, up from the bass stand; a long walk from the parking lot. I was getting some nice fish there. I was fishing right alongside Ralph Sherman who works down at the grain store. He had told me some good stories about fishing up there. Well, all of a sudden, I heard him screaming: "I can't believe this! I can't believe this!" I was on my favorite rock. I came all the way in. I said, "You all right?" "Yeah, yeah," he answered, "You won't believe this. Look at this." The night before I had lost some fish. His fish had a whole bunch of nylon line in its mouth. It had my leader, and it had my hook, and it still had my eel that I had lost the previous night. And Ralph had caught it with his favorite plug. He was getting very frustrated because he couldn't get that plug out of the fish's mouth because it was so tangled up.

Something like that made the night special, but I still didn't get my fifty-pounder. Well, the next night I finally caught my first fifty-pounder. That was in 1978. So I was very proud. The next three years in a row, I caught a fish weighing about fifty pounds, with one exception.

I was up at Squibnocket, again in the fall. Two nights in a row I caught fifty-pounders. The third night I had one on that felt much more powerful. It took me a *long* time getting it in; it made several runs. It made three very long runs. I was very concerned about my line holding up. It was lip-hooked; not gut-hooked. If it were gut-hooked, it wouldn't have fought as much. This one gave me a good fight. And it was at a tricky spot.

Finally, I got it in. This fish measured about fifty-four inches long. It had a gut on it like it had swallowed four or five ten-pound tautog. It was just massive. When I got it home, my wife took pictures. We weighed it in the garage. I got on a bathroom scale to get my weight. Then I grab the fish in a bear hug. The fish weighed sixty-three-and-a-half-pounds. She looked at me and said, "Do you want to mount it?" "Nope," I said. "I'm not going to mount it. I'm going to sell it." At that time it was either sell it or mount it. I didn't sell it for the money. I just sold it because I thought, "There's a bigger one out there." Now I think maybe I should've mounted that fish. That's the biggest striper I've ever caught.

I caught these fish around the Squibnocket area, Gay Head, and Long Beach—all after the Derby. I wanted to get a big one on the North Shore. So I said, "I'm not going to go to the south side for a year. I'm going to go to the North Shore and stick it out." I stuck it out that next year, and I got some forty-pounders but no fifty-pounder.

So in 1981 I fished the south side again. I was at Squibnocket. I had a fish on. It was brutal. Big waves; a heavy surf. Squibnocket is brutal in a heavy surf. I was on a rock. This fish came up with a wave, hit me below the knees, and knocked me off the rock.

The fish was still on. I knew it was hooked. I still had my rod. My waders were filled with water. I had an awful time getting up again. I wouldn't let go of my rod. Luckily I was between the rock and the beach. I was a little concerned about the undertow taking me out beyond that rock. If I went beyond that rock, I'd be in deep trouble. I'd have to let go of my rod, the fish, everything! I'd have to swim for my life! I think that was one of the times that I was very, very scared. I was all alone. There was nobody around. All these things were running through my mind. "Should I really go for this fish? Is a fifty-pounder worth it? Is it a fifty-pounder?" I didn't know, but I knew it was big.

Finally, I grabbed the fish. I gave the fish a bear hug, I put my hands in his gills and then I was back on my feet. For a while, though, when I had him hugged like this, I went under again and I was completely wet. I lost my favorite fishing hat, soaked my light, and ruined my waders, because they got pierced by the dorsal fin.

I got him to the beach and I thought, "That's a nice fish!" When I got home, the fish weighed fifty-four-and-a-half pounds. That was it for the year. I didn't go back anymore. I was lucky.

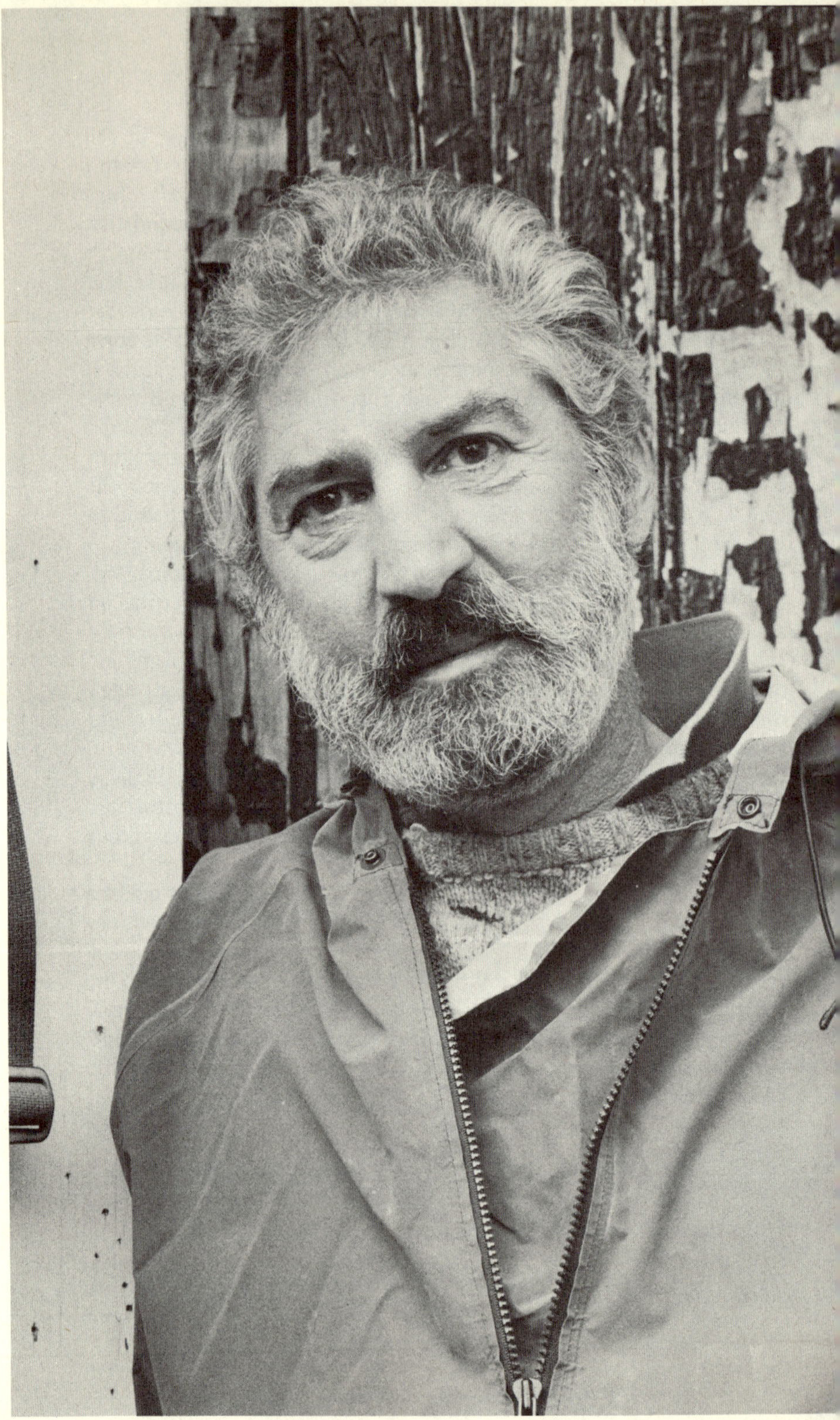

4

Roberto Germani

Roberto Germani is called by the sound of the surf. Strange forces from the ocean tides generated by the earth, moon, and sun pull at him constantly, distracting him during his deepest sleep. The forces call him to the shore, where he wanders between the high and low water marks. Transfixed by onrushing waves as they break over the offshore bars, their swirling waters carrying mysterious creatures and flotsam, he will step off into the surf zone.

His fixation with the sea's edge is an obsession. As a man possessed, he often reminds me of Christine Gordon in the 1943 horror classic, I Walked With a Zombie. *The wife of a rich plantation owner on a Caribbean island suffered a strange malady. She would often sit up suddenly in her bed, rising out of a deep sleep. In a trancelike state, she would open the doors leading from the house, disappearing into the jungle, drawn closer and closer to the zombie masters who call her with their voodoo dolls and drums.*

Roberto is almost without willpower to his callings. Unseen striped bass and bluefish pull at him day and night—voodoo fish in the hypnotically beautiful waters that surround the Vineyard.

ROBERTO GERMANI

His lack of willpower was noted by sportswriter Les Boyd in the May 30, 1979, edition of The Providence Journal:

Bob Germani has been getting out of bed at two every morning, dressing quietly and leaving his room.

His van, loaded with surf rods, lures, waders and all the other paraphernalia of surf fishing is waiting in the parking lot outside the building.

An hour later he can be found somewhere in the white water that rims the Rhode Island shoreline, casting for striped bass and bluefish.

Nothing unusual about that. A lot of guys get up early to go surf fishing.

But not from hospital beds.

He didn't go this morning. He couldn't persuade his doctor that he ought to be out surf fishing on the very day he is scheduled for surgery.

When I was a little boy, I used to see surf fishermen on the beaches of Rhode Island. It seemed like a nice thing to do. I hoped that I could try surf fishing one day. Years went by before I had the opportunity. I was about forty years old, and I had just returned from living in London. I asked two old friends of mine, who were surf fishermen, to take me. I said, "Show me what the hell this is about. This is a childhood fantasy of mine."

The first place I went fishing was in Tiverton, Rhode Island, with my buddy Vinnie. I used a ten-and-a-half-foot Berkeley rod with a little spinning reel. My friend Eddie showed me what plugs to get. This particular day I used a blue-and-white Atom swimmer.

We went out on this rocky outcropping late in the afternoon. I caught a striped bass that weighed about eight pounds. Catching this fish stirred something very primal in me. I became obsessed. I was hooked on surf fishing. I immediately devoted all my spare time to fishing. It seemed to fulfill some long unmet need going back to when I was a little kid and said: "This is how adults play."

I've always felt as if I'm in the wrong century. I would like to have been born a thousand or twenty thousand years ago. I'm very idealistic. I'm a very primitive sort of person. If I could have chosen when I was born, I would have said, "Put me in the middle of a rain forest and let me wear a feather in my head. I'll take a life span of thirty-five." Surf fishing satisfies my primitive needs. I've always loved the marine environment. I feel like I'm married to the lip of the sea.

I started fishing every day. I would go after work, or I'd get up at two in the morning and go before work. My obsession was so strong that I couldn't find a fishing partner who could keep up with my pace. I couldn't find anyone willing to devote every minute of their spare time to surf fishing. So I went alone, trying to teach myself by watching where other fishermen were parking their cars. When I found other fishermen I would observe what plugs they were using.

I went fifty-six days without catching another fish. I started fishing at Beaver Tail and worked my way down toward Narragansett Pier. At Beaver Tail I saw a guy catch what I now know is a bonito. I saw the fish and I saw how long it fought. Just the sight of someone else catching a fish drove me on.

Eventually I discovered Matunuck Beach and Deep Hole. It turned out to be one of the best places in Rhode Island to fish. There are mussel shoals that dry out twice a day, causing an algae bloom. The incoming tide floods in with nutrients; it's almost like a cauldron of plankton soup. The water swirls around with baitfish and crabs. When the tide drops all the crabs go underneath the rocks. When the water rises they come out looking for food. It was a very busy place because of that. I caught some nice fish there. One morning several years ago, I caught two thirty-one-pound stripers. Those were the last two bass I kept. I still catch them, but I don't keep them.

Deep Hole can be a treacherous place to fish. To get to the offshore bar most guys fish the bottom half of the tide. You have to wade across a trough of water that's close to chest high. Then you go way out—about one hundred-fifty yards. When you're out there at low tide it's like an island. When the tides come in, two wave formations meet, which causes a good amount of white water. Most guys would fish the bottom half of the tide and get off the bar. Once you went out there, on the top half of the rising tide, you were committed to stay there for that whole six-hour period. A lot of things could happen in six hours: you could get tired; you could get injured; you could fall down and break your wrist. Now you can't get off for six hours because the wave action is pretty rough. It also has a rocky bottom. We'd call the rocks bowling balls. They were all smooth and they moved sometimes. I was always worried about my footing. It was a great place for fishing, though.

I was fishing Deep Hole on a stormy night for bass with an eleven-and-a-half-foot rod and a two-ounce mackerel popper. I used poppers at night because swimming plugs would get pushed in by the waves. It was hard to get the desired action on the swimmers, so I used poppers. I'd work them across the side of a wave. If you fished there long enough you knew how to read the water.

That night, using the mackerel popper, I felt a good-size strike. I thought, "I've got a big bass on!" I would work it in a little bit, and then it would go back out. I'd pull and pull. I'd open the drag all the way and let it run. I fought that thing for maybe a half hour, and didn't know that it wasn't a fish. At first light I saw that I had hooked into a gill net. The tide had brought it around me and I was surrounded by it. I said, "How am I going to get out of here?" When I tried to move off the bar I went down in this gill net. I said, "Now I'm in trouble." I'm holding a rod in one hand and trying to get up, and I'm being pushed this way and that way, by the waves. I thought I was going to die. I struggled to get up. I took out my fishing knife and started hacking at this gill net. Finally, I cut myself free. Then the sun got brighter and brighter and the tide started dropping, and my panic went away. But I cut that gill net up from end to end.

About seven in the morning, the owner of the gill net arrived. He was coming to fetch his net because he knew the storm had taken it and he figured that it would end up where I was fishing. When he saw what I had done to it, he said, "What is going on here?!" "I cut this thing to shreds," I told him. "You ought to know better than to leave a net out in weather like this."

Gill netters also used Deep Hole because it was so productive. In certain weather, it's not a good idea to set the net because it most likely will break away. This guy just didn't give a damn.

ROBERTO GERMANI

In those days most guys kept all the bass they caught. Out on the bar, the fish were usually gaffed and put on a 20-foot-long metal chain stringer. This allowed you to keep fishing, instead of taking the fish all the way back to the beach. These fish floating on stringers at night proved to be a great shark attraction.

Andy Ray, a great fisherman, was out there at night and he was bumped in the leg by something. He looks and thinks he sees an oil-soaked section of a mast in the water. So he kicks it with his leg. And he told me, "About a minute later, *boomp!*" He gets bumped with this thing again. He said, "Oh, this damn log!" He kicked it again, and pushed it with his foot to get it out of the way. He tried to kick it in another direction so the tide would carry it away. He said about a minute later he got another bump on the leg from this same thing. He kicked it again, and it didn't move away instead a tail made a tremendous splash next to him. He said he lost all his cool. He didn't know what he was supposed to do.

When two guys are out together at Deep Hole, if they see a shark they walk to the shore back-to-back and sideways with the butt end of their long rods in front of them to poke the shark off. Andy Ray was alone though. Sometimes when he'd kick it, the shark wove and took a whack back with its tail. Andy estimated that the shark was eight or nine feet long. That's enough to spook you at night. Eventually, it just went off and left him alone. I think the rubber waders may have blocked the human scent and the shark lost interest.

I fished other areas in Rhode Island, including Newport, the Sakonnet River and Point Judith Light. Point Judith Light was discouraging and uncomfortable. There are a lot of square boulders so you can lose fish there very easily. The water's always got a mean chop to it. A lot of guys bang their noggins there. It has a reputation for giving guys bumps and bruises. I did most of my fishing alone at Deep Hole.

I moved to Martha's Vineyard in 1982. I was supervising a detox, a twenty-bed facility for alcoholics in Providence. It was a high-pressure job. Most guys lasted a year. I did two years there. Every day I would drive forty miles to fish at Matunuck in the morning and at night. I was fishing seven days a week. There was no stopping me.

ROBERTO GERMANI

After my Jeep got stolen in Providence, I decided to move to the Vineyard. I had fished the Vineyard surf many times with Greg Joannidi, a teacher at the high school. I told them at work I was leaving. When I first got here, I painted houses and fished the rest of the time. Now I've arranged it so that work doesn't conflict with fishing. I drive school buses during the winter, which gives me four or five hours in the middle of the day; during the summer, I drive the night shuttle, which gives me every day on the beach. I've designed my employment to fit my fishing.

Sitting on my fishing workbench, in a small wooden box that once contained cheddar cheese, I have several gleaming cobalt-chromium dentures that once belonged to the former patients of retired Vineyard Haven dentist, Dr. Maxwell Lewitus. The unusual combination of clasps, palatal bars, white porcelain teeth, and pink acrylic does not resemble any baitfish known to modern marine science. I plan, someday, to drill two small holes in the metal. I will attach a clasp with a barrel swivel to one end and an O-ring with a No. 4/0 hook to the other end, transforming these formerly hard-working prostheses into a new lure—The Choppers. For the nondiscriminating bluefish that may have lost some of its razor sharp teeth in previous encounters with ocean debris, the temptation to lunge for my new Choppers lure may prove to be irresistible.

I was fishing the Cape Poge Gut with a bunch of guys. We were on the north side of the opening across from North Neck. The bluefish were on the other side. We had a contest going with experimental lures. There was a long kitchen wooden spoon and two plastic toy boats. Later we tried a piece of chorizo, which is Portuguese sausage.

My toy boat was black, four or five inches long and two-and-a-half or three inches wide. It had a little man in it and a black-and-silver friction engine in the back. The other boat was about seven inches long and three inches wide. The wooden spoon was twelve to fourteen inches long. Using screw eyes and treble hooks we managed to rig them as lures.

With our big rods rigged with regular poppers we managed to draw the bluefish closer to our side of the Gut. When we saw them getting into range, we all fired the spoon and boats. It was weird because it was a calm day and there was no wind. The spoon didn't show up well in the water, but the two little boats did. As we're reeling them in, a bluefish hit my boat from behind. I could see it clearly. We all screamed; it was like watching a mini-horror show. The little plastic head of the driver went flying off in one direction and the friction engine somewhere else. We fished for a while longer. I think the total fish caught were: small boat, five bluefish; big boat, three bluefish; and kitchen spoon, one bluefish.

Then we decided to try the chorizo. So we took a heavy piece of monofilament, drove it down through the piece of sausage, tied a treble hook on the end of it and cast it out. The bluefish wouldn't touch it. And it was meat.

The next day I took my toy boat to East Beach. There was an old man there fishing alone. He pointed and said, "They're right here." There were a lot of bluefish there. I walked up to him and showed him my toy boat lure. I said, "Do you want to see me catch a fish on that?" And he said to me, "You catch a fish on that, I'm going home!" I said, "Are the fish close?" He said, "Yeah." I said, "Get ready to go home." I threw it out there, and on the first cast a bluefish nailed it and I landed it.

I finally retired the boat, because it was cracking up. Glue and tape could barely hold it together. That shows you, I guess, that on certain days bluefish aren't discriminating at all, and then there are times when they are.

One evening, me, Eddie Amaral, and a couple of other guys were fishing inside Cape Poge Pond just before sunset. The bluefish would only hit a five-eighth-ounce yellow Pencil Popper. We got a blue popper in the same size but it wasn't what the fish wanted. Someone tried a yellow-and-pink Atom popper without success. Nothing worked but that one size and that one color. That's all the blues would take—a five-eighth-ounce yellow Stan Gibbs Pencil Popper. So, bluefish can be as selective as any other fish.

Bluefish were also very selective on flies during the great bluefish blitz of 1984. We had blues up on Lobsterville Beach running fifteen to twenty pounds. The world-record, fly-rod bluefish was taken that year.

The bluefish stayed in the waters off Lobsterville for weeks because the sand eels were there. It was one of those once-in-a-lifetime things. It was the best surf fishing for blues that the Island has ever seen and probably ever will. They were all big fish.

The flies people were using were white, white-and-green, and white-and-silver. One day, the fish kind of went off those colors. Arnold Spofford decided to use a red-and-yellow fly and he started getting them. He said, "Match the hatch," and laughed because that's what trout fishermen say. A couple of nights before, though, he creamed the fish on a small yellow-and-red Rebel. So he just made up some flies on that color idea. He's one hell of a fisherman. He caught four and I caught none. Because of the frustration I was going through, he gave me one of those flies. On my first cast I had a fish. The fishing stayed like that for four days. It had to be red-and-yellow. Then at the end of the fourth day they went back to taking the standard white or white-and-green.

On November 9, 1984, I was flyfishing and caught a thirty-five-pound bass at Dogfish Bar. I knew there were big fish there because I had seen bass defecating in the water. There are a lot of guys who won't believe this, but I learned this a long time ago. When the water's calm and the water's right, you can see a bass defecating. It's mostly oils, with other things mixed in. When a bass defecates it shows as a tiny, tiny circle in the water. If it's very windy, you are not going to see it. The water has to be almost pond calm. The material comes out of the anal vent. It creates a perfect circle because it's coming up from a single point. It's not going to be an irregular shape, unless the water is rough. The tiny circle expands until it's about six or seven feet in diameter, then it dissipates. It doesn't last that long either.

I remember telling some guys from New York about this the next day. They were down on the beach catching blues. I said, "There's bass around here. I've seen them crapping." Some of the guys laughed. They said, "Oh, Germani lost it now. Roberto's mind is gone. You know, he's talking about seeing bass crap!"

But I learned this from a guy named Manny Rose. Forty years ago there was a story and a picture of him in the *Boston Herald*, "Forty bass over forty pounds in one night—Manny Rose." This guy had been watching bass for years. He showed me that trick one night when I was still in Rhode Island. He said, "Don't forget that. Because where they crap is where they're going to stay for a while." I don't know if it's true or not, but he said it.

So, I'd seen the bass defecate up there, and I say, "Oh, good, there's some fish in there." I guess if you see enough of them you can tell what is a big bass and what is a small bass because obviously their size is going to determine the volume of their waste. So I started fishing there pretty heavily. I'm not one to go out fishing in total blackness. I like to start an hour before sunrise. I won't spend much time in the pitch black because then the visual element is gone, and it's like being blind. That spooks me. I like to see the fish. That's why I like to use floating line when I flyfish. And so, I got this one bass that weighed thirty-five pounds. I know that it weighed that much because I happened to have a small scale with me.

One of my theories, which applies to all fish but particularly to bass, is that when they take a fly they often don't even know they're hooked. When they've got a big Danny plug in their mouth, they know something's up. They can even see it sometimes. With a fly it's different. It's almost like you have to romance the fish, putting him into a dreamlike state. So you don't really fight the fish. What you do is kind of mystify him and, as you mystify him, you get him tired, and as he gets more tired and more mystified, he gets into a dream. When he comes to shore, he isn't that alarmed by the whole thing.

I always use plugs or flies. I could never get into baitfishing. I don't like dealing with bait. It's too inactive. Fishing with an eel or something on the bottom is more like fish trapping. If flyfishing is hunting, then baitfishing is trapping. With baitfishing you may wait for the event to happen, rather than actively seek it. I'm too much of a high-energy person to just sit and watch a rod. I probably love fly-fishing so much because of the movement. I love the different elements of flyfishing. There's the aerial element where the line goes out through the air. That's almost an art form. Sometimes I get carried away. I make arabesques in the sky. It's like playing. Then there's the liquid part because fishing is really dealing with the interface of the air and the water. Then there's the fluid part—the water part. How the fly comes back and how the line goes stripping through the water. It's almost like flyfishing is fishing a handline with a fly rod stuck on it.

Although practical conservative fishing techniques will provide successful results, some fishermen seek new ways to frustrate themselves.

In 1947, the Vineyard Gazette *reported the following fish story:*

> A novel method of fishing was being practiced during the week by John Rogers of Cambridge, who took advantage of the prevailing offshore wind to use balloons to carry his line and lure over the water. The balloons used were of fairly small size, say about twice or three times the size of the familiar toy carnival and circus article. They were of various colors, yellow, red and so on, and, aside from the matter of utility, made a pretty sight against the sea.
>
> Ingenious and spectacular as the balloon method was, Mr. Rogers did not make any important catches. It was ironical that his son, arriving for a much shorter stay and using conventional methods, took a good-size bass. . . .

Combining the antiquated heave-and-haul technique with the availability of a modern but well-worn conventional reel, Roberto seeks to increase the challenge of hooking and landing bluefish and bass.

The heave-and-haul technique was popular before saltwater bait-casting multiplier reels were mass produced in the mid-1800s. These reels were expensive. Not all fishermen who wanted to purchase them could afford to do so. For these fishermen heave and haul continued well into the early 1900s.

In the early 1800s a chunk of bait, such as crab, lobster, menhaden or shrimp, was commonly used. After placing the bait on a large hook the fisherman would swing the line around his head and heave it into the surf, then handline it back to shore.

ROBERTO GERMANI

On the beaches of Martha's Vineyard, in 1915, Captain Percy Daniel West would use the heave-and-haul method exclusively, not switching over to rod and reel until the late 1920s. I spoke with Percy several months before his death in September, 1986.

"The bluefish and bass would come in close to the beach," he said. "I would twirl this fine linen line with a tin squid on the end. We wouldn't use bait, but would use a bright shiny squidder. I would pull the line in hand over hand. The line was about 300 feet long. It was a hell of a job getting it out. Not many people could get it out 300 feet. Every time you cast it out you had to have it neatly curled on the beach or it would tangle. I didn't use gloves but sometimes my hands got burned. You had to play the fish very carefully. I liked going out to Wasque and the openings near Wasque. I would go as often as I could."

I think every guy who has fished long enough has always wondered, "What would it feel like to have a fish on a handline?" That's the ultimate when it comes to intimacy. As an intimate weapon, a handline is a step above a fly rod because a fly rod is a handline with a rod stuck on it.

When I started handlining, I used fifty-pound-test squidding line. I also like to use a stripping basket like the kind used in flyfishing. It helps prevent the line from tangling as you twirl it around your head in progressively wider circles until the weight of the lure helps it reach the ideal velocity for releasing it into the water. If you tried to do this with the line coming directly off the spool it would either overrun itself or knot up. Thick monofilament turned out to be too hard to handle. It was always in these big lumpy coils. So I finally thought, "Why not use a fly line section in front?" I've got a whole bunch of used fly lines. I like the idea because I use a floating fly line. Now I can throw a plug out and I could leave it there. My final rig was thirty yards of eight-weight floating fly line, with a three-foot, fifty-pound-test monofilament shock leader attached in front. At the other end I tied on seventy-five yards of fifty-pound-mono backing on an old conventional spool that I wear on a specially designed rubber belt around my waist. I pull the line in hand over hand and take up the slack with the reel spool.

Sometimes this would work at Wasque. There's a section at

Wasque where the water goes out, then part of it comes back into the middle about two hours into the west tide. There's an edge where the water runs in different directions. So I throw a big swimming plug on the water that's moving west, but the fly line is floating, which keeps everything on top. The moving water is causing a big loop in the fly line, so the plug can actually stay in the same spot. I've had plugs stay there and swim for ten minutes. It's like keeping a kite in the air. If you really like to do some lazy plugging, that's the way to do it.

You can also handline live bunker. The technique I use here is a little different. I've got this long section of fly line; at the end of it is a piece of monofilament with a little hook. The hook's in the fish's back. The fly line is actually holding up the monofilament. You can watch where the bunker goes by keeping an eye on the floating fly line. The line keeps the weight of the hook off the fish so it swims upright. It works! And it's exciting.

What I learned from my handline fishing is that you could fish with a pencil as long as you've got the proper feel and other tackle. A rod is used to get the lure, plug or fly out a certain distance and give you a certain amount of control bringing the fish back. But it's mostly for getting it out there. The best kind of rod would be something heavy enough to get the distance you're looking for; then on the retrieve, God would hand you a four-weight fly rod and you could take the fish in.

Some observations I've collected on surf fishing are:
Francis Endicott, in 1897, wrote in "The Striped Bass" in American Game Fish:

> *What matter it if our catch does not rise above the dignity of pan-fish, or even if the proverbial "fisherman's luck" should fall to our lot? We have a day spent in the glorious autumn weather, breathing the balmy air of the Indian summer, tempered and softened as it comes over the salt water, until we feel an exhilaration which will show itself for many days after in a renewed activity of mind and body.*

ROBERTO GERMANI

Roberto Germani, in 1979, Providence Evening Bulletin:

> *I think we're different because we get off on the primitive aspects of the hunt. . . . You're right in the middle of the fish's environment, you're in its territory. Becoming one with the water is as much a part of the experience as catching a bass. I never leave the water unsatisfied, even if I don't catch a thing.*

We need certain things to live, for sustenance; we need air, water, and food. We also need things for the mind. Fishing is so important to me because it gives me insight into myself. I spend a great amount of time alone. Unless you're the type of person who needs a fishing buddy, you're going to spend many hours in dark, mysterious places where forces that have been long submerged and long forgotten come to the fore. You're going to get frightened for no apparent reason. You may see apparitions. You may feel insignificant.

Just being on the way to fishing somewhere is a beautiful experience. Catching a fish is the bonus. One morning I was fishing with a friend at Nauset Beach on Cape Cod. We actually saw a picture of eternity. There was just this first light and a cloud formation; and it hit us both at once. We said, "Damn it, there it is!" I shouldn't say a picture representing eternity, it was a picture of eternity. It was fantastic. I remember another time walking along Nauset, watching a pod of Pilot whales moving along quietly. I wasn't catching any fish. But I wouldn't want to have been any place else.

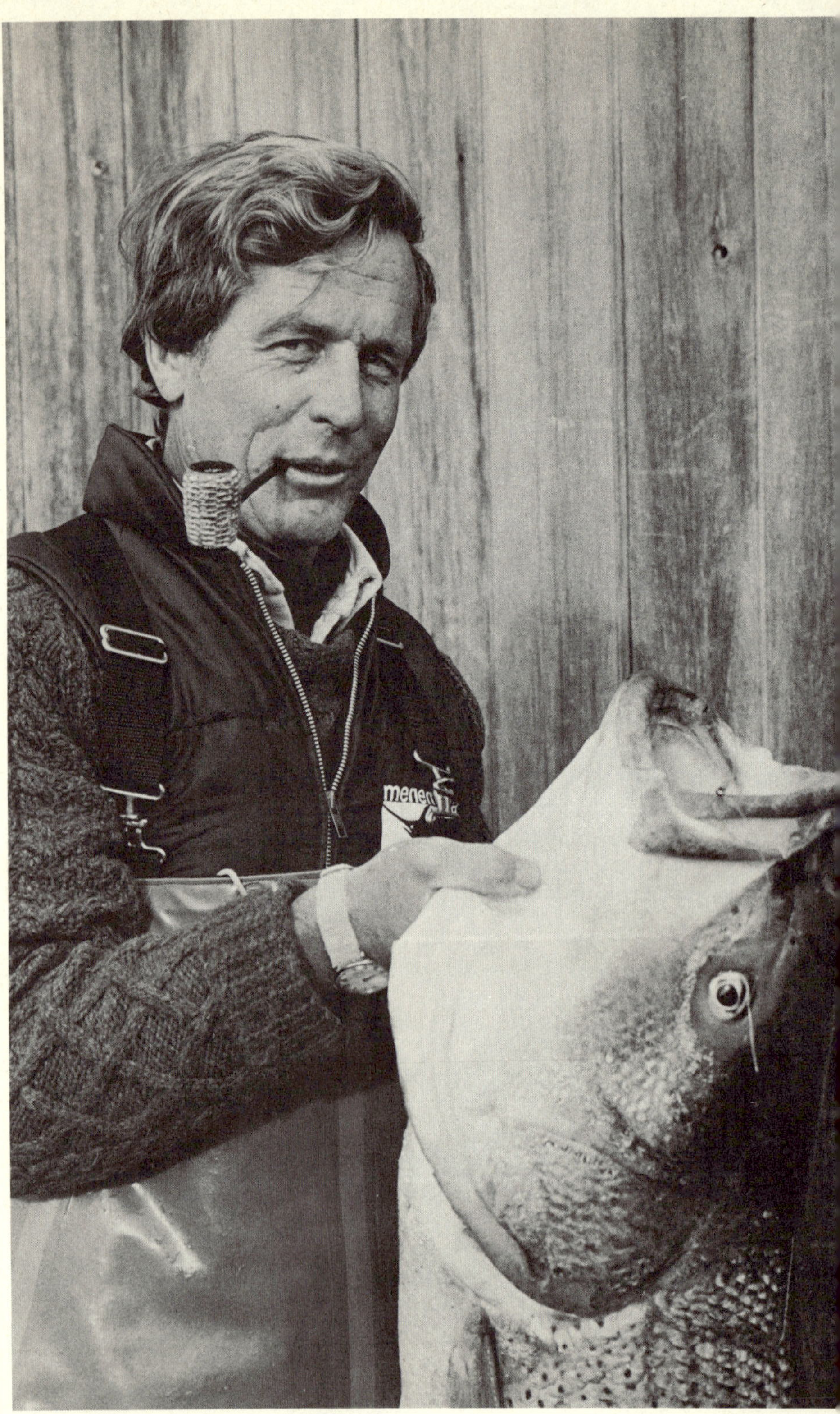

5

Kib Bramhall

I don't like fishing alone on a pitch black night with cloud cover overhead and a fog bank creeping slowly toward shore. I am, therefore, sometimes willing to sacrifice some of the secrecy of my favorite fishing holes to share the camaraderie of a surf-fishing friend. The security of this companionship helps ward off the distress I feel when the rocks seem to move and dune monsters call from their lofty perch behind me.

Fishing alone, on a night when the fog was thick, Kib Bramhall wandered the beach with a dying flashlight, clutching his rod and tackle. The opening in the dunes that marked the foot-bridge over Black Point Pond at Quansoo was not visible in the engulfing darkness. His senses were alert as he sought out the path that would take him to his Land Rover to escape this cameo appearance in an imaginary horror film. Without forewarning, he was bumped rudely in the small of his back by a blunt object. His heart racing, he turned to defend himself against the stout moist nose of a lost sheep that had wandered down from a nearby farm.

Kib loves to fish alone in the middle of the night when it's so black you can't see your hand in front of your face. In November 1962, while on the staff of Salt Water Sportsman, he wrote an article called "The World of The Night Surf," in which he extolled the virtues of night fishing: "To its devotees, night surf fishing is more challenging, more rewarding than its daylight counterpart. It produces more stripers. And bigger ones. Its aesthetics are taken from an altogether different frame of reference and they are intensely poignant."

Kib roams the beaches from dusk to dawn. The blackness of night feeds a fever that burns daily until the fall migration draws the fish from Vineyard waters. When the fish leave, he suffers severe symptoms of withdrawal. His restlessness, as he paces the house, eventually subsides. Thoughts of dark beaches of the past season soon turn to dreams of future battles.

My early days of surf fishing are probably responsible for my fanaticism. When I was a kid I spent the summers on the Jersey Coast where my grandfather had a large house right on the dunes. He and his six children ran a season-long surf-fishing contest among themselves. In the house was a fishing room, where the tackle was stored. It also had a blackboard on which was posted daily and weekly fishing scores.

As a very impressionable kid of seven, I learned that success in surf fishing was the keystone to prestige and popularity in our family. I tried to join in as soon as I was big enough to wander down to the ocean and fish.

My most poignant memory of those years was a day in 1939 or 1940 when most of the clan was out bottom fishing for bass, which is how we generally caught them. I walked along the beach with a tin squid and caught my first bass right in front of them. I can still recall what it was like walking along seeing some terns diving over a spot in the water and casting to it, and getting the fish. It's one of those memories that's indelible in my mind.

I didn't get to the Vineyard until 1945 because the family was basically located in New Jersey, and we didn't have enough gas to get here during the war. My mother's family was here during that summer, though, so my mother and I came up to see them right after V-J Day. The Jersey Shore immediately ceased to be an important place for me. I fell in love with the Vineyard. I began fishing here on my own, and with my father, in the late forties. In those days we used to fish almost entirely at Wasque Point. I would go out there on my bicycle; I'd go on the Chappy ferry and bicycle out on the dirt roads and walk down to the Point. When my father was here, we would drive out together.

Sometimes there was an opening; sometimes there wasn't. But we didn't have a Jeep, so we went by way of Chappy. In those days, we usually had the rip to the two of us. If another person came, we would consider it an insult. It was amazing how different it was then. It wasn't really the good old days, but the fishing was good. We would catch more bass than you'd catch there now, and we'd take bluefish and an occasional weakfish. The bluefish were few and far between and not big; a four- or five-pounder was huge!

The first weakfish I caught up here was in 1947 at Wasque Point on a Ferron Jig. The Ferron Jig is a block-tin squid—the Hopkins of those days. The next weakfish I caught was in 1977—thirty years later. The species just went into a total decline in these waters during the interim.

Probably the most amazing thing that happened in those days was when a woman named Sheila Rice foul-hooked a sturgeon from the beach at Wasque and landed it. It was estimated to weigh one hundred-eighty pounds, which is an awful lot of fish to land in the surf.

Another memory of those early years was a September day when I bicycled out to South Beach and walked down to the Katama Bay opening, which I often did when I didn't want to fish at Wasque. A couple of gentlemen who had a vehicle took pity on me. One was Tom Osborne. I can't remember the other guy's name. They had hired Steve Gentle to fly them to Muskeget to go bass fishing for twenty-four hours, and they invited me along. I was just fourteen. Muskeget is an island just off Nantucket. You can see it from Wasque on a clear day. It's a small sand atoll that had a dilapidated fishing shack on it. So we took off from Katama Airport the next day, my parents having given me reluctant permission to go.

The three of us were dropped off at Muskeget. We unpacked some camping supplies and lugged them to the run-down shack and then started fishing. We caught a lot of striped bass that were about twenty pounds. We got them all on metal. The next morning we fished again and caught some more. That's when the plane was supposed to get us but it was too foggy. We had run out of food, except for a case of beer.

The plane finally did come and get us the following day. We loaded all the bass and ourselves aboard and tried to take off. We couldn't get off the water because of the extra weight of the fish. So we had to go back and unload some bass and make two trips out of it.

One of the interesting fishing experiences that happened to me was in the early fifties. One evening I was invited to go fishing with Tony Gaspar, Percy West, and Ralph Grant, who were my heroes. They were the hard-core, all-night, successful bass fishermen of those years.

I ran into them one night down at Katama opening. I guess it was Tony who asked me if I'd like to go fishing with them. They wanted to explore South Shore. I said, "Of course." I went in Tony's Jeep. There was one other vehicle. We went to Edgartown Great Pond opening. It was still light. We were fishing Ferron Jigs, and we got into a school of sharks that were hitting metal. I don't know, to this day, what they were. They might have been Dusky sharks, but they were big. It was a blitz like a bluefish blitz. We'd cast and get a shark. We broke one rod and just stripped the gears right out of three reels, and lost any number of Ferron Jigs. I think we landed one! It was devastating. I've never seen the like of it.

We kept thinking the next fish might be a bass or a bluefish. There used to be many more sharks in these waters than there are now. Fishermen very often ran afoul of them.

One night, for example, I was fishing at Gay Head with Buddy Oliver and Stan Gibbs. Stan hooked a substantial bass on a darter, played it for a while and got it most of the way in, when a shark came and bit it right in half. He got a little more than the head back.

I also hooked a very big shark at Wasque. My father was with me; he was bottom fishing and catching sea robins. There were sharks that kept coming in and finning right next to the beach. I grabbed one of my father's sea robins and put it on a large hook and threw it right in front of a shark as he was cruising by. He grabbed it and stripped all the line off the reel in seconds. When he came to the end of the spool, he jumped clear of the water. I'm sure it was a Mako. It was a very spectacular and very short-lived battle.

When we got through with the sharks and picked up the pieces of our broken tackle, we decided there couldn't possibly be any bass at Edgartown Great Pond opening because there were too many sharks. So we went to Tisbury Great Pond opening. And there we got into some bass on plugs. It was the first time I had ever hooked a bass on a plug. These lures were large wooden swimmers. The fish I hooked wasn't particularly big, but I panicked and tightened up and broke him off. It was a memorable night, though, because it was the start of something.

I think it's amazing how good fishing will make even the most seasoned fisherman so excited he can barely function. The classic example that I remember happened in the mid-fifties up at Pilots Landing. There was a school of very large pollock that would come in during the early mornings, and they'd hit metal. These were big fish—fifteen to thirty pounds. They were showing and acting like bass. There was one man who was fishing the Derby from off-Island who got so excited at the sight that he backlashed time and again, finally, snapping his jig off. He sat on the beach, and his hands were trembling so much that he could not knot on a new lure. We called him the "Trembling Man."

I saw him several days after this incident, fishing down at Anthiers Bridge. When I reminded him of the pollock, his backlashes, breaking off the lure, and not being able to tie it back on, he immediately started trembling again. The memory of it was so intense that it affected him in an extreme way.

There used to be so many pollock in the late autumn here that there was a Pollock Derby that ran the week after the Striped Bass and Bluefish Derby ended. It centered around Menemsha and Gay Head and was run by Manuel Lima, an ardent and respected fisherman. His gas station in Edgartown was also a tackle store. It became headquarters for the fishermen. To enter the Derby, everyone would fork up, say, five dollars; and it was a winner-take-all pot. It wasn't formal, but it was popular.

KIB BRAMHALL

Over the years Kib has fished with many of the legendary characters of surf fishing, including Frank Woolner, Hal Lyman, and Al Reinfelder. None, however, fascinated him as much as the eccentric, sophisticated, and secretive Sergei de Somov, the Mad Russian.

This is a story about the Mad Russian, whose real name was Sergei de Somov, and his wife Louise. They fished up here for a number of years from the mid-fifties 'til the late sixties or early seventies. Louise won the Derby in 1954. She and Sergei had driven their Jeep down to Zacks Cliffs at low tide and parked in a crevice of the dune where no one could see them. They fished for a good long time and didn't get anything so they decided it was time to go home, but the tide blocked their way and they couldn't get out. Because they had nothing better to do and still had some bait, Louise put on some sea worms and a sinker and bottom fished to wait out the tide. And that's when she caught her fish. I think it was a forty-five-pound striper.

Sergei was a fascinating man! I wrote a story about him for *Salt Water Sportsman*, "Phantom of the Surf," because he was so mysterious and secretive in his ways. I wrote: "The Mad Russian is a topic of conversation wherever surfmen gather on the Northeast striper coast. His skill at beaching bull bass would, by itself, be enough to ensure his fame in striperdom. The added element of mystery enhances it tenfold. Many regard him with an awe akin to that commanded by the ancient deities. Others simply respect him. A jealous few protest that his fishing skills are no more than ordinary, and that his elusive tactics are merely designed to mask that fact from fellow anglers."

For many years, literally nobody saw him fishing. If he saw headlights coming in the distance, even if he was in the middle of a blitz, he would pack up and leave. He just had this thing about making himself mysterious, which he did very successfully. His peak accomplishment was winning the Derby three years in a row—in 1963, '64, '65—always with a fish that weighed at least fifty pounds. No one else has ever won it for bass three years in a row.

I would sometimes fish with Sergei when he wasn't fishing seriously at his secret spots. We would go in daylight just to have fun. When it came to serious bass fishing, though, nobody fished with him.

One day he saw a plug that I had bought in a tackle store in Paris that had been made in Germany for tuna fishing in South Africa. It was a great big swimming plug that was rigged with two No. 8/0 single hooks—no trebles. It looked very good to me. I couldn't resist, so I bought it and brought it home. I showed it to Sergei, and he said, "Ah, Kib, that's a very serious looking plug. May I borrow it?" And I said, "Of course." I was flattered that he wanted to use something of mine.

He reported a couple of days later that he had taken a lot of school bass on it, and would like to borrow it a little longer. I rather reluctantly agreed. He ended up winning the Derby that year with my plug that had come from France. He gave me a photo of the fish that he caught. I never did get the plug back. He died shortly thereafter, and Louise wouldn't give it to me. She just kept everything that had to do with him.

Fishermen aren't as secretive now, because bass fishing isn't what it was. Bass fishing bred a type of fisherman that simply doesn't exist today and won't until the bass come back in a big way. It's very hard to say exactly what Sergei did to preserve this aura of secrecy because he was so successful at it. He would simply show up at Derby headquarters with eye-popping catches. No one had seen him make the catches. He never said where he caught them. A lot of people felt that he was doing something illegal, which, of course, wasn't true.

He was a gentleman, and just a very good fisherman. He would spend hours during the daytime walking the beaches of the Island looking for holes, bars, and bait. By the time he finally went fishing, he had it figured out. He used gigantic tackle—free spool tackle with sixty-pound-test line.

The second time he won the Derby, he arrived on the Island approximately the day the Derby began. The next day he drove down to Derby headquarters at about nine-thirty in the morning. He walked in and shook hands with everyone, including Ben Morton, who was running the Derby in those days. And then, more or less as an afterthought, as he was walking out the door, he said, "Oh, would someone come out here and help me with something?" He had a fifty-four-pound bass in the trunk of his car. He wanted someone to help him carry it in. He was very casual and calm about the way he did that.

He always wanted to break the world record. He made several of his plugs. He sawed the butt off one of his rods and made a popping plug out of it.

He remained a mystery to the end, except for the fish he caught on the plug he borrowed from me. That morning he was fishing on South Beach near Chilmark opening at first light. There were witnesses to that catch.

He was the son of a Russian diplomat. He spoke five languages. He was an old-world gentleman who would lapse into French when he got excited, all of which added to his color.

Fishing for striped bass in recent years, I balanced a compulsive drive to catch and take a big fish to the taxidermist with the desire to conserve this troubled species by either releasing them or no longer fishing for them. The addiction of surf fishing for stripers, however, is difficult, if not impossible, to withdraw from.

Few fishermen have stopped their pursuit of this status symbol of the surf. Most conservation-oriented philosophies matured slowly, often after hundreds of trophy-size stripers had been successfully landed. The fanatics who filled their trucks during the past four decades began to see a lessening of the catch in recent years. This decline led to an increased awareness for the troubled fish.

Al Reinfelder was an innovative surf fisherman who exemplified the conflict between being a "hungry," which he described as someone who wanted "fish and fishing so bad you can't sleep at night for dreaming of it," and a conservationist, which he became before his death, when he helped form the conservation group the Striped Bass Fund, Inc.

Back in the late sixties I was fishing in Florida under one of the bridges that go down the Keys near Islamorada. I was trying to catch snook or tarpon. I ran into a guy from New York and we got to talking about striped bass fishing. He asked me if I'd ever heard of a lure called the Alou Eel. I said I hadn't. He said I should know about this development. So he gave me the address of Al Reinfelder, who was making it. When I got back to *Salt Water Sportsman*, I wrote to Al and told him I would like to try a couple of his lures. Soon I received a selection of Alou Eels. When I tried them, I started catching bass from the beach and from my boat.

An Alou Eel has the right motion and the right shape, and very often it will certainly outfish plugs and rigged eels. One night, between Dogfish Bar and Pilots Landing, I was casting in the midst of a bunch of fishermen who were fishing live eels. I took the only bass and I took it on an Alou Eel. That's an unusual, and not representative, example of what it can do. But it's a wonderful lure.

Al had to see what was happening up on the Vineyard with his lures, so I invited him up. He joined me in fishing various South Shore openings, and did very well. Around that time, he invented a lure called the Bait Tail, with his partner Lou Palma. It's sort of a glorified jig using soft plastic instead of feathers. He also developed a method for fishing bridges with this lure, which was very revolutionary. He had a lot of bridge fishing experience on Long Island. One night he said to me, with Lou there, "Let's go catch a bass off Anthiers Bridge with the Bait Tail."

We went to Anthiers, and what he showed me was something that I had never thought about, and which most people wouldn't believe possible. His method of fishing a bridge was to stand on the up-tide side of the bridge and lob the Bait Tail up into the tide. It sank to the bottom, then bounced back toward him, with the tide. When the lure got to the shadow line formed by the bridge, if the fish was there, that's when it would grab the Bait Tail. The full force of the tide is working with the fish. We're fishing the "wrong" side of the bridge. The bass immediately wants to go under the bridge, and it's got all the tide working with him.

In order to make this method work, we had to use extremely heavy tackle. We were using conventional stout rods with forty- to sixty-pound line and the drag screwed up all the way. When a fish hit, we would try to hold its head above water so that it couldn't get any purchase and swim under the bridge. We were holding a bass which could be any size at all, and most of them were very big. We were just holding its head above water until it exhausted itself.

The thrashing sounds that were made by this fish were amaz-

This is a rare posed photo of Sergei de Somov (left), pictured here with Kib Bramhall in 1960.

ing. It was like a series of cars falling in the water. We were either successful in keeping its head above water and eventually exhausting the fish (then we'd walk on shore and bring it in), or else it got its head under water and went under the bridge and cut us off. That's about the sum total of the method. I tried it myself several times and had some success with it. But the heavy tackle aspect of it eventually wore thin. I don't do it anymore, but I'm sure it could be done today.

Al was a "hungry." He was one of those guys who wanted a lot of bass and he wanted the biggest bass. Of all the great fishermen who had been hungries, he was as hungry as any of them. After he had been fishing on the Island for three or four years using Alou Eels, plugs, and Umbrella Rigs, which he also was instrumental in inventing, he stumbled upon the method of fishing live menhaden for bass. One year he discovered that there was a school of live menhaden in Tarpaulin Cove on Naushon. He let Spider Andresen and I in on this secret. He offered to show us a system of striped bass fishing that he hoped God would forgive him for introducing.

There were no menhaden here in those days. They've made a big comeback in recent years. I think that was the basis of the Columbus Day Blitz. The menhaden simply showed up along the beach and good fishermen, or opportunists, figured it out.

Once the menhaden got thick here, the bass began to smarten up a little bit. It was no longer so easy to catch them on live bunker. In the early days, in these waters, the fish hadn't seen a live menhaden. They just went bananas over it.

Al, Lou Palma, and I caught many, many big bass that way. I think it was probably one of the instrumental factors in Al becoming a conservationist. He began to feel guilty for having taken so many stripers. He saw that the species was in trouble.

He eventually devoted a large portion of his time to conservation efforts to save striped bass. But he wasn't always that way. Neither was I. I haven't kept a bass in six or seven years. But I used to be one of the rod-and-reel commercial fishermen. I used to catch a lot of bass and sell them. I got a lot of money catching bass. I don't really feel guilty about it, but I would never do it now. In the days we did it, there seemed to be no end to the numbers of bass. We never even thought about depleting a limited resource, because it seemed unlimited.

The species is in very serious trouble. One can only hope that the conditions of the water in the Chesapeake are cleaned up sufficiently to help make stripers spawn successfully. But, bass have always been cyclical.

There's no way to know what caused the early cycles of abundance and decline. Therefore, it's hard to compare them. However, now, with all our scientific techniques, we do know that while bass do spawn in the Chesapeake, their fry are not surviving. And we can be *pretty* darn sure that this is being caused by pollution. Acid rain and runoff from chemical fertilizers used on farms didn't exist in the past. If the species were to simply vanish, we would all be guilty of a serious crime. I think it's incumbent upon everyone in the fishing community to try and do whatever he can to keep the species viable.

During the Derby, bottom fishing at Stonewall Beach with Sherm Goldstein, I landed a nice striper of about thirty pounds. It put up a good fight, working me down the beach to just before the rocks jut out onto the point. After removing the leader from my line, I placed the fish against the steep embankment of sand that formed a small cove behind me. Although I was trying to keep the fish out of my way, I was also trying to hide it.

Soon after my catch, headlights blazed in the parking lot and two fishermen approached me. Their bait buckets and tackle clattered in the quiet of the night. "Anything happening?" one of them said. "No, it's been very quiet," I said. With a look of discouragement, they turned and left the beach. Perhaps to try another quiet spot.

One of the things I've always found most colorful about striped bass fishing is the lengths to which fishermen will go to keep secret the whereabouts of their catches and their methods.

Here on the Vineyard, I think that one of the things died-in-the-wool bass fishermen are most careful about is concealing drag marks on the beach. It's the sign of an amateur to leave drag marks, because any knowledgeable bass fisherman who is trying to find fish will see this. It's very recognizable. Good fishermen brush out the marks with their feet or even a broom.

It's also very amusing to see the lengths people will go to mislead others about where they've caught their fish—everything from outright lies to driving to various places where there are no fish because they know someone's following them. If you tell the truth about where you've caught a fish, people very often won't believe you. If you want to keep your spot a secret telling the truth is almost as successful as telling a lie.

In my own case, perhaps the most amusing example occurred about twenty years ago. I'd been fishing at Squibnocket and Stonewall Beach with Dick Hathaway and Ted Henley, and a couple of others, and no one had caught anything. Everyone left and went straight home, except me. I happened to stop at Anthier's Bridge on my way home; and I caught a forty-eight-pound striper there. I was pretty proud of that fish. The next day I told anybody who wanted to listen about this big fish. In fact, there was even a picture of it in the *Gazette*, as I recall. And I didn't lie about it. I said I caught it at the Big Bridge. I went back there the next night and nobody was there.

The following day several fishermen asked me, "Where'd you really catch that?" I said, "I caught it at the Big Bridge." They said, "Come on. We know you were up-Island. You were seen at Squibnocket; you were seen at Stonewall. We went there the next night and you weren't there. Where were you?" I said, "I caught it at the Big Bridge." And they still wouldn't believe me. I had that place to myself for two or three weeks. No one even looked! They simply wouldn't believe that I was telling the truth. So, very often the obvious is the best disguise.

In the 1870s, anglers used Atlantic-salmon fly rods when fishing for striped bass. Many of the flies used to land salmon, including the Scarlet Ibis and Durham Ranger and especially the Silver Doctor, were successful on stripers. Twelve separate tying steps using such exotic feathers as guinea fowl, golden pheasant, and pintail duck gave the Silver Doctor a beauty stripers couldn't resist.

Saltwater flyfishing didn't increase in popularity along the East Coast until about 1947. On the Vineyard, few fishermen attempted the sport until the late 1950s. Arthur Silvia, a respected Vineyard flyfisherman for thirty years, used to fish alone so often that he finally tried to get his brother interested. Arthur said, "I never saw any other flyfisherman for a good twenty-two or twenty-three years. I got my brother Eddie started in 1967, but he soon dropped it. He wanted an easier way to catch big fish." In the late seventies Arthur, along with Bruce Pratt, stimulated the interest of Kib Bramhall, who was longing for a new challenge.

According to Joe Brooks in The Complete Book of Fly Fishing: "Saltwater fish seldom, if ever, feed on real flies which have fallen to the surface of the ocean, and there is no aquatic hatch similar to that of a fresh water stream or lake, and therefore there are no dry flies tied for salt water. Rather, flies for the briny have been designed to imitate such common forms of ocean-going fish food as minnows, crabs, shrimp, small worms of the ocean, sand fleas, and so on, and saltwater flyfishing is therefore almost entirely confined to streamers, bucktails and popping bugs."

Joe Brooks felt the only way to catch big stripers on a fly in the New England surf was to throw big six-inch popping bugs into the ocean. Kib, however, caught a huge striper on a yellow Lefty's Deceiver, a deadly streamer fly developed by Lefty Kreh.

Back in the early sixties at *Salt Water Sportsman*, I was given a saltwater fly rod, reel and some flies by a manufacturer to try to get me, and possibly our readers, interested in the sport. I tried it a little bit and caught a couple of bass. But I quickly dismissed it as an esoteric exercise. The rod I had was a tarpon rod, and you could've cast an Atom plug with it. It was very heavy. I felt it was an uncomfortable, graceless activity. I put it totally out of my mind for at least ten years.

Then, in the late seventies, I had come to a point in my life where the challenge of fishing was not as formidable, and it just wasn't interesting anymore. I knew I could catch fish on bait, eels, plugs, and jigs. I could use either conventional or spinning gear. There was nothing new anymore. I found myself losing interest in the sport, which absolutely horrified me because it had been what made me tick for almost my whole life.

I started hearing about a couple of the fly-rod fishermen on the Island, namely Arthur Silvia and Bruce Pratt, who were both catching large striped bass on flies. I thought, "My God, that is a challenge!" I set about teaching myself how to cast a fly. I got some equipment that was better suited to the sport, and I began trying to get into it.

What really whetted my appetite was a morning at Lobsterville in July. I'd gotten up very early and gone up there with my fly rod. Through my binoculars I saw a guy hauling in a fish way down the beach. So I went down; and it was Arthur Silvia. He had two or three bass weighing between eighteen and thirty pounds on the beach. He was hooked up to another, which he duly landed. I began casting quite near him.

The bass that Arthur was catching with his fly rod were about eighty feet off the beach. I couldn't reach them. I simply couldn't cast that far. I ended up sitting down and just watching this man perform. He's a consummate fly caster and a consummate flyfisherman. I was *astounded!* He could put a twenty-pound bass on the beach in six minutes with tackle that would be considered medium weight. I was determined to learn how to do this myself. So I kept working on my casting. I kept fishing at Lobsterville, and I finally did get a fish one morning.

That same autumn, I heard that the second biggest bass in the Derby, going into the second week, had been caught by Bruce Pratt on a fly. Here he was, competing with a fly rod against all of the people who were using conventional and spinning tackle, and *beating* almost all of them. I wanted to find out what he was doing, so I began fishing in the same area, over on Chappaquiddick. I started talking to him. He was very helpful. He ended up making me a rod, and showing me things about how to fish and where to fish that I never would have known otherwise.

No matter how much I learned there was always more to learn. It was always very hard to catch big bass on a fly. Bruce was almost totally responsible for my catching the bass that won the Fly-Rod Division of the Derby. It weighed forty-two pounds and thirteen ounces.

I caught it on the last night of the 1981 Derby, the first year they had a Fly-Rod Division. I knew that Bruce had been flyfishing for bass on Chappaquiddick near Cape Poge. The last night of the Derby I went out there and ran into Bruce. He told me that the night before he had lost a bass that he thought was in the forty-pound class. He'd had it on for more than an hour. The fish had taken line, then stopped, taken line and stopped. Eventually it stripped the line. Bruce showed me where this had happened. He wasn't feeling well and was going home. So he said, "You fish right here and use one of these." He gave me a yellow Lefty's Deceiver. He said, "It's going to be too bright for a white fly tonight; use the yellow one."

I actually started fishing at five in the afternoon. There were quite a few of us fishing there with fly rods. We kept fishing until about three in the morning. Nothing had been caught except a couple of small fish at dusk. Everyone decided to go home. I was simply too tired to drive, so I sacked out in my car for an hour-and-a-half or so. I got up around four-thirty and started fishing again. The big fish hit at a little past five.

The fish hit very close to the beach and immediately ran off almost all the line on my reel. I had one-hundred-fifty yards of backing, and I was well down into it. I thought about what had happened to Bruce because when the fish had run off his line, he'd stopped and waited. I knew that if that happened to me, the fish would get a second wind and then take the rest of my line. So, when it stopped, I kept a bend in the rod, held my hand on the spool so it couldn't move, and took a couple of steps backward. I could feel the striper's head turning around. If you do that to a fish you've sort of gotten it into its head that you're going to win. I think I beat its spirit a little bit. And I was able to regain some line before it made another run that was significantly shorter. I did the same thing at the end of that run—kept a bend in the rod, took a couple of steps backward, and turned its head around. I kept doing that. Those are the tactics I used—very brutal and strong tactics. It killed the fish in about twenty minutes. I owed it all to Bruce. It was his place, his fly, and he taught me most of what I know about saltwater flyfishing, along with Arthur Silvia.

I think many people use a too big hook when flyfishing for stripers. If you read books on the subject, which aren't really current, they'll tell you to use a No. 3/0 or No. 4/0 hook for striped bass. It's been my experience that a No. 1/0 is all you need. It's big enough to hold a fish. They'll never straighten the hook out as long as you keep a bend in the rod. Because of its smaller size, it has a lot less wind resistance so it's easier to cast. It's also less visible, so it's easier to fool the fish.

Another thing about flies is that you should not tie them with too much material. Store-bought flies tend to have too many feathers, too much bucktail, and too much Flashabou; it's just too big a package. They're attired to sell fishermen rather than to catch fish. The one exception to that is big bluefish; they like a big bulky fly.

For everything that we catch around here, I think the Lefty's Deceiver is one of the best, all-purpose saltwater flies. But there are plenty of others that catch fish. Anyone who ties their own flies is constantly experimenting and coming up with new patterns that work. If you had to pick one that was consistently successful, though, it would be the Lefties.

I think if you could use only one color, white would be it. If you could use two, then have a white fly and a yellow fly. If you start getting into mixing colors, then something that's white underneath with hair on the top that's either green or blue is effective. Now there are all sorts of new materials, such as Flashabou, which add a lot of seductive glitter to a fly. There's nothing to be lost at all by putting that in.

I bend down the barbs on all my hooks because I think the hook penetrates to its bend far more quickly and readily. And it makes releasing fish a cinch. I highly recommend bending the barbs down, not only on flies, but on any lure.

For bluefish, it's a good idea to use a shock tippet. Some people prefer wire; some heavy monofilament. I have gone to eighty-pound-test mono because the blues rarely chomp through it. I also think it's a little more aesthetically pleasing to have monofilament rather than wire on the end of your fly line. But that's strictly a personal preference. I don't think one is more effective than the other.

The greatest fly-rod bluefishing that occurred on the Vineyard was in fall, 1984, at Lobsterville when a number of world records were set. The fish ranged from ten to twenty pounds, and they were hitting flies regularly. I think it's the best bluefishing there's ever been. It just went on day after day and week after week. It was nighttime, daytime, anytime. People with no experience would come up there and catch huge fish.

I think the fish were migrating, coming down from Maine, where they'd spent the summer. When they arrived on the North Shore of the Vineyard, they found conditions to their liking. There was plenty to eat. The sand eels were thick. The weather was warm. There was just no reason for them to move any farther. They just hung out.

Bluefish very often aren't a great fly-rod fish. They'll dog it a lot. They often won't make long runs. On flies up at Lobsterville that year, though, those fish were taking off with a hundred yards or more of backing. Time and again they would do this. Then they would jump. They put on the best display I've ever seen. They jumped, they made long runs, they were tenacious, and they were big beautiful-looking fish. Some people said they looked like Atlantic salmon—very full-bodied and healthy.

Striped bass flyfishermen usually hate to see bluefish because they'll not only beat a bass to the fly, but they'll often bite through your tippet unless you're using very heavy shock leaders, which I don't like to use when I'm bass fishing. These blues were an exception; they were a welcome addition to our fishing. I hope it happens again. A lot of people showed up in 1985 with fly rods waiting for a repeat, but it didn't happen.

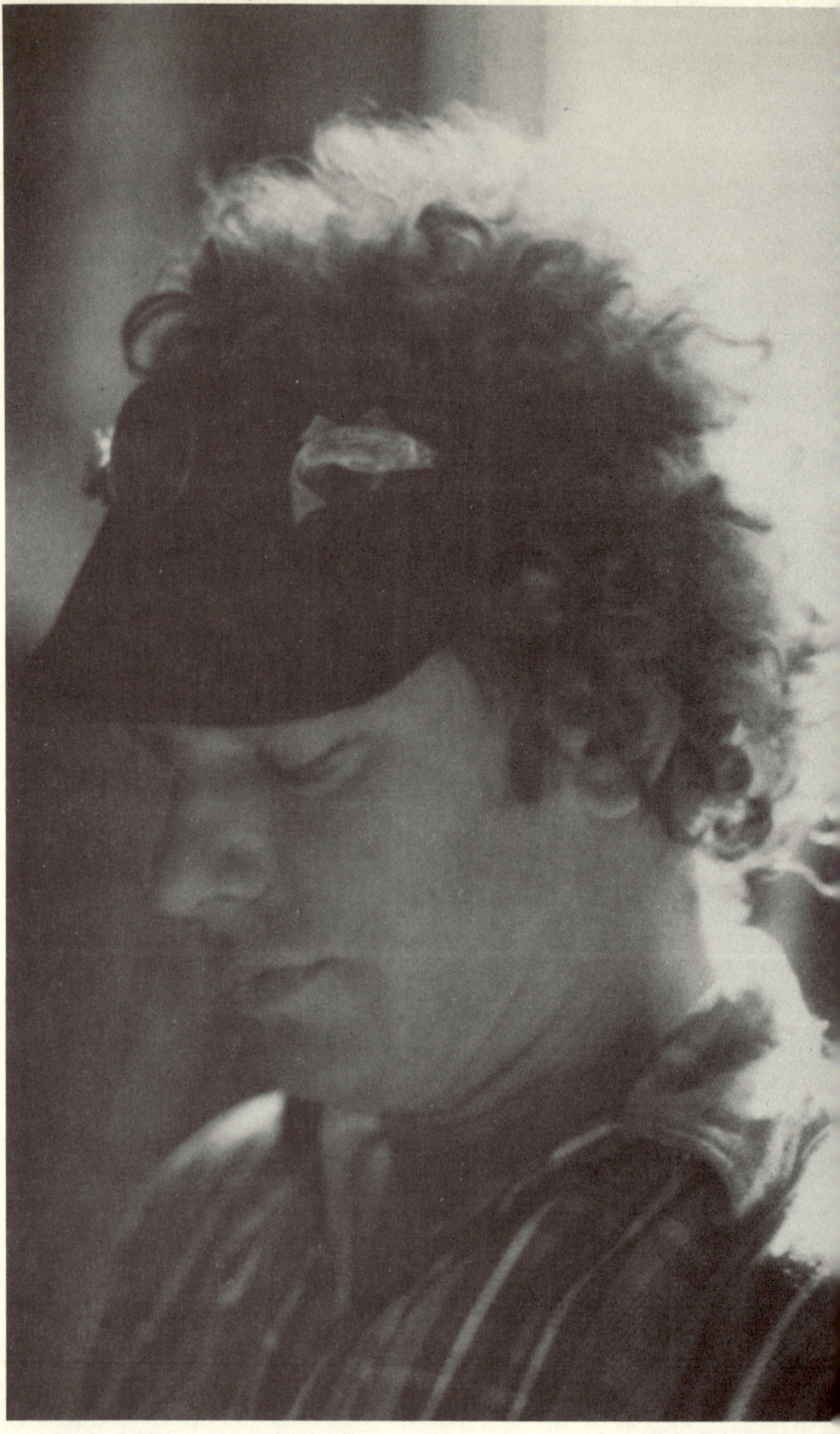

6

Richard Landon

News of an unusual fish story travels over the Vineyard fishing grapevine with the lightning speed of the most scandalous gossip. These stories have travelled from Gay Head to Oak Bluffs before the fish has had time to stiffen.

One such fish story involved the sixty-eight-pound yellowfin tuna caught by Dan Colli. On October 30, 1986, Collie hooked and landed his tuna while surf casting near Wasque. The fish hit a Spofford's Ballistic Missile and made four long runs before being beached. Yellowfin are usually caught from boats miles offshore. No one in the Vineyard fishing community could ever remember a yellowfin being caught from the beach. The grapes were popping off the vine as fishermen spread this story.

In the late 1960s, Dick Hathaway hooked a giant sturgeon in the Wasque rips while fishing for stripers. Estimated to weigh two hundred pounds, Hathaway lost the fish after a half-an-hour-long battle.

Another story that spread rapidly was the landing of a fifty-six-pound fourteen-ounce striper on six-pound-test line, at Gay Head

RICHARD LANDON

by Dick Landon of New Haven, Connecticut. What fascinated fishermen, and set their tongues wagging, was that the catch was made on such light tackle. As news of this striper spread, so did the rumors.

The best rumor had the five-inch lure pass into the throat of the fish and out the gills. The fish supposedly tossed and turned, wrapping itself in the line like a cocoon. Rendered helpless, Dick could then work the fish to the beach. None of this was true, but it was fun speculating how a thirty-one-year-old stranger could beat out all the seasoned Vineyard fishermen.

I was born on March 23, 1950. I grew up on the Barrington River in Rhode Island. It's an estuarine river which runs through Warren and into Narragansett Bay. Not far from our house was a bridge which crossed the Barrington, where my older brother and I used to fish for cunner, silversides, and mummichogs. No one taught us how to fish. We tied our own knots and used nails and bolts for sinkers. I never caught a striped bass from the bridge, but I did catch a five-pound tautog. That fish was one of the high points of my early fishing. For a few years, in the fall, we caught small bluefish, only we called them "skipjack."

When my family and I moved from Barrington in 1962, my salt water fishing temporarily came to an end. We spent some time outside of Greenville, Maine, where I did some freshwater flyfishing. I didn't start again until around 1974 when I visited Martha's Vineyard. So, there was a hiatus in which I never went saltwater fishing. I didn't put the time in and there was no one to teach me the rudiments involved.

I came to the Vineyard to help some friends construct a writer's studio in Gay Head. In lieu of payment, we asked the owners for continued access to their summer camp. While we were building the studio, though, we didn't fish; we didn't know how. A year or two went by before we used the camp to go fishing. I borrowed a fishing rod from a friend in Vineyard Haven and took it to Jack Koontz at the Chilmark Chandlery. I showed him this old, cheap glass rod and said, "What could I match with this?" He sold me a Daiwa 7000.

At first, we only fished at Lobsterville Beach. We would get there at six or seven every evening and usually catch three- and four-pound bluefish. After fishing several weeks, I caught a small striped bass. Then we began to explore other sections of beach, like Dogfish and Pilots Landing. We began to catch a few more stripers, again fishing only in the evening—never after dark—and using only poppers.

It took several more years to learn important fishing basics. We learned in several ways. One of my friends, Joel Radding, has a science background. Joel likes to read technical information. He was the one who learned about tying knots. We weren't tying good knots early on. He read books about fishing equipment and techniques and passed the information on to the other guys. With his technical sense and my intuitive sense, the two of us were able to figure out quite a bit.

Joel started fishing at night. He began to fish the tides. He would pass the information he gained on to the rest of us. The first time he fished a northeaster off Gay Head the storm came at low tide. He had fabulous fishing, catching many large stripers in a spot where we previously had only caught schoolies. He called me early that morning and came up to the camp with about a half-dozen fish in the thirty-pound class, which was a real watershed for our little group. That was the kind of information we shared. The next month or so I would look for the same conditions and fish the same spot. One morning there were large bluefish, stripers, and even some bonito there. I haven't seen bonito off Gay Head since that morning. An old-timer I met on the beach said he had caught them off the point before. His name was Oscar Flanders and he was a great fisherman. Oscar taught me a lot about fishing Gay Head. There was a story circulating that Oscar had a telescope in his Gay Head house that he used to check the conditions of the sea at first light. If things didn't look right to him, he went back to sleep.

The summer after I lived on the Vineyard, I moved to New Haven, Connecticut. Every year I came back for a few days in the spring and again in the fall for the Derby. In the fall I fished with my old fishing friends. Curiously, as the stocks of striped bass began to dwindle, our fishing improved. We were developing into better fishermen, so we were catching more fish. During the late 1970s it was hard to believe the stories we were hearing about a dwindling striped bass population. Our jobs were marginal or non-existent at the time, so we were selling fish and counting on the income to buy tackle and food.

Without Joel Radding, my fishing history would be non-existent. Although my interest was always there, Joel encouraged me with his knowledge and enthusiasm. He is a mainstay at Gay Head, and often haunts the beaches until the end of November. He recently bought a fourteen-foot, two-handed fly rod. They're used in the British Isles for certain types of salmon fishing. He uses it in heavy surf conditions. He was known for his cars, and owned an unusual assembly of old vehicles, one of which was an old Chevy Bel Air that haunted Gay Head like a mean ghost. Now he uses a 1968 green Rambler for his fishing vehicle.

The Connecticut shoreline is protected from the pounding Atlantic surf by Long Island. Between Long Island and Connecticut is Long Island Sound. Many stripers swim along the Atlantic side of Long Island; preferring to migrate and feed at Sandy Hook, New Jersey; Montauk, New York; Block Island, Rhode Island; and Cape Cod, Martha's Vineyard, and Plum Island, Massachusetts. The Sound's connection to New York Harbor and Hudson River stripers, however, gives Connecticut a large population of school stripers, and they keep light tackle and flyfishermen busy.

In Connecticut I don't do much fishing because I don't have the time. When I do fish, I fish a little estuary inside New Haven, where the West River flows into the harbor. I usually go so I can keep a sense of the quality of water and the type of life that's there. On one side of the West River is a mountain of garbage covered with sand; it must be twenty stories high. This fill is leaching into the river. On the other side is a junkyard with a collection of rotting automobile parts and heavy steel equipment of all sorts. This lines the river from New Haven Harbor up about one-half mile on each side. There's a little bit of eelgrass in different sections, and there's a dam across it, which allows the Yale rowers to practice their sculling. The river is polluted. At one time there was extensive farming upstream. Quite a bit of stuff is still being dumped into the river.

On any evening outgoing tide I can catch quite a few striped bass, and they'll range from twelve to twenty-four inches long.

Sometimes I fish from the trestle that crosses the river. Amtrak trains travelling between Boston and New York come by every fifteen minutes. They whiz by me, horn tooting, about two feet away, as I brace myself against the side of the trestle. Few people fish here.

The bass feed on grass shrimp and herring. There's a small herring run into the West River. At low tide there's an even flow and the herring can make it through the dam. I talked to people at Yale hoping they would put in a fish ladder, but so far there haven't been any results.

One evening I went down to the river, and I noticed the water was thick was mummichogs. They were breeding along the shoreline, up against rusting metal, the dump, and in the eelgrass. There must have been millions of mummichogs along the shoreline. Because they were breeding, their colors were a mixture of green and iridescent olive and yellow. It was a beautiful thing to see.

Connecticut has few long sand beaches. There isn't much classic surf fishing. Fishermen mostly fish the estuaries, the rivers, the jetties, and rocky outcrops. There are many stony islands off Milford that are popular with bass fishermen. The bass caught are usually small Hudson River fish. About twenty-five percent of the fish come from the Chesapeake, providing some large fish, and seventy-five percent come from the Hudson River. There's a lot of boat fishing up and down the coast and quite a bit of night fishing in the lagoons and estuaries when game fish move into the shallows. There are light-tackle enthusiasts and flyfishermen who catch striped bass, bluefish, and weakfish.

When the sixteenth-century philosopher Francis Bacon said, "God hangs the greatest weights upon the smallest wire," he could have been referring to Dick Landon's 1981 Derby winner—a fifty-six-pound fourteen-ounce striper caught on six-pound test. The fish is the second largest striper to win the Derby since its inception in 1946. Only Dick Hathaway's sixty-pound two-ounce fish, which was taken in 1978, was bigger.

This is the story of my 1981 Derby winner. That fall I came to the Vineyard with a few friends. One of the first things we did was walk the beaches. We had learned enough about surf fishing to know that beaches change and that holes develop and move. At some places, each season and each week within a season, the beach changes dramatically. We were walking the beach near Zacks Cliffs, just up from a buoy resting in the sand, when we spied a deep hole. We called this area the "Bop." It was between Zacks Cliffs and Philbin Beach. We began fishing there that evening and had good luck. During the next three or four nights, before I caught the Derby winner, we were catching a lot of weakfish. We were catching ten and fifteen weakfish a night, plus some small bluefish and small bass. We would fish there in the evening and in the morning, with more success in the evening.

There was also an incredible accumulation of baitfish, including silversides and sand eels. We could see them every evening being pushed up against the shore in large numbers by both the tide and the game fish. Rarely had we ever seen larger amounts of baitfish in Gay Head.

Because the game fish were small, we were using light tackle. We had caught any number of small bluefish and bass and weakfish on six- and eight-pound test with small rods and spinning or conventional gear. During the previous few days there was a north wind blowing, coming at our backs over the dunes so the surf was quiet. The tides were improving and the moon was growing full.

A group of New Jersey fishermen was fishing near us. They're one of the few groups of people we saw regularly on this section of beach. We showed them some of the tricks we knew and talked to them about how we fish that area. Another group from New Jersey was keeping undersize bass. As a result of that, someone gave their tires a good slashing one evening. There were a number of four-wheel-drive vehicles up in that area that had a difficult time getting out.

I remember going out on a Thursday, after waiting for the tide to improve. The tide was growing flood, and dusk was coming. We usually ride all the time, but my friends had the itch earlier and had taken the truck. We still like daylight fishing. It's something I find difficult to get away from.

I decided to walk down to the beach with my small rod, hoping and expecting to catch the same kinds of small fish that I had caught before. A friend of mine, Bill, was fishing on one side of me and Joel was on the other. A couple of New Jersey fishermen were also near me. I thought I had the inside position on this hole. Although people were fishing nearby, they weren't fishing it well. It was twilight. There's very little depth perception then.

About that time we saw Hank Schauer walking down the beach. He's an unmistakable form—a great tall fellow, walking quickly, big rod over his shoulder, always dressed to the nines. Hank likes to stop and talk. I'm sure he has any number of friends up and down the beach, and is willing to make more. He usually parked near Zacks Cliffs and would walk to the Gay Head cliffs and back. He told me he hadn't caught any fish in weeks. That was a continual story of his, but I didn't always believe it. I remember seeing him one day at a cottage he was renting with a friend. The two of them had about twenty bass laid out on their front lawn. He's a good fisherman. He saw we were catching a few fish, but he was restless and wanted to continue walking. As he departed, he said, "As soon as I go, you're going to do real well. The gloom cloud is scattering."

I continued fishing into the evening. It was getting darker. I was casting a five-inch Rebel that I modified by removing the center hook and upgrading the front and rear hooks with a better quality larger hook. The Rebel had a black back and gray sides. I was using a short glass rod that I made shorter by cutting off the top six to ten inches. That gave the rod quite a bit of backbone. The total length of the rod was just more than five feet. I was using a small spinning reel, a Daiwa 1600 and what I thought was eight-pound test, which proved later to be six.

I had caught about eight weakfish and several blues. At one point early on, there was a tremendous boil to the left of the plug. I didn't tell either of my friends, who may have been five or ten yards from me, that I saw this thing. This was at the very first light of moon. Something very large had come after the plug and missed it completely.

I fished this hole like I would freshwater. I cast, let the plug sit for several seconds, and then begin dabbling it and shaking it around a bit. Then I begin a slow retrieve, stopping to allow it to come to the surface. Somewhere in the middle of one of these casts a very large fish hit the plug, took it, and headed east along the shoreline. The immediate run of the fish must've used seventy-five or a hundred yards of line. I had about two hundred-fifty yards of line on the reel.

It was hard for me to tell how large a fish it was. I had previously caught a striper in the low twenties on this particular rod and light tackle. This fish felt a little bigger, and at other times a little smaller. I began to get concerned because I was losing a lot of line. I had backing on the spool—some old monofilament, and that was exposed now. I had between thirty and fifty yards of good line left. I remember that the fish had pulled me up. I had come up out of the hole. I was walking the fish, even as it was taking line, to cut back on some of it. This was not easy to do at night because the beach was covered with cobble and stones to the east and there were some large rocks out in the water. I had the position of the rocks memorized, having fished there so often. You can't let your line rub on them, or all is gone.

At some point, as the line was still going out in this initial run, I had to make a choice—one I don't like to do—and that was to clamp down on the drag a degree or two. It's something that's not supposed to be done and it's something that's dangerous to do while the fish is running. I didn't think I had any choice at this point. This fellow from New Jersey, who is a good fisherman, walked with me a bit, hoping to see the fish, although it was quite some time from being landed. He told me not to touch the drag. We debated even as we walked along. I had decided to tighten the drag. I said, "I think I ought to." When the speed of the fish diminished slightly due to the drag of more than a hundred yards of line being pulled through the water, I tightened the drag. The fish continued to run, and suddenly at one point it stopped.

When the fish was out there, it held its ground. It was in some current. With the pressure of my stubby rod, I think I was able to help stop it. When I tightened the drag, it seemed to lose some of its steam. My early experiences taught me you can get a striper fairly quickly after the first run. Its strength is sapped and you can work it pretty hard. I began to work the fish in as much as I dared. The fish came easily at that point. Obviously it was a little tired. I worked it in a lot. And with some pulling again, it made a few short runs. Over the next fifteen minutes I was able to work it within fifteen or twenty yards of shore, but it was still out of sight, still in the dark, still with the occasional rock about. I had it close, but I had taken too long. In that time of working the fish rather gingerly back to shore, it had regrouped, and then started on another long run. It took out another fifty to seventy-five yards of line with a strong surge running back in the same direction. I had the rod braced up as much as I could against my body to put extra pressure on the fish.

When the fish stopped after its second run, I started to worry about the line catching a rock. I was able to slowly work it in again. I was fully expecting another surge of power and a long run, but it didn't happen. When I got it close to shore I had to contend with the waves. Even though we were in the lee of the wind, there were gentle swells. When the fish was ten yards out in front on the other side of the breaking swell, I quickly thought of the best way to bring him in. It wasn't a bad swell. It was about two feet high, but strong and something for me to worry about.

There's a point just off West Chop Beach Club, where I didn't want to land at, because it is much more stony. So I continued to move west toward a sandy location. I didn't want to land it on the cobble. The tide was still up. I worked it closer, and on my first attempt to bring it in on a wave, I wasn't successful. The fish still had enough strength to pull out line again. It worked itself out another few yards, and I brought it back in. The second time, I brought it up into a wave, and that wave kicked it up on the shore, on a nice sandy stretch.

I don't like to stay too close when I'm putting a fish onto the beach. If the rod is too close, it doesn't give the line a chance to stretch, in case there is any last-minute maneuvering by the fish. The fish laid on the sand, and I was able to hustle down and grab it by the gill, at which point the line broke.

The Rebel didn't pass through the gill as was rumored. The first hook had caught in the lip and the second hook caught the gill cover. Later in the evening I had taken the plug and placed it back on the side of the gill just to keep it out of the way.

I wasn't using any terminal tackle. The line was tied right to the plug. It really is a good way to go if you're willing to take a chance. You always get the best action from an imitation minnow with a direct tie. I don't even use an O-ring. I don't like the action they give the lure.

I caught the fish around eight that night and I was down at Derby headquarters by nine. I took the rod in with me to show the tackle to the people at the weigh-in. It was all very exciting.

The next morning I still had the fish in the trunk of the car. I decided to go back to Gay Head where I ran into Hank Schauer. I said, "Hank, do you want to see something? I had a little luck." I opened the trunk of the old '68 Rambler and, shamefully, against a tire jack and a spare tire, was this fish. And there was Hank, standing tall over it with a strange look on his face.

Early one morning, in the mid-1970s, I fished the south side of the Gay Head cliffs, about fifty yards east of Southwest Rock. Although the water can be cloudy—filled with reddish-brown clay that washes from the cliffs by the action of storm tides and torrential rains—this morning the water was clear. Sand eels, crabs, and sand dabs were visible feeding and resting on the sandy bottom. My hopes of catching a striper increased as several swirled in front of me. The sight of their broad tails and thick powerful bodies made my heart race. I had trouble containing my excitement. My senses were acute and the palpitations that caused my chest to vibrate like a bass drum in a marching band made me susceptible to being easily startled. Suddenly, a large striper swam toward me. Sensing my waders, it swerved sharply to the left and continued behind me, almost hitting the back of my legs. I was so unsettled that my casting became erratic and my concentration was shattered. I never caught a bass that morning, even though I could look one in the eye.

Fishing at Gay Head, in low-water conditions, strange things can happen. There are often fish feeding right around you. The fish grubble around in the rocks feeding on crabs and worms. I've seen tautog and striped bass feeding this way. The stripers often stick their tails out of the water. Sometimes I'm able to catch these fish. On calm days I use light tackle, even though there are many barnacle-covered rocks. On days with a heavy surf running, I use heavier tackle.

One morning I was fishing with Joel at Gay Head. A fish went for my plug within fifteen yards of me. It made a swirl and a splash and then continued to head in—having missed the plug. This fish continued at a kilter. It didn't move straight through the water but it moved off to one side and then barrelled in. It came in and put a rub right onto my thighs. As it grazed by it went farther inshore behind me and then righted itself, regained its composure and strength and then shot back out to deeper water.

I think fish get disoriented after hitting a plug. Even though they miss the hooks, they still feel some tension or a sudden pull and it sends them into a panic. I've seen fish hit close in and continue straight in more than once. I've caught striped bass that have all but beached themselves after hitting the plug. They get confused. When they hit the surf, the surf obviously aids in their propulsion onto the shore.

It's always unnerving being bumped by a fish. One night when I was fishing at Dogfish Bar I almost got bumped by a shark. I had waded into the water and was fishing out on the bar. A few feet from me, a large shark came cruising by. A large fin, showing at least twelve or fourteen inches above the water, came right by me. Being a rather crazy and sometimes foolish person, I thought there was some chance it might take a plug. I put two or three casts in front of it, without success. I was frightened, but I stayed in the water and continued to fish. Later, it struck me that I may have been a little foolish not to get out of the water.

Whit Manter has often impressed me with his success in catching large and numerous bluefish and stripers and keeping his catch a secret. He has never shied away from putting in his time on dark cobbled beaches in the middle of the darkest nights, often in dank miserable weather. His talent at keeping his fish hidden was undoubtedly passed along by his grandfather, Daniel Manter, who had the following encounter with Steve Bryant at the Tisbury Great Pond twenty-five years ago. "Anything happening?" asked Steve. "Yup, I caught one bass," replied Daniel. "Where is it?" "You're standing on it. It's buried."

The first year I fished the Derby, around 1975, I was a novice in every sense of the word. A friend and I came to Pilot's Landing and walked over the bluff onto the beach. We saw a young fellow fishing with a number of rods, and each one was lined up on the beach in a sand spike. He struck me as a very serious fisherman. I thought he was baitfishing. That was my first, rather crazy, thought. All the rods were reel to reel.

We fished up and down the shore not far from this fisherman. We saw him pick up one rod at a time, use it for a while, and then put it back and grab another one. My curiosity got the better of me, so I approached him and introduced myself. This fellow told me he was practicing. He was going through each one of his rods and learning its quirks. Some of them were old rods, some of them looked newer. He was running through their motions and mechanics. There were different plugs, including poppers and swimmers. I learned years later that it's more difficult to pop with conventional gear than spinning gear. This fellow had two or three spinning rods and three or four conventional rods. He would work right through all of them again and again. I said, "What are you doing?" He said, "I'm practicing for the Derby." And this was Whit Manter down at Pilot's Landing. I learned over the years that Whit is a serious and dedicated surf fisherman. He had his mind set on winning the Derby.

Whit opened a whole curtain for me on the Derby. He showed me that the Derby is a serious event for a lot of people. The next four weeks were going to be very intense for some of those fishermen. He also showed me that fishing in general can be taken seriously, which I had never done before. It was only because I found out that one could approach it with a serious attitude that I became a quality fisherman.

Encounters with nature's creatures are common when surf fishing. Many times I have seen deer standing in a field, frozen in fear, sniffing at the exhaust from my intruding vehicle. The only owl I ever saw in the wild was while I was on a fishing trip to Wasque. A barn owl sitting on the limb of a dead, wind-bent tree near the sloping dunes of Katama. The closest I've ever been to a skunk was at Lobsterville, when one approached my tackle bag as I was changing lures by flashlight.

RICHARD LANDON

Dick Landon also had some encounters with creatures other than fish. Walking with Joel in a heavy fog below the Gay Head cliffs, the two were dive-bombed by birds protecting their nests. At the time, these unseen attackers reminded him of hostile spirits guarding sacred fishing grounds. A seal feeding on bluefish and a fulmar in the sky gave Dick lasting memories of nature's surprises. All these encounters remind me of something many good surf fishermen say: "There's more to fishing than catching fish."

In fall 1984 I was fishing along Moshup's Trail near the West Chop Club with Joel. There had been all sorts of jumbo blues along the south shore. These fish were ranging from eighteen to twenty-four pounds. Joel had real good luck. He had started fishing the week before I arrived on the Vineyard, and was catching these large blues on a fly rod. Some of them weighed as much as eighteen pounds. The first night I arrived we fished Gay Head in a northwest wind that was really blowing. We were using heavy tackle and caught blues on almost every cast. You just could not get away from them. It was exciting fishing. We lost tackle. We brought in fish that we weighed on the beach, then released. While we were fishing and catching these bluefish, we saw seals in the surf. There were maybe three or four of them cruising back and forth. I didn't see any fish in their mouths, but it appeared they were feeding hard.

The next day, the wind had died. We returned to the same spot and started catching twenty-pound bluefish on light tackle and fly rods. I borrowed Joel's fly rod and he took my rod with a Daiwa Mag Force 35-A reel. He hooked what felt like an ordinary blue for the day—around fifteen, sixteen pounds. Suddenly, something very big hit that bluefish and began taking off unbelievable amounts of line. There was a heavy chop in the water. It was not easy to see, although it was full daylight. At the end of his line, twenty to thirty yards out, a seal surfaced with a big bluefish in its mouth. The seal had Joel's fish and was diving and surfacing with the bluefish in its mouth, heading out to Noman's Island. That's when the line snapped—two hundred yards of ten-pound test. I don't believe the seal was hooked. I think the seal had the blue and the blue had the hook. These were not little harbor seals, either. I would guess they weighed two hundred to two hundred-fifty pounds. They were really big critters.

One fall I came here to fish by myself. Every evening I would go out fishing. I would usually walk the beach from Philbin to Gay Head and cast as I walked. At Philbin Beach one evening I looked up into the sky. On the horizon there was a dark speck. It might have been a bird of some kind. But it caught my eye. It seemed quite far away, yet close at the same time. I could not get a distance on it and I could not get a fix on what exactly was up there.

I stood my ground and didn't fish and watched this thing. It was coming closer to me and it was getting large. The wind was southwest and blowing right in my face. After ten minutes, I could determine it was a kite without a tail. I could not for the life of me figure out what was holding up this kite, unless someone was way out in a boat somewhere else in the world at the other end of this line. I stayed and watched.

Soon the kite came near the beach about a hundred feet above me. I was able to spot the kite string, and entangled in the string was a bird. Somehow the bird was supported by the kite, even though the bird was being dragged along the surf line through the ocean, banging each wave, just being pummelled. The kite was now behind me blowing up over the dunes into Gay Head. I was able to run down, grab onto the line, and let it slide through my hand until the bird was pulled right up to me. It was a small, gray-masked bird, called a fulmar. I was able to get it untangled and the kite went blowing back to Gay Head again. I made a home for the gull in the dunes. It was a little battered, but it had no cuts or a broken wing. I left it in the tall grass up on one of the bluffs. After staying with it for a few minutes, I continued my fishing. I went back to check the gull and, as soon as I touched it, off it went! It was healthy and strong. It just needed a rest. Frightening it one more time sent it off.

I don't fish in New Haven. I fish on the Vineyard where I stay a hundred yards from the surf and I can hear it all night long. I used to fish here eight hours a day for weeks at a time. That was before I had my family. I don't spend as much time fishing because I want to spend more time with them. But my family's getting older now. I've taken my four-year-old daughter bluefishing. She's caught fish and finds a lot to like about fishing. My wife even picked up the surf rod for the first time recently. So, we may spend more time on the Vineyard, and other things could happen.

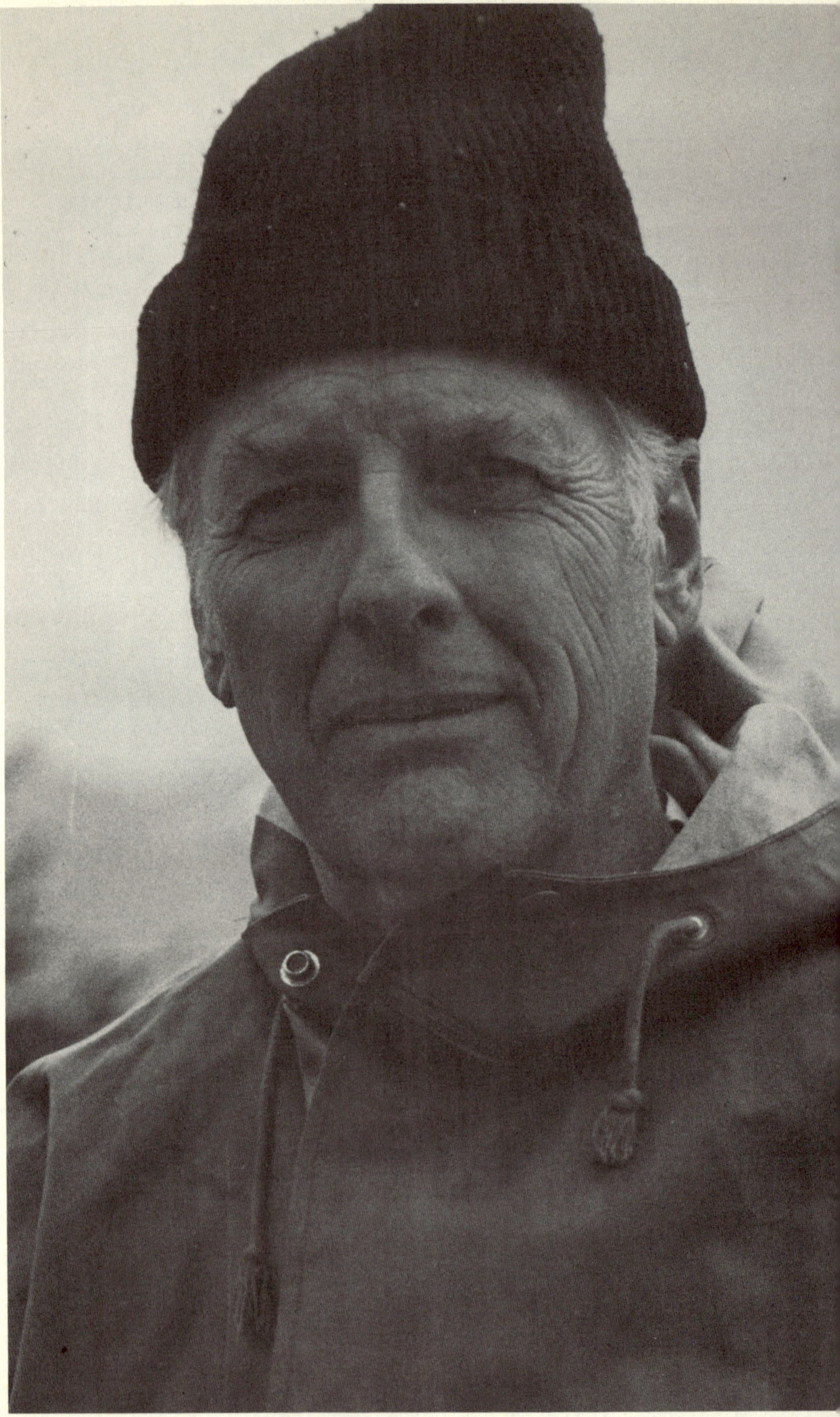

7

Hank Schauer

My early days fishing the surf were filled with frustration and joy. I appreciated being outdoors, and occasionally I would luckily catch a fish. I had little knowledge of tides, lures, or drag systems.

The neophyte often performs strangely when attempting to land a fish in the surf. At Wasque, I saw a fisherman stop reeling when his fish was still fifty feet offshore. Substituting body movements for a few cranks of the reel handle, he backed up so far onto the beach that he stumbled into the dunes, disrupting several resting terns.

It was a gaff, an unnecessary tool for the beach fisherman, that led to my first encounter and long friendship with Hank Schauer. As Hal Lyman and Frank Woolner point out in their book Tackle Talk: *"Perhaps it should be emphasized that gaffs are not necessary on a sand beach, where game fish can be landed high and dry."*

I was landing a nice bluefish at low tide behind the Gay Head cliffs early one morning. As I was gingerly weaving it between the exposed rocks toward a safe perch on the beach, my friend Sherm Goldstein splashed into the water, gaff in hand. As the mighty war-

rior plunged his fierce-looking weapon into the helpless bluefish, a distinctive voice yelled out, "What are you guys doing? Don't you know how to land a fish? You don't need a gaff!" At first defensive, and slightly offended, Sherm and I soon realized that this was Hank's way of saying "hello." Hank Schauer is a knowledgeable surf fisherman who communicates his knowledge by grumbling and gesticulating.

I started surf fishing on the Jersey shore in 1938, when I was ten years old. My grandfather gave me a Calcutta rod with a reel that didn't have a drag. I had to thumb the spool. The early fishing I did was baitfishing. We raked calico crabs and fished off the jetties. He used to tell me to go down to the beach when it was dead low water, so I could find the holes cut in the bars. He was trying to teach me to read the water. Many people just blind cast. They make a million casts and hope that one hits a fish on the head. We tried to do it a little more scientifically. I had an expert teacher.

Grandfather taught me how to bottom fish the calico crabs, using four-ounce pyramid sinkers. In the spring, the crabs would shed. We used shedder crabs and soft crabs. We would pull the shell off the shedder crab and rig it just like a natural crab. If the hook came out the back, we'd cover the hook with a claw and tie it on with rubber thread. You could rig it so they'd look just like a crab sitting on the bottom. And of course the bass are swimming around looking for natural bait. Bluefish and weakfish love them, too. In those days, though, weakfish were scarce.

My grandfather had a shack in Long Beach Island, New Jersey, and we used to go there and fish Barnegat Inlet for weakfish. There was a lot of baitfishing going on, but lures were also used. The primary lure was a metal squid dressed with feathers. There was no bucktail. Nobody used bucktails in those days.

This fellow named Brauer, who was Coast Guard Chief of Sandy Hook, was making some crude homemade plugs. His plugs are now collectors' items. One of them, oddly enough, was a Flaptail. He used copper to make these Flaptails. They had sort of a scoop nose on them, and they would make a commotion. They were surface plugs. He also made a jointed plug with a nose on it that swam across the top of the water. They were hand-carved and hand-painted, but they worked. The first twenty-pound bass I ever caught was on one of Brauer's Flaptail plugs.

There were guys who fished with eels in those days and they caught big fish. And there were some big fish caught by baitfishermen. I never caught any big fish until later on. I really got into surf fishing when I got out of the Marine Corps in 1947.

I was fishing locally in Monmouth Beach and Sea Bright—places like that. Then the Korean War broke out. I got called back into the Corps again and was there for a year. When I got out of the Marine Corps, I started working at Sandy Hook for the Army. Sandy Hook was a fisherman's paradise.

Sandy Hook, New Jersey, sits on the end of a skinny finger of land jutting into the Atlantic and pointing toward Rockaway Inlet and New York Harbor. It reminds me of the tail of a dog which, given the opportunity, would wag between Staten Island and Brooklyn, splashing in the water of Sandy Hook Bay.

The United States Coast Pilot, *published in 1940, describes some of Hank Schauer's favorite fishing spots, including Tower A jetty, although it is not specifically named.*

> Near North Hook Fog Signal there is a Coast Guard station, a storm-warning display station, and two tall observation towers from which coastwise and foreign vessels are reported to the Maritime Exchange in New York City. These observation towers and a large black tank to the southeast are the most prominent objects on the northern end of the hook. Southward from these are some houses, and Sandy Hook Lighthouse.

The Navy bunker at Katama Beach, built during World War II, was the Vineyard's contribution to fishing holes marked by military installations. Once set back from the ocean in a three-sided mound of earth, creeping erosion toppled it into the sea. The currents swirling around the scarred old block of concrete dug deep holes, making it a popular and productive place to bottom fish.

I met some old friends from high school who were going down

to Sandy Hook to surf fish. Their names were Paul Siciliano and Butch Toth.

We would all go out together, and drop somebody off from the car at various spots to find the fish. We had jetties named First Jetty and Tower Jetty. The Tower Jetty had a big observation tower at one time that was used for trying to spot German submarines during World War II. Brauer would sometimes get reports on the bass from submarine spotters. He'd get a telephone call, "There's a school of bass down off such and such a point." He would buzz down there to fish. He caught many fish this way. The Tower Jetty was famous for its bass fishing. It was nasty to fish on. You could only fish on it at low water, because the rocks were slippery. We used either boots with creepers or golf cleats in them. We would walk out and fish the point. On the north side of the jetty there was a nice pocket where the fish would trap the bait.

We would let one guy off at the First Jetty; the second guy we would leave off at the Tower Jetty; the third guy would take the car and he would go up to what we called the Cove—Spermacitti Cove, —and fish there. When we found the fish, we would compare notes. The next night, we would all go back to the area where someone had found the fish. We started fishing in early May, and we would fish right on through the fall. This was from about 1952 to 1958.

Once in a while, we would leave two guys off at one place, especially if there were four or five of us. One night Butch and I got off at the Tower Jetty. We always agreed that if somebody got into fish, he would blink his flashlight. We left a couple of guys off at the Cove, and Butch and I were fishing the Tower Jetty. Butch was a real big guy and he was a weight-lifting champion in New Jersey and even coached some Olympic people. Well, Butch and I were fishing, and I guess we caught a couple of fish on the Tower Jetty. We had arranged that at a certain time of night the car would pick us up. We came back to the car, and the other guys opened the trunk. They had about twenty bass in the back of the car from the thirties down to about twelve or fourteen pounds. Butch was livid about this whole thing. Butch was always claiming they'd signalled without batteries in the flashlight.

They were only about a half a mile from us. The contour and structure of the beach was such that, if you signalled, you'd be around the corner and you couldn't see. It was a stretch of beach similar to Gay Head. If you're around the corner of the Head toward Pilot's Landing and the other guy's up near Southwest Rock, he could signal all you wanted and nobody would ever see the light.

Finally, I got in the back of the car with Butch. He had a wart right on the top of his ear, so I just touched the wart on his ear and I said, "Now, Butch, calm down." He growled at me and said, "Shut up. These guys didn't signal me!" He wanted to kill somebody.

Eventually we got kicked off the beach at Sandy Hook. They made a missile site there. I was transferred from my job at Sandy Hook down to Fort Monmouth. The government people at the Hook wouldn't let us fish there anymore. So I bought a boat—a twelve-foot aluminum boat with a 7½ horse-power motor. We used to carry the boat over the sea wall and push off into the surf, and fish the Hook anyway. We would run down there in the middle of the night and fish all the rock piles and bars—only we'd fish outside in.

Most of my fish were caught on rigged eels in those days. I'd get home from work, gulp down my supper, and meet this friend of mine. We'd carry the boat over the sea wall and launch it. We'd fish Tower Jetty and First Jetty. We caught lots of fish this way.

Around 1930, Ned Nordeen, a New York fisherman, learned about rigged eel fishing from a Rhode Island fisherman, Art Clarke. Ned took this information back to New York. It wasn't long before rigged eel fishing techniques spread to New Jersey in the early 1940s.

When we first started using eels we would throw them on the cement to stun them and rig them while they were still alive. I said, "This is a crazy way to do this," because they would still wiggle around.

I found a solution of Kosher salt and water would kill and preserve the eels. You could keep them longer that way. I would change the solution after all the slime came off the eels and then put them in a fresh solution. That made them much easier to rig.

I made eel needles from welding rods. I would take a piece of light steel rod, about ten inches long and a sixteenth of an inch thick, hammer one end down and drill a hole through it. The other end was sharpened to a tapered point.

I used forty-five-pound-test, braided nylon line to rig the tail hook, which was a No. 5/0 or No. 6/0. The two ends of braided nylon attached to the tail hook were pulled through the eel, with the needle, until they came out the eel's mouth. The tail hook was posterior to the anal opening, and the open end of braided line is out through the eel's mouth. That line is used to tie the metal squid, with its front hook, onto the eel. I also use button cord to tie the eel's lips down to the front of the metal squid. I would wrap it around ten times and tie two square knots. I would sear the knot so it wouldn't fray.

I started using regular lead to make the squid molds because block tin was too expensive. I found a mold of a flat squid that had a curve in it. This doesn't allow the eel to sink down to the bottom. When you reel it, it swims up toward the top. Now I use wire instead of braided nylon because the bluefish are around more. Some fishermen said wire kills the action of the eel but I disagree. The eel swims just as good and looks just as natural with wire.

Some good eel fishermen fish the rig slowly, letting the eel go down on the bottom. I fish it just like a plug. I reel fast, keeping it on top of the water. Some fishermen use live eels, but I prefer the rigged eel. The rigged eel is easier to keep out of the rocks. A live eel can get down in the rocks and get tangled up and make a mess. In the middle of the night, you don't need a mess.

We had a good mullet run at Sandy Hook in the fall of 1954. The fishing that year was excellent. There's a beach down on the Hook we call Officers Beach. It has a beautiful sand bar right off the point. The mullet used to come out of the rip and run down the beach in schools. You could see the mullet. They'd make a Vee on the top, and you knew they were there. Sometimes patches of mullet would cover an acre. The waves would curl across the bar and roll into the beach. There was a deep cut on the inside of this bar. The fish would chase bait right across the bar in through this cut.

One exceptionally clear day just two of us were fishing on the beach. The waves were rolling across the bar, and a patch of mullet

HANK SCHAUER

was coming along. The sun was at such an angle that you could see right through the wave. The wave made a big tube, and you could see what was in the wave. There were striped bass swimming in this wave, just like a line of football players, charging, trying to kill the quarterback, chasing the mullet. These bass were all different sizes. There were hundreds of them swimming through the curl of the wave. They were chasing the bait into the white water. We would put a plug out, and as soon as it hit the water, you'd have one of them.

I think I caught most of the fish that day on these Heddon Torpedoes. They were a deadly plug. They were very thin and had a propeller on either end. They had these little tiny hooks. You had to fish with a very loose drag, otherwise a fish would straighten the hook right out. The plugs went right across the top of the water and made a commotion like an injured fish. Heddon makes a lot of fresh water gear. Actually, these plugs were designed for fresh water.

Heddon also made a variation of the Torpedo called the Injured Minnow. They were flatter and looked like a fish that was swimming sideways. They had a prop on both ends and a tail hook and belly hooks, and they came in different colors.

Back in the fifties, Jersey had a limit, ten fish per day, eighteen inches from the fork of the tail to the nose. We never kept fish that small anyway. We would always throw those little ones back.

Hank Schauer ran into Sergei de Somov while fishing at Sandy Hook. Conceding that Sergei was a great fisherman, Hank also found him aloof. According to Jerry Jansen, who fished with Sergei in New York, and Ralph Grant and Kib Bramhall, who fished with Sergei on the Vineyard, Sergei was extremely secretive but also friendly. Perhaps Sergei was too busy fishing to socialize with the Jersey Shore fishermen.

We had a guy who used to fish the Hook all the time, who was quite well known up on the Vineyard. He was called the Mad Russian—Sergei de Somov. He won several Derbies on the Vineyard. He was a very secretive guy and he fished at the same jetties we fished. If he ever saw you coming, he would walk off the beach because he didn't want you to see what he was doing.

HANK SCHAUER

One night I walked up on him and he didn't see me coming. It was in the middle of the night. He was fishing on the end of a jetty, and he was using plugs that were like a lead-weighted clothespin. He would cast them out and reel just as fast as he could, making that plug go right across the top of the water. It was like a Spofford's Needlefish, only it was a wooden plug. He painted them black for fishing at night, and red-and-white for daytime fishing. He didn't fish too much during the day because he figured the percentages of night fishing were always best.

One time, early in the morning, when things were slow, we were sitting up on the sea wall. Along comes the Mad Russian. He was down in the surf and we couldn't see what he was doing. He was a long way off. He usually wouldn't talk to other fishermen. He wasn't a very friendly guy. Well, this time he walked up the beach and he humbled himself. He said, "Would you fellows mind giving me a hand? I have a few fish down here. I can't pull them any farther. I'm pretty tired." So we went down and he had about ten fish, each more than thirty pounds, on a stringer.

He used to bury fish on the beach. He would put a stick in the sand to mark them, then he would go dig them up, put them on a stringer, and pull them off the beach. The rope was half-an-inch thick. He would tie one fish onto this rope, string the rest of the fish on top, and drag them through the wash. You can just imagine dragging three or four hundred pounds of fish for two miles. He was a big guy; he was just leaning into it, and he couldn't move them. So, we went down there and helped him carry his fish up.

He bought a brand new Chrysler one year from the proceeds of the fish that he caught. This is on the Hook. He caught a lot of fish. He was a dedicated fisherman. As far as I know, he just used variations of these little weighted plugs. He would often fish a jetty. I watched him several times when he was unaware of my presence. He would go out on a jetty and fish the inside first—right in back of the break of the wave. He'd make three casts out there. Then he'd go to the middle of the jetty, and he would fan cast—casting to the north, east, and west. Then he'd walk out to the end of the jetty and he would fish right off the tip, over the broken rock. He'd make more casts out there because he felt the fish would be out there. Then he would go around to the south side. If there were no fish off that jetty, he would walk up to the next jetty. This was his method. He was a tireless fisherman. The guy would fish all night. He'd start at dark, and he'd quit at dawn. Not too many people will fish like that today.

On a day when the bait was kept nervous and alert by sporadically hitting bonito, I was fishing next to David Duarte on the west Menemsha jetty. The day was sunny and the sea was calm. No salt spray was coating the rocks, which are often slick in bad weather. Several boats were anchored or trolling near the jetty crowding the jetty fishermen as they cast. Problems arose if a fish was hooked and made a run toward the boats, because the fishing line could easily wrap around an anchor line.

David hooked a bonito that made an immediate run for the anchor line of the boat off the point of the jetty. As David yelled for them to pull anchor and move out, we had the distinct feeling from the boat fishermen that we were intruding in their ocean. They did pull anchor and David did land his fish, but not without some sore tempers and unnecessary excitement.

Hank experienced the battles between jetty and boat fishermen. In the early 1960s, Sandy Hook had the largest concentration of striped bass guides in New Jersey. Milt Rosko, in Secrets of Striped Bass Fishing wrote: "The Sandy Hook trollers fish along the peninsula as well as in Raritan, Sandy Hook, and Lower New York bays. One of the most famous spots is the tide rip at the point of Sandy Hook."

Commenting on the jetty jockies, who fish from Manasquan Inlet to Sandy Hook, Rosko noted that "most anglers move from jetty to jetty until they hit into a concentration of feeding bass. As fishing of this type is rather tiresome, you'll ususally find two groups. One group doesn't mind the exercise and fishes with lures, while the other takes it easy and fishes with natural bait, waiting for the fish to come to them."

Hank Schauer doesn't mind the exercise, and he is too restless to baitfish anymore. Hank has gone from calico crabs on the bottom to rigged eels and black-backed Red Fins on top.

I was fishing on a jetty with my friend John Paremely. The

trollers would come in real close to the beach. Guys on the jetty would cast across the trolling lines. One of these guys in the trolling boat had apparently hooked a fish, and the fish had run across the end of the jetty. John cast out there, and, as he was reeling in, the other guy's line got wrapped around his plug. So he started pulling the line, and he pulled in this twenty-six-pound bass that was hooked on this other guy's lure. He pulled it right into the surf.

The guys on the jetties were constantly at war with the boats that were coming in too close. We had this anti-trolling lure. It was a pyramid sinker with razor blades in each corner. About twenty inches up from these razor blades was a tennis ball. The line would go through the tennis ball and connect to the pyramid sinker. When the boats would come in too close and troll along the jetties they would usually have four rods out. We would cast our anti-trolling lure right across the top of their lines. Then we would reel in fast and the razor blades in the sinkers would cut the lines. You'd see one rod after another go up slack.

It was a real war. Nelson Benedict wrote about it in the *Newark Star Ledger*. One of these boats was trolling wire line and hooked this tennis ball sinker arrangement and brought it in. They found out what was cutting their line. Benedict's column, in the following Sunday paper, attacked the guys on the jetties for doing bad things to the trollers. But these trollers on the boats were coming in and fishing too close.

I also fished the jetties with Little Eddie. Little Eddie was a slight built guy. He was a nutty striped bass fisherman who often fished morning, noon, and night. He loved to cast these big doodle-bug lures. Another one of these boats came in and fished right on top of us. Well, Eddie put on a big doodlebug and cast out there. A freakish thing happened. It hit this guy's radio antenna and just churned right around the antenna. Eddie reared back and was reeling this boat right into the jetty. The boat was about a thirty-foot powerboat. The guy throws it in gear and starts pulling away. It looked funny. Here's Eddie fighting this thirty-foot boat with a doodlebug wrapped around its antenna. Of course, the guy pulls out and contacts the Coast Guard. The Coast Guard came down to the jetty and wanted to know what was going on. So we told them. And the Coast

HANK SCHAUER

Guard got out there with a bullhorn and told the boats to leave and let the people fish off the jetty.

Hank Schauer stalks the fifty-pound striper like Captain Ahab pursued Moby Dick. Although the intensity of his obsession may vary from year to year, the relentless drive never completely leaves him. Captain Ahab lost a leg during his first encounter with the great albino whale; Hank lost a little bit of his sanity during his first encounter with a fifty-pound striper that escaped.

Jerry Sylvester, who used to fish with Francis Bernard, also lost a large fish that he kept thinking about, second-guessing himself until the day he died. Wondering whether he should have used a plug instead of an eel, he wrote in Salt Water Fishing Is Easy: *"Well, I have fished for so many years that I have acquired the ability to judge the weight of a fish on my line to within a few pounds. . . . Should you get a fifty-pound fish, or over, on your line it will feel as though you had tied into a loaded cement truck going downhill. . . . In my years of fishing for striped bass I've caught quite a few that weighed from forty to fifty pounds and I've come to know the feel of a heavy fish on the line. So it was not too difficult for me to gauge the weight of the one I lost. I repeat, in the eighty-pound class."*

When the opportunity presented itself to fish on the Vineyard, Hank made the necessary arrangements. With dreams of the fifty-pound striper lulling him to sleep like sheep in fish clothing, Hank set out for Gay Head and Squibnocket.

One of the most fantastic and memorable days I've had fishing was at Gay Head during a driving northeaster in the late 1970s. It was the last day of the Derby. The rain was almost falling horizontally it was blowing so hard. I went down there around four in the morning.

The tide was running strong; the waves were washing over the banks by the windmill, and there was a tremendous backwash. There were weakfish, bluefish, and bass in close. They were all in schools in different places. I was running up and down the beach trying to find where the biggest bass were. They were swirling—tails coming out of the water. I'd see a big tail, and I'd throw a big swimmer out, crank the reel two turns and the swimmer would disappear. I'd be on to a fish. The fish all weighed in the high twenties. I was tagging them and putting them back in.

Everybody on the beach had fish. Some fishermen were concerned about getting to the Derby weigh-in station before it closed. I wasn't concerned about weighing in fish. All I was concerned with was catching fish. There were some fantastic bluefish. I think the biggest bluefish in the Derby was caught right at that spot. And one of the leading bass was caught there that day. I don't even know how many fish I caught, but I caught a lot of fish that day. I caught bass, bluefish, and weakfish. The weakfish were running eight to twelve pounds and the blues ran up to twenty pounds.

It was a really violent storm. There was a young boy down there fishing with his father. And his father wasn't paying attention to him. The kid had a big fish on, and this wave came up in back of him and was washing him right out to sea. When I saw this I grabbed him right by the seat of his pants. He had a fish on, and I pulled him up onto the beach. I told his father, who I became friendly with later on, that he'd better watch his son or he was going to be out at sea on the end of a bass.

That day the weakfish were over near the Southwest Rock. They had the bait trapped in this little pocket, and they were running the bait right up onto the beach. You could see the weakfish finning. They'd hit a pocket of bait and then come right out of the water. It was a fantastic sight. The bluefish were right out in front on the bar. The bass were in this great big pocket, right inside the big rock on the flat. And they were chasing the bait about. I could see their tails come up. Sometimes I could even see their dorsal fin.

There weren't that many people fishing down there that morning. There were two people who had fished all night. They left early because they had to make two trips down to get their fish and drag them up the cliffs. I was fishing with a friend of mine. And there were a couple of guys from Long Beach Island, New Jersey. One guy won the Derby that year with the biggest bluefish. It was nineteen pounds, six ounces. There was another fish caught that night that was eighteen pounds, by a friend of his who said, "I got the Derby with this bluefish." And his friend beat him out the next morning with a nineteen-pounder.

HANK SCHAUER

I went down to fish Philbin Beach in Gay Head one night in the fall, 1981. A couple of guys I know—Dick Landon and Joel Radding—were fishing down there. So, I fished a while alongside them, back and forth, up and down the beach. I walked up to Dick and said, "Well, the gloom clouds are going to leave, so I'm going to go up and fish Zacks Cliffs, and you guys will probably catch fish, when I go."

I saw him the next morning and he said to me, "Hey, Hank, I want you to see something." So I said, "Did you catch a big fish?" He said, "I caught one twenty minutes after you left." He was using about a five-foot freshwater rod with six-pound-test line. Twenty minutes after I left he hooked this fifty-six-pound striped bass, right in the backwash, and landed that fish. I went up to his car and he opened the trunk, and here was this tremendous fish. It turned out to be a Derby winner. I fished right in that spot, which proves you can't beat luck! There's got to be a certain amount of luck, catching a fifty-pounder.

I can remember talking to Don Honig, the doggie doctor. I mentioned that I was fishing around Squibnocket. I fished half the night up at Squibnocket. I even went back in the morning and fished there. After all that time I put in, running myself into the ground, I had caught one thirty-one-pound striper. Don had a friend visiting. The next morning it was raining, so his friend wanted to sleep. Donnie called me up and said, "My friend didn't want to get up because it was raining in the morning." So they got up at eleven o'clock in the morning and went out to Squibnocket, and this friend of his caught a striper in the fifties—right in this very place where I was fishing.

During fall 1987, Hank Schauer caught two fifty-pounders, on rigged eels at Stonewall Beach. The gloom clouds parted. Hank said, "I always fish hard but just didn't have the luck. I spent many years trying different tides and techniques and spent countless lonely hours on the beach to catch those fish. It was worth every minute and I wouldn't have wanted it easy. Things that come easy are never appreciated.

"Stonewall, with its slippery bowling ball rocks and deep drop-offs, is one of the most difficult places to land a fish on the Vine-

yard. I felt even more satisfied catching my first fifty-pounder at Stonewall. I'll never forget that first fish, suspended in the curl of a large breaker, at dawn, with the sun touching the horizon."

Fishing in Deal, New Jersey, Hank Schauer reached the end of a humpback jetty at low tide. The large rocks in the middle of the jetty, covered with velvety green moss and jagged barnacles, had fallen into the ocean years before, creating a twelve-foot gap. Hank caught two stripers and was concentrating on catching more when the rising tide cut him off from shore. Hank did not panic. Instead, he tied his fish to a twenty-foot-long rope, put his rod in his mouth and swam doggie-style to the safety of the inner jetty rocks, where he climbed up and pulled in his fish. A bystander watching from the beach said, "I'm not drinking, so I believe it. If I had a drink, I would think I was seeing things."

I've got a long love affair with the striped bass. It goes way back to when I first decided that just catching fish and killing them wasn't the only way to go. They used to net them in New Jersey. They netted them right in the spawning season when they used to go up the Mullica River. I've seen thousands of pounds of fish, that couldn't even be sold, rotting on the ground. It was a sinful thing. Everybody became a netter—milkmen and everybody else. We raised a lot of money, hired lawyers, and went down to the State House in Trenton to put a stop to this type of fishing. Finally, we got them to stop gill netting striped bass in New Jersey.

I contributed my bucks, but I didn't have much money at the time. I went to many meetings. They were still netting them in the Chesapeake Bay tributaries in Delaware, and netting was still permitted in New York. We felt frustrated. Now, fortunately, people have gotten wise and said, "Well, let's protect this fish."

I've seen a lot of beautiful sunrises and sunsets. I love to fish in the pouring rain. I love the nights. It's awesome to look up in the sky at night and see billions and billions of stars. I used to sit on a rock and pray. I would thank God for making me part of all this.

Frank Woolner reads the water at Gay Head in 1957.

Nelson Bryant's old fishing tackle reveals a history of lures.

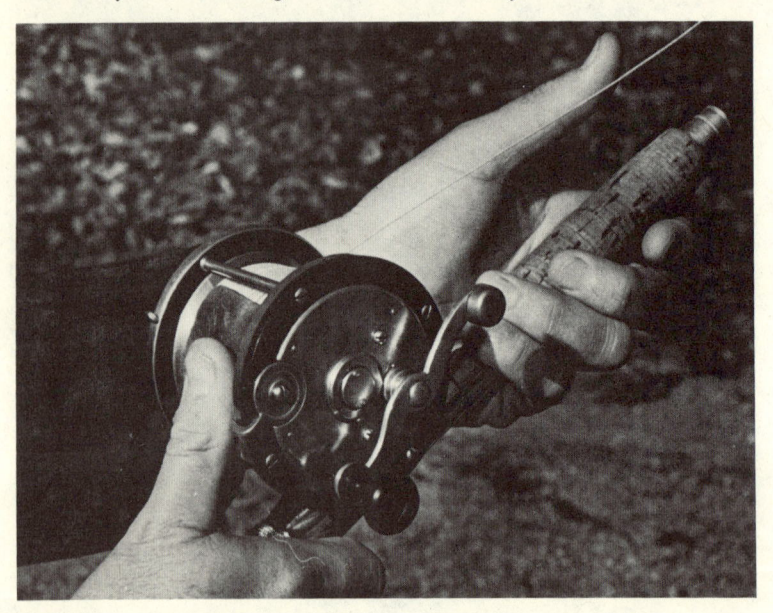

The early surf-fishing reel boasted a thumb stall (it did not have an adjustable drag) and linen twisted Cuttyhunk line.

This assortment shows the contrast between early squids, molded out of lead and/or tin and today's squids made from nickel or chrome plated.

Hal Lyman, publisher emeritus of *Salt Water Sportsman,* is a pioneer of modern surf fishing.

Dick Hathaway lands a bluefish taken on an Atom Popper.

A 1957 photo of Oscar Flanders (left) and Buddy Oliver caught them discussing fishing strategies at Stonewall Beach.

Ray Metcalf, at age sixty-nine, poses with his derby winner—a fifty-one-pound, fourteen-ounce striper.

Percy West (left) and Ralph Grant display their catch at the 11th Annual Martha's Vineyard Striped Bass and Bluefish Derby, 1956.

Buddy Oliver stands on the rebuilt bass stand at Squibnocket in the mid-1950s.

This channel opening into Tisbury Great Pond is usually dug out by hand in order to mix fresh and salt water together, thereby obtaining the correct mix for healthy oysters. At one time, oxen were used on the beach to help the channel.

Cooper Gilkes III (center) is pictured here casting a fly into the surf at East Beach on Chappaquiddick.

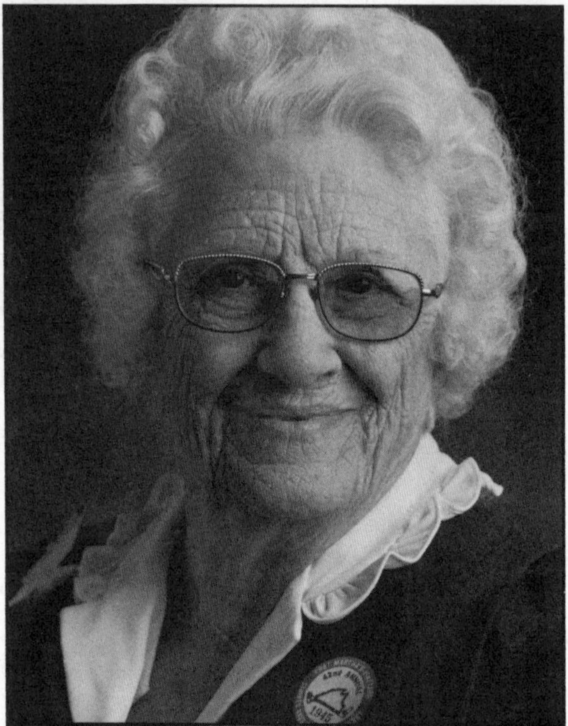
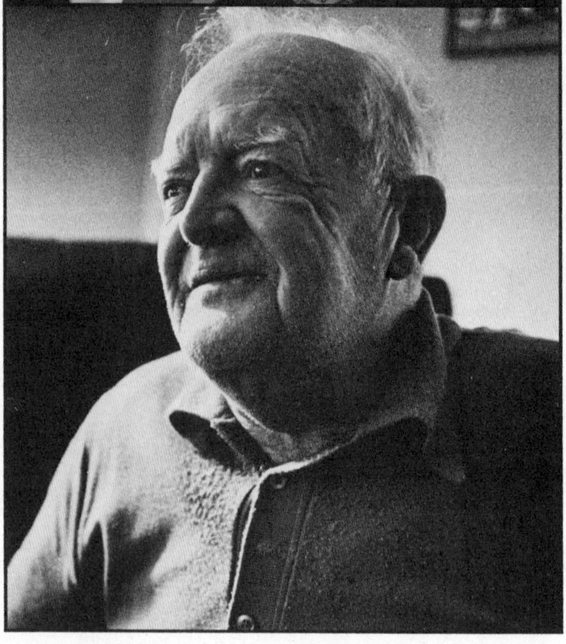

8

Ray and Bernadette Metcalf

The old masters of the Vineyard surf-fishing fraternity began a tradition of fanaticism, manic behavior, sleepless nights, and poor eating habits that they unknowingly passed along to future generations. These fever symptoms started with fishermen legendary for their success: Buddy Oliver, the Grant brothers, Percy West, Gus Amaral, Sergei de Somov, Oscar Flanders, Howard Andrews, and Ray and Bernadette Metcalf.

Like most fishermen, many members of this group were secretive about their techniques and favorite spots. Even their families didn't know where they caught fish.

Some of these old-timers, however, fished mostly for fun. Sharing their knowledge was as satisfying as catching a big fish. Nature's beauty and dangers were the stimulants that kept them awake.

While other fishermen found peaceful solitude at night on

nearly inaccessible beaches along the varied coastline of the Vineyard, Ray and Bernadette Metcalf fished during the day where anyone could see them. The challenge of catching big fish was secondary to the joy they shared being together.

R.M.: I was about thirty years old when we moved to the Vineyard from Fairhaven, Massachusetts. I would go after mackerel and scup in Fairhaven. Ten years after I moved here, they started the Derby. My friend was in it. He enticed both Bernadette and me to join. We won many trophies, reels, and plugs.

In those days we could go anywhere and fish and not have anyone follow us. You didn't see No Trespassing signs like you do today. I had a Jeep and I could go way down the beach with it. We always had the same gang like Tony Gaspar and Monty Wells.

B.M.: When they caught a ten-pound blue at the time, it was a big fish. A friend once came over with a ten-pound blue. I said, "Oh my goodness, she has the biggest blue we ever saw!" Now a ten-pound blue doesn't mean a thing.

R.M.: I like to use a No. 7/0 hook, with a four-ounce lead, an eighteen-inch leader and a piece of butterfish. I put my pole in a sandspike and sit in the Jeep. I may even have a cup of coffee or listen to the radio. When I see my pole bend, I've got time to run and grab it; by that time the fish has swallowed the bait. Many guys who bottom fish lose their fish because they pull the bait right out of the fish's mouth. The idea is to let him swallow it.

B.M.: Ray worked until four each day. I'd have dinner ready. The minute he'd come in he'd say, "Let's go!" We'd pack the Jeep and stay until it got dark. We came home just to go to bed. We'd get our work done during the day.

R.M.: We'd go surf fishing when we had the time. That was it. Regardless of the time, like the day I got my Derby winner—in the middle of the afternoon, the tide was wrong, the water was dirty—*everything* was wrong! If you saw me going, you'd think I was crazy.

Fishing's just pure luck! That's all. A lot of people would say to me, "Hey, Ray, where's a good place to go fishing?" I'd say, "If I knew, I'd be there."

B.M.: I've fished since I was a little girl. My grandfather taught me how to fish in Fairhaven. We had a cottage there, and I used to go fishing with him. He taught me to fish for bluefish. I always liked the low tide when it was just about to turn in. Every time I caught a big fish, it was at low tide.

We used to fish for tautog and bluefish. I never heard of bass when I was a little girl. We didn't hear much about bass when we first came here either.

R.M.: Every minute we had, we'd go fishing. That was it! Come home from work, unload some of the tools out of the Jeep, load the fish poles and gear and we're off.

B.M.: We like to fish for butterfish at the Edgartown town wharf.

R.M.: When the butterfish were running, the fellows would fish off the end of the wharf for bonito and false albacore.

B.M.: There's been large numbers of bonito these last few years down at the wharf. The kids catch them. A seven-year-old girl caught one this past summer.

R.M.: I'd give the butterfish to the guys fishing for bonito. They'd hook them right through the back with a treble hook and float them out. Boy, those bonito used to hit them!

B.M.: One Saturday morning we spent two hours at the wharf. Cooper Gilkes III, Ralph Case, and a bunch of men were fishing for albacores. We spent two hours sitting there catching small butterfish for them to use.

R.M.: Down on the wharf butterfishing one time, a young couple, newlyweds, were watching me. The wife was getting such a thrill watching me, I said, "Here. Try it." So I let her take the pole. Well, by God, she caught one! Her husband couldn't stand it; he had to take the pole. Well, between the two of them, they admitted they had the best time of their lives.

My technique worked well. On the bottom of my line was a treble hook. About two inches above it, I'd have a single hook. I'd put my bait on the single hook. When the butterfish would nibble at the bait, which was usually squid, I'd give the line a little jerk. The treble hook below the bait would come up and snag the butterfish.

B.M.: Many women first say about fishing, "I don't think I'd like that." I remember when Monty Wells married a girl from Boston, she used to say, "Oh, I don't like fishing."

One day Ray and I took her. Ray gave her his rod and she

caught a fish. That was it! She was hooked. She came back and said to her husband, "I think I'm going to get a rod." "Well," he said, "I thought if you caught one, that would happen." Then she came fishing with us and her husband. We had grand times. So it doesn't take much to get women interested. They may say, "Oh no, I can't do that." But if they catch one, then they're hooked.

R.M.: One day Bernie went down to the Herring Creek with her girlfriends to get some quahogs and came back with a big bucket of oysters. When she came in she said, "Gee, I never heard of oysters down there." So I was talking to the boys downtown one day. One of them said, "Oh yeah, I put them there to salt." He got them from the Great Pond and put them in Herring Creek to salt.

B.M.: He got them from the pond but the bag busted in the creek. We were quahoging and I said, "I got some oysters." My friend said, "Bernie, you're dreaming!" I said, "I've *got some oysters!*" So they quit quahoging and we picked up oysters. We came home and I cooked the oysters. Then Ray heard this guy say, "I put a bag there to salt them. I got them in the pond where it's not very salty—they were in fresh water." So we had a nice meal of oysters.

R.M.: Bass is my favorite fish to catch. Bluefish will give you more of a fight. But finding bass is the fun. If you went every day and caught one, it wouldn't be the same. Somedays you don't catch any; it makes it better.

Down at the hole where we'd fish, it seemed like we'd always catch three skates, then the bass or blues would come in. We always seemed to catch two or three skates before we could get a bass or a blue. Some people say if the skates are there, you might as well pack up and go home, but that's not a good idea. I'll tell you one thing, though. If you're fishing and you see seals breaking water, go home. They chase all the fish away. Also, when you're fishing and you see the fins of a sandshark, go home! They're bait chasers. We never left on account of catching dogfish, though. You might catch a dogfish; and next thing you know, you've got a big bass.

B.M.: I always say there's a cycle. Before we had the bluefish, we had all the flounder we wanted. We'd catch two at a time. We'd bring great big buckets of them home. We were catching flounder all along the south side. The flounder—oh, the flounder! When the blitz of bluefish came in, we didn't see them anymore.

RAY AND BERNADETTE METCALF

R.M.: I have a bait trap to catch mummichogs. I'd put a trap down off Atwood's Circle with a little bread in it. We would go back in an hour and have all the bait we could use. Little mummichogs are the best bait there is for flounder. Sometimes if we were in a hurry, we didn't wait for the trap; we had a net and we'd go to the creek and seine them.

B.M.: I think when the cycle of bluefish goes out, the flounder's going to come back. It might take quite a few years, but I think that's what's going to happen.

The unrelenting surf changes the shape of the Vineyard in subtle ways. Sand is often moved off beaches, exposing countless rocks of different shapes and sizes. When conditions change, sand moves back onto the land, as if thousands of trucks appeared in the night dumping their secret cargos.

More than six thousand years ago, during the time of the glaciers, Cape Poge Pond did not exist. There was no South Beach and no Katama Bay. The bar ending at Norton's Point and partitioning the Atlantic Ocean from the Bay had not yet been formed.

When the Norton Point bar finally did form, establishing the southern boundary of Katama Bay, it was often breached by pounding waves breaking through the gritty sand. Maps from the late 1800s show west and east openings of the bay. The former was near Mattakeset; the latter near Wasque.

Many of the old-timers who fished the area in beach buggies took the Chappy ferry from Edgartown. This approach would give fishermen a direct route to Wasque and the east side of the openings. Often small skiffs were kept on the beach to cross the opening, gaining access to fishing spots along the Norton Point bar.

As the openings closed and reopened again, deep holes would temporarily form offshore. Baitfish, striped bass, and bluefish would lurk in the coolness of the deep water.

In the early 1940s when both openings were closed, a deep trough was present offshore. Bernadette Metcalf, with a keen eye she developed while frost fishing for whiting with her grandfather, was drawn to this one special hole. Its dark undulating waters formed a mysterious pool filled with the ingredients for a bouilla-

baisse. It beckoned to her like an ice-blue swimming pool on a blazing summer day.

R.M.: Bernie's the one who really found what later became known as Metcalf's Hole. This was about forty years ago.

B.M.: I'm the one that found it; I'm the one that fished there first. I always walked the beach a lot.

R.M.: We'd park and she'd walk.

B.M.: As I was walking I saw this bar offshore. I said, "This looks like a good place to try fishing."

At the time Katama Bay was not open to the ocean. It had closed recently. The spot I liked was near the old opening. The sand bar was formed by the water running out across the beach and a deep hole was created between the beach and the bar. I thought, "Now when those rips come over that area near the bar, the conditions should be good for catching fish."

So, I started to fish and I caught some. It didn't take long before Ray and some friends saw me. We stayed there to fish. Most people would go right by us to fish at Wasque. We caught loads of fish at that spot.

One day Ray, my brother, and my sister-in-law were sitting on the tailgate. The tide was extra low. They had stopped to eat lunch. They said, "There's no fish. It's too low." I thought to myself, "That's all right. I'm going to try." I went down the beach a short distance and I caught a great big eighteen-pound bluefish. I put my rod under my arm. My father taught me to whistle with my fingers; so I whistled to them. As I was pulling it in, they said, "You must have seaweed." All of a sudden, I pulled this great big fish in. Then they came over and we caught three or four more big bluefish. Remember, the water was very low, so it doesn't always go by the tide. The blues are there at different times. They might be there at high water; they can be there at low water.

R.M.: You could see a dark spot in the water where the hole was. The water running out from the old opening cut a trough out there. That was it. That's the spot that became Metcalf's Hole. We wouldn't go to Wasque anymore. We'd just park there and fish all day.

B.M.: That was our spot. We always went there. After we

found that spot, I don't think we went to Wasque twice. Some of the guys called it Metcalf's Hole. They'd say, "Oh, the Metcalfs are always there." When they told somebody to go fishing, they'd say, "Go fish in Metcalf's hole." So, they named it that.

R.M.: You'd laugh. The day after I caught my big Derby winner in 1974 at Metcalf's Hole. You couldn't get within a mile of it. Fishermen were lined up there like flies at a funeral.

On a crisp June morning about twelve years ago, I fished Pilots Landing with Sherm Goldstein. Although steamships stopped discharging passengers long ago, access to the beach is still possible along a deeply rutted and winding ancient way. A moon tide that was running unusually high caused the surf to cut into the brownish clay cliffs, turning the water close to shore the color of coffee with cream. The dirty water was discouraging, but the other conditions were ideal. Sherm remembered that striped bass are primarily bottom feeders. The action of the surf stirs up the sand and rocks driving crabs, sea worms, and sea clams from their hiding places. Casting a white bucktail jig twenty feet out and bouncing it along the bottom, he landed three stripers weighing between fifteen and twenty-five pounds on three consecutive casts.

Dirty water, wrong tides, and gale-force winds can keep many fishermen at home. Undaunted by less than ideal conditions, Ray Metcalf plunked a butterfish in his favorite hole and caught the Derby winner in 1974—a fifty-one-pound fourteen-ounce striped bass.

R.M.: Back in 1974 I was fishing with Bernie, my brother-in-law Fred Castonquaye, and his wife. We were down at Metcalf's Hole. Fred got on a big fish. The rest of us all reeled in, to give him a chance. The fish would work its way in and out. Finally, it got close enough to gaff. When I gaffed it a wave hit me and filled up my waders. So I pulled his fish high and dry and I said to Bernie, "Well, I guess I'll take off my waders and dry off in the sun and fish again." "Oh no, no, no. You've got to go home and change your clothes," she said. It's about half past two—bad time of the afternoon to fish. I went home to change my clothes. When I came back, I caught the Derby winner.

I didn't see anything special in the water. I was bottom fishing with butterfish. Everything was wrong. It was the middle of the day and the tide was low. I put the rod in a sand spike and we're sitting there talking. Then the pole bent right over. Of course, I ran like the devil, grabbed it and made sure he had it down good. Then I started to reel him in. People say, "How long did it take you?" I don't know how long; all I was worried about was my line parting. I went up and down the beach with that son-of-a-gun. He was fifty-five inches long and his girth was only twenty-six inches—long and thin.

There were people following me up and down the beach. They could see it was a big fish. This was one time people couldn't say "your wife caught it." I had proof she didn't.

You know a mistake many fishermen make? When they get a big fish on, and the thing comes right up within five feet of them and all of a sudden they say, "Oh yeah, I'll fix that so and so." And they tighten up their drag! The worst thing in the world they could do! The next time the fish comes in and starts to go out, he keeps right on going out because he snaps the line.

I set my drag before I throw anything out in the water. I bet if you go in my shop now and try my reels, you'll find each one is set.

I don't know how many times my Derby winner came in close and then made a run. I was getting tired of reeling but I didn't touch that drag. I kept saying to myself, "Don't touch that drag!"

B.M.: And I kept saying, "You better let him go 'cause you're going to have a heart attack." Ray was halfway in the water. I was scared.

R.M.: I wasn't going to let go. But five more minutes; he would've had me in the water with him. I was very tired. I was walking up and down the beach trying to work him in.

Finally, I got him in close enough for Bernie to yell, "It's a striper." What a beautiful sight it was—right in the crest of a wave.

B.M.: The sun was shining right on those stripes. He'd come right up to the top and then he'd swoop down again. Oh, he was tough!

R.M.: Oh yes. That was a beautiful sight. But I'll tell you one thing; it was more beautiful when I had him high and dry up on the beach!

B.M.: There were some people way down on the point. They saw us with spy glasses. When they saw him pulling in that fish, they all came down to watch.

R.M.: I had a white oil cloth that I put down on the tailgate of the Jeep; I put our fish on it. I had my big one, my brother-in-law's big one, which turned out to be almost forty pounds, and three or four good-size blues. When I turned on the paved road on the way home, I noticed a car following us. When I drove in the yard, he followed me in the yard. It was the police sergeant. He said, "Boy, that is the most beautiful sight I ever saw!"

The first thing I heard when I got to the weigh-in station was, "Your wife caught it!" They all holler that every time I bring one in. Inside the weigh-in station there's a table to put the fish on. There was some guy ahead of me with a fish, but mine was getting heavy. So I said to the guy, "Do you mind if I put this on the table?" He turned around and looked. The fish's mouth was right in his face. They guy jumped right off the floor! He got out of my way. When he saw my fish, he walked out. He wouldn't weigh his in.

Downtown Edgartown used to have a chalkboard in the old Turf and Tackle Store. They put the leaders' names on it with the weight of their fish. I ran into one of the guys and he said, "Hey, Ray, I see somebody beat you!"

"Yeah. What'd they get?"

"I hear it's a sixty-pounder."

"Oh yeah."

So, I walked by the store and looked at the board. Sure enough, the name Paul Kelly was on the board with a sixty-pounder. Paul Kelly never even knew what a fishing pole was. It turns out the guys did it just to tease me. The guys were standing in the back and when they saw me looking, they laughed like crazy! But, boy, when the guy from the fishing club saw it, he made them take it down.

The next day, I went back to the same spot. It was a zoo! It was a jungle. I went by in the Jeep. I could see there were no fishing spots and the guys were joking and saying, "Get lost, Metcalf; we're here!" No one caught anything.

RAY AND BERNADETTE METCALF

B.M.: You were sixty-nine years old then and the boy that took third was fourteen. Never in the past has there been such an extreme age range—a youngster and an old-timer.

R.M.: That was funny. The first and third prizes—a senior and a junior. That's the best part of the fishing. I love fishing for the fun, and especially for the kids.

B.M.: Ray won the Governor Francis Sargent Award for the heaviest striper during the Derby and the Sergei de Somov Memorial Trophy for seniors. He also won a trip for two to the Azores. But we didn't accept the trip. Ray loves to stay on the Island.

R.M.: Bernie wouldn't fly unless she could drag her foot on the ground. We accepted some prize money instead.

Lost fish stories give the fisherman an opportunity to exaggerate the size of the fish. Not having seen the fish, the fisherman can pick a weight, usually in the poundage of the largest fish ever caught, and excitedly tell his friends about the big one that got away. When the fisherman tells this story, however, he should keep in mind that "lost" fish are sometimes found.

Arthur P. Silvia told me the lost fish story of Bucky Rhodes, which took place in the early 1940s. Bucky was bottom fishing near the Tisbury Great Pond when he had a tremendous hit. Because he wasn't paying attention, his rod was pulled from its sand spike, across the sand and into the ocean. This gave Bucky the perfect opportunity to fantasize and brag about a fish so large that it swam away with his rod. The next day Bucky returned to the beach where he met a congenial policeman who was vacationing on the Vineyard. For relaxation the cop had decided to do a little bottom fishing. When he retrieved his rig to check the bait, he snagged a foreign object. The object was Bucky Rhodes' fishing rod with the fish still hooked on the line. The cop reeled in the fish and gave Bucky back his rod. The fish was a twenty-pound striper, which the cop took home for dinner. Dreams of a seventy-pounder quickly faded for Bucky Rhodes.

R.M.: I'll tell you a good one. One day my wife and I were fishing on a Sunday, and I caught a forty-two-and-a-half-pound bass.

When I brought him ashore, there was a plug stuck in his head, and a lot of line wrapped around it. Harvey Ewing, the reporter, was there and saw it. So he put the story in the *Standard-Times*. The next day Kib Bramhall came over and said, "Ray, before I see it, was it a Reverse Atom plug?" Then he asks if the leader was tied with what they call a perfect knot. I remember he used to pull the knot with his pipe stem. Everything he said was right. He hooked onto it on a Thursday at Squibnocket and then his line parted. There's a lot of rocks up there. I caught it on a Sunday off Katama at Metcalf's Hole.

He was plugging. I got it on sea clam. I did give Kib his plug back.

B.M.: The bigger fish he'd give to the nursing home and other places like that.

R.M.: I'd give all the big fish away.

B.M.: We never sold fish. We used to give them away to all the neighbors. There were old people on the other side of the street, and we'd furnish them with fish. It never went wasted.

Bottom fishing squid near Goff's an anonymous fisherman had two rods in sand spikes. Because it was late and he worked hard at his job, he decided to take a little nap. When he awakened, one rod was gone; the drag marks in the sand reminding him of some bizarre snail race. The remaining rod was bent over straining against the weight of a bluefish that was effortlessly stripping line from the reel.

Bernadette Metcalf almost lost her fishing gear during a picnic when a big fish jerked it from her sand spike. As it headed for storage in Neptune's locker, she put down her sandwich, lunged, and grabbed the butt, just before it disappeared.

B.M.: I was fishing with Ray, the postmaster Mr. Wilde, and his wife down at Metcalf's Hole. I was sitting on the tailgate of the Jeep with Mrs. Wiley watching my rod, which I had in a sand spike. While I was having a sandwich and coffee, Ray got onto a fish. All of a sudden, *my* rod starts to go down the beach! I thought I was going to lose it. I said to my friend, "No use running after it because it's going too fast." Then it stopped, so I started to run after it. When I picked it up I tried to set the hook, but I fell over a steep embankment head first into the water. I held my coffee cup in one hand and my rod, with the fish still on, in my other hand. Ray heard the others shouting, "Bernie, Bernie." He looked back and saw my white shirt sticking out of the water. So he came running, and he just picked me up by the back of my shirt and hauled me out. After that, I just thought, "Well, I'm going to get through fishing."

My mind was numb, from being in the water. Sometimes they say we can save ourselves, but I don't think so. My head was under the water. But I held my cup and my rod. Ray said, "Reel!" My reel was full of sand, which made the handle difficult to turn. It was squeaking away. But I pulled in a twelve-pound bass. I went to drink my coffee, but it was a cup of saltwater. I never gave up on that fish. Even though I was soaking wet, I held my ground.

R.M.: I'm sorry to say I can't walk the beach like I used to and cast like I used to. I have to be careful I don't strain myself. I've had the shingles for more than eleven years. Now I've got some gout.

B.M.: Last year he went to fish. He had a bluefish on and had trouble with the shingles. A fellow had to help him. So, this year, I guess the fishing is over.

R.M.: Oh, well. When you get to be eighty, you're bound to have troubles.

When Ray Metcalf died about a month after we shared fishing stories in his living room, he was eighty years old. The Reverend George F. Almeida, pastor of St. Elizabeth's Church in Edgartown, included his own fishing story in the eulogy:

> *Fishing was one of his greatest hobbies. Many times you would see him and his dear wife fishing at the wharf. One day he wasn't catching fish. Someone in a fishing boat came along and gave him a large fish for his bucket. The next day a woman with a fishing pole asked Mrs. Metcalf if she had seen the gentleman who had caught the large fish yesterday. "Oh," she said, "He lied. He is over there. He did get the fish here, but he didn't tell you how he got the*

fish." *Many episodes like this will be written about Raymond and his lovely wife, Bernadette."*

B.M.: This young couple comes along. I'm on one end of the wharf, and he's on the other end. They came over and said, "Where could we fish without going in a boat?" I said, "Down at South Beach." "Well," she said, "There's a man who was sitting here yesterday who caught a great big bluefish." So I looked at her. I said, "Is it that man down at the end of the wharf?" She said, "Yes." "Oh," I said, "That man lies terribly!" She looked at me and said, "Well, he said he caught it here." I said, "I don't think so. He said he *got* it here." Everybody was laughing. It was fun.

Ray used to say that he was the biggest fish I ever caught. We were married for almost forty-nine years.

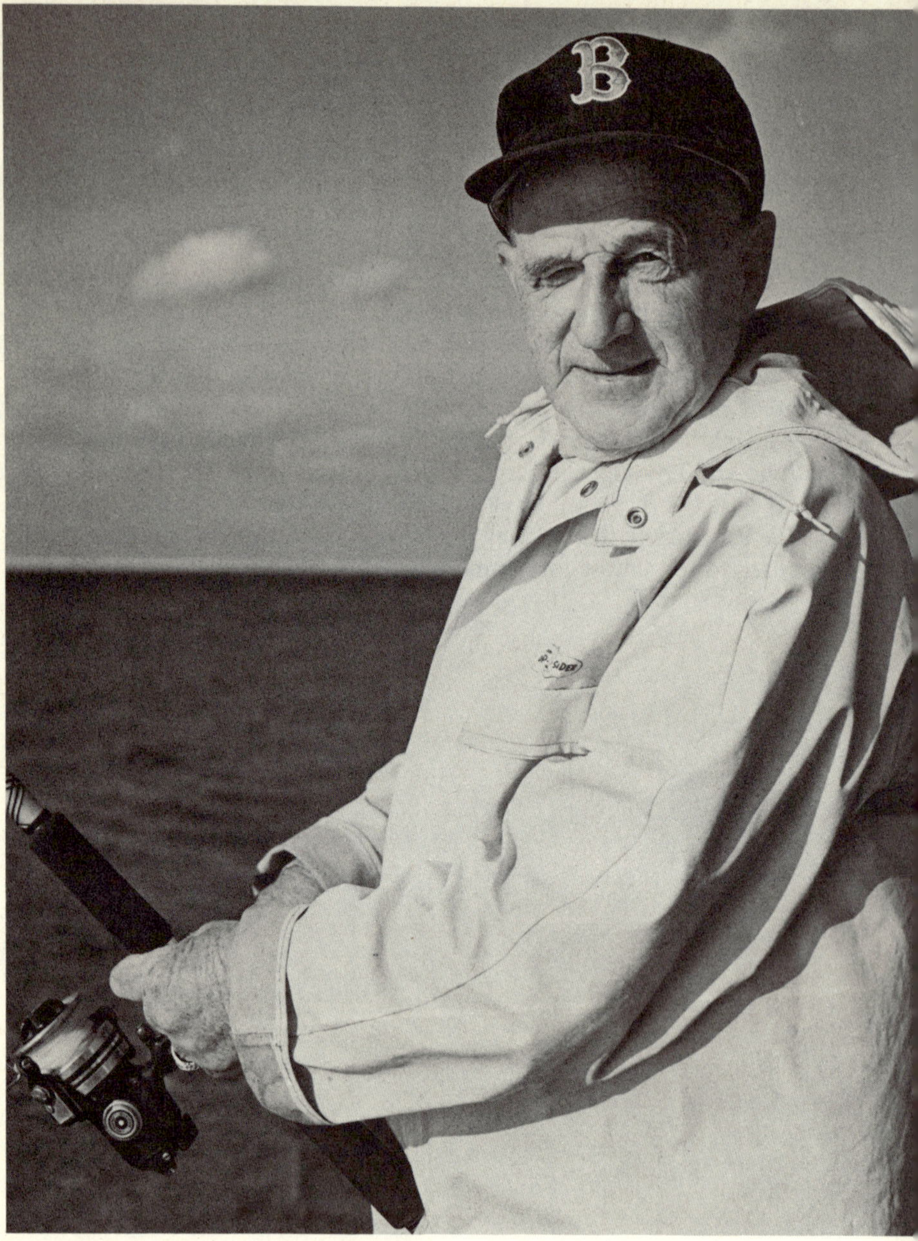

9
Ralph Grant

I first heard about the fishing exploits of Ralph Grant from my friend David Finkelstein. David and I often fish the Wasque rips on Chappaquiddick. Like most surf fishermen on the Vineyard, we fish Wasque during the last four hours of the falling or west tide. We prefer a southwest wind working against the tide.

During a period of northeast winds and rough seas, David and I decided to give Wasque a rest. A few days later David called. "Did you hear about Ralph Grant?" he asked. "He went out to Wasque during the middle of the day, in the northeast wind, on an incoming tide and caught stripers and bluefish. He was the only one on the beach."

I have learned much about surf fishing over the years so I try to follow some of the basic principles of tide and time. The Ralph Grant story, however, reminded me again that the rules of surf fishing are loosely enforced. The fish certainly couldn't care less about the theories of fishermen. This wasn't the first time I had the feeling that the fish were laughing behind my back as I stayed home and waited for the "right" conditions.

RALPH GRANT

Ralph, alone or with his brothers and friends, often dominated the surf-fishing news. Articles in the Vineyard Gazette *and the New Bedford* Standard-Times *during the late 1940s and 1950s document some of Ralph's successes:*

>1948: "Ralph Grant caught 26 bass with brothers Mansfield and Ken at Katama."—Vineyard Gazette
>
>1949: "The Grant brothers, famed for their hearty creels, made another killing totalling 237 pounds ... at Squibnocket."—Vineyard Gazette
>
>1950: "... Ralph Grant of Edgartown took four big ones in a row.... With Ralph on Monday was Bob Pond of Attleboro who caught two big ones. Bob is manufacturer of a well-known line of plugs and there's no bet as to which kind he was using."—Standard-Times

The first time I ever fished I went with my brother Mansfield at Eel Pond in Edgartown. We both had conventional reels. It was at night. We couldn't see what we were doing. About the third cast I got this good strike. So I said to my brother, "Oh boy, I've got one on." He said, "Play him, play him!" So I said, "Okay." I played him. And I'm working like mad for about ten minutes and I didn't seem to be getting anywhere. Finally, Mansfield shined a flashlight on my line. I was hooked into the side of the marsh about ten feet in front of me.

This was about 1940. Surf fishing on the Island wasn't very common in the 1930s. Steve Gentle and I used to go down to Katama. He had a Ford rigged up with large tires. This was before the time of Jeeps. The Smith brothers would come down to do some heaving and hauling. Once in a while they'd catch a bluefish. They'd use about a hundred yards of line and coil it on the beach. At the end of the line was a leader about five or six feet long with a large lead jig on the end of it. The jig probably weighed six ounces. They would swing it around their heads, get it going good and then cast it. They'd retrieve it by hand and curl it on the beach.

Steve and I went down there with rods and reels. I had an old reel; I don't know what it was. But Steve had a good rod and a vom Hofe conventional reel—one of the first good fishing reels ever made. We caught plenty of bluefish using Ferron Jigs. The Smith brothers just laughed at us. They looked at the rods and reels and said, "What are you doing with those things?"

A few years later, a fellow named Harry Clark was fishing down at Katama with this odd-looking pink plug, about six inches long. He didn't do too much with it, but I liked the looks of it. So, I went home and sawed down the leg of a chair. It was large in the center and tapered down. I put a hook-eye in the large end and a tail hook on the other end. I went down alongside Harry Clark, who was using Ferron Jigs that day, and I caught two fish to his one with this strange plug. So, Steve Gentle knows about this and he starts calling it my famous Chair Leg Plug.

Then my brothers and I got to be very avid fishermen, so we bought an old 1940 Chevrolet Sedan. We put big tires on it. We were very good at finding new places to fish. One of the places we found was called the Mussel Bed, which got to be famous afterward.

The Mussel Bed was at Squibnocket. Nobody ever surf fished there before. The reason I know that is because John Lamborn had started what they called the Squibnocket Fishing Club up above the Mussel Bed a bit. We'd go in and stay at the Mussel Bed. We caught a lot of fish—just us three brothers. And John Lamborn got wind of us catching all these fish. He's trying to find where we're fishing.

We'd hide the Chevy Sedan in the bushes. When we caught a fish we would put it in the trunk of the Chevy. Lamborn would go by and never see us with fish. One day, just as we're getting ready to leave, Lamborn comes driving around the corner, his headlights shining right on us. He said, "Ah, there's where you sons-of-a-gun are catching all the fish." After that the place became well known. Crowds of fishermen would go up there. So, we said, "Forget it; we're not going to go fish in a crowd."

A few years before, we had bought a piece of beach up at Stonewall Beach to get this gravel up the beach. While we were around there doing our work, I said, "This looks like it might be a nice place for fishing." So, when the crowds drove us out of the Mussel Bed, we started going up to Stonewall Beach. I've seen acres of fish break in there. In fact, that's where I got most of my big catches of fish.

There was a bowl there on the left side of the point. The bait seems to hang in that bowl as it comes across the shoal. I liked to fish it on the east tide—the rising tide.

We were at Stonewall catching a lot of fish. People heard about our fishing again, but they couldn't find us. So, Al Doyle, who was a very good fisherman, made up his mind he was going to catch us.

One night we saw headlights behind us. We knew someone was following us, but we didn't know it was Al Doyle. But, we went like mad. I turned quickly into the Stonewall Beach entrance and turned the lights out. He went zipping by. He never did find us. Later when he saw us, he said, "You sons-of-a-gun, you caused me a lot of work. I got on the wrong road. I took down stonewalls and everything trying to find you guys. I never did."

I always told my brothers, "Now listen, we've got a good spot. Let's not ruin it. Let's not go in there during the day so they see us. We'll go after it gets dark and they won't be able to find us." So it goes along nicely about two weeks. All of a sudden my brother Mansfield, on a nice Sunday, said, "Ralph, I think I'll take a run up to Stonewall to see if there's anything doing."

Unknown to us, Charlie Lima and Doc Amaral decided they would circle the Island in a boat to look for us fishing on the beach. Charlie told Doc, "We're going to find out where those guys are. So, we're going to get a boat and we're going to go around this whole Island, and we're going to find those guys." So, they're out in the boat looking through glasses and they spot Mansfield. Lima said, "There they are; they're right there. That's where they're getting them! Right there." So that was it. That let the cat out of the bag. They finally found us. But afterward we kept heading down-Island to the east, looking for good spots.

This was about the mid-1940s now. We had gotten a Jeep. We would drive up the beach to Rum Runners Rocks. We ran into a lot of fish there. It seemed that the fish were working down the beach all the time. So we wouldn't have to make long drives on the beach, we were lucky enough to get a key to a nearby gate from Al Pacherhill. And we used to go through the gate, lock it and then we'd just drive over to the rocks.

George Arnold's nephew was following us one night. We turned in there and locked the gate. Once I locked it up, he couldn't get in. He wanted to get in where we were really badly. The next time we went in, we couldn't get out. That son-of-a-gun had gone and bought a lock. He put another lock in the chain, so we couldn't get out. He got back at me. We had a tough time getting out of there because we had to drive all the way down to West Tisbury to find another access.

Another night I was fishing with Percy West at Rum Runners Rocks. We were catching a lot of fish. In fact, one night at the Derby headquarters, I don't think there had been a fish turned in when Percy and I came in with thirteen or fourteen bass—the biggest kind of bass. And Dick Hathaway, who won the Derby in 1956, was there; Dick wanted to know where we got them. Well, we didn't tell him. Maybe we told him a lie or something. He said, "Well, I'm going to catch them." So he and a couple of his buddies are by Alley's Store. They were waiting for us to go by. We went by, and we saw them in there. So we go like a son-of-a-gun, and we turned in on the road to Quansoo. They weren't in sight. But they were driving along and saw how we smoothed the dirt up one side when we made that sharp turn in the road. So, they found us then, up at Rum Runners Rocks.

Bob Pond and I got to be good friends. He makes the Atom plugs and he was one of the founders of Stripers Unlimited. He would come down to the Island from Attleboro and go fishing with me. He'd say, "You find out where they're hitting, and I'll come down." So I'd call him up, and he'd come down. He'd come down off the boat with his waders on, and his flashlight around his forehead, all set to go with his rod and reel in his hand. I think he copied his popping plug from what I told him about my Chair Leg Plug. In fact, he made the Atom swimmer with the faceplate in the front. When I told him about my Chair Leg Plug, he took this Atom swimmer and turned it around and, where the faceplate was, he put hooks on the back. That was the same as the Chair Leg Plug.

In 1985, bunker were the primary baitfish along the Vineyard's coast. The large schools of sand eels that were partly responsible for the exceptional bluefishing of the previous fall did not return. This fall the blues wanted the oily bunker, making bluefish difficult to catch on either plugs or flies.

On a cold fall day in November, after the Derby, with the wind howling out of the northwest and the sky gray, using a No. 4/0 weighted treble hook, I snagged a bunker from the basin. After carefully removing the snag hook I would double hook the bunker on a live-lining rig—one hook behind the head, the other in front of the caudal fin. I gently cast the bunker into the outgoing tidal waters from the end of the Menemsha jetty and it soon attracted two bluefish. One blue hit the front of the bunker, the other hit the tail section. I was fighting two bluefish, each ten to twelve pounds, pulling in different directions on the live-lining rig. Eventually the fight proved too much for one wire leader, breaking off at the crimp, allowing one fish to escape. I landed the other blue after a respectable fight.

Double-headers, catching two fish on one cast, do not happen frequently. When Ralph had his first double-header back in 1963, the story was reported in the Standard-Times *of New Bedford: "One of fishing's rare events occurred here Friday night when a veteran Edgartown angler beached two 10-pound striped bass on one plug during a single cast."*

About twelve years ago, I went down to the west side of the Tisbury Great Pond opening. We had just opened it to the ocean probably three or four days before. I had noticed that after it was open for three hours, schools of herring were going in. So I said, "Well, this would be a good place to catch some bass." Percy West and a couple of other guys were over on the east side fishing away; they didn't seem to be doing anything. And so, all of a sudden I got this heck of a strike.

I was casting a small popping plug. The hooks are probably three or four inches apart. And this is kind of hard to believe. I fished for about twenty minutes fighting to get what I thought was one fish in. And lo and behold when I got the plug on the beach, there were two bass on it. Both weighed about twelve pounds. One had the tail hook in his mouth and the other had the front hook in his mouth. They were so close you almost had to pry them apart to get the hooks out of them. I don't know how in the world the second one got hooked.

The only other time I heard about something like this involved George and Joan Arruda. They were fishing when Joan caught a bass and a bluefish on the same plug. George and Joan used to go fishing all the time; they never missed a day going fishing. This was about twenty years ago. They used to go down way past Wasque. They would go over on the ferry and go across the Dyke Bridge, and then head down and go down to what became known as Arruda Point. Just before you get to the jetties there's a point that makes out on the Edgartown side. That's where they fished. On certain tides, a rip forms. The water will go across the shoal and into the deep water. The fish will hang just on the edge of the shoals and the deep water, so you cast out there where the shoals and the deep water meet. Evidently, that day, bass and blues were feeding together.

The Arrudas fished there for years, and then all of a sudden they never went fishing again. Year after year, and almost never missed a day. All of a sudden they quit. I don't know why. I often said to George, "What did you quit fishing for? You know, you used to be a fixture down there at Arruda Point." And he said, "Well, we just didn't want to fish anymore, that's all." No reason. They got the point named after them by Foster Silva in the late 1960s.

There was a picket fence at Wasque. Fishermen were shoulder to shoulder, rods high in the air. Fishing lines arched gracefully in the air when plugs carried them to their intended spot. Crossovers were frequent, though, because the fishermen were crowded into a small area. When this happened, the fishing line looked like string attached to a downed kite hung up in the branches of some towering pine tree.

Fishing next to Steve Amaral, I unintentionally cast over his line while he had a fish on. My line wrapped itself into a curious variation of a surgeon's knot, which effectively ended Steve's fishing. His line soon parted with a sickening twang; fish and lure both were lost. If looks could kill, I was dead. I could only offer Steve another lure and stay out of his way.

Dick Hathaway is a wonderful fisherman and a very excitable guy. We were fishing to the north of Wasque Point. Mr. Leland, who owns the house up on the hill, came down with a bunch of other guys. So Mr. Leland's fishing away, and he's in everybody's hair. You see, he owned the beach. He figured he could do what he wanted. So Hathaway gets a nice fish on. As he's playing it, Mr. Leland comes down and casts right across Hathaway's line; breaking it.

Dick Hathaway was irate. And, by and by, Leland got a nice fish on. He's playing away, and Hathaway goes up with his jackknife and cuts Leland's line. "Did you see what he did?" Leland says to me. I said, "Yeah, I saw. But he lost his fish on account of you, so he was getting even." Leland decided to leave the beach after that.

A year before this incident, Hathaway was working with us at Grant Brothers. He was just a young fellow. I don't think he'd ever been fishing before. But he says to me, "How about you guys taking me fishing tonight?" We said, "Sure. We'll take you."

So we took him down to Katama. Katama Bay was open at the time. The opening had worked down to the east and was way down near Wasque Point. There was pretty good fishing there. So, we went down on the Chappaquiddick side because it seemed to be best. We went over on the ferry with the car.

Nobody's doing very much. Hathaway probably had been fishing for about ten minutes and he hooks onto this fish. He finally got it in. He was so excited, he got it right up in his arms. He's patting it and he says, "Oh, baby, look at that!" Hathaway's first fish was a thirty-five-pound bass.

The first light of day shone on Ray Houle as he cast an eel into the Tisbury Great Pond opening. His legs, entombed in waders, were sinking into the soft sand, as the surf washed around his knees. A honeycomb of foam covered the sand at the surf line, littering the beach with skate egg cases, seaweed, and jellyfish bodies.

The fin of a shark was visible cutting through the ocean. Approaching from the east, near the shoreline, the shark was closing in on the bait coming out of the pond opening. Along with Ray's eel, the baitfish were tempting the shark.

Although Ray didn't want to hook the shark, because he feared his reel would be stripped of 150 yards of thirty-pound-test line, the shark proved to be too fast. It hit the eel without reducing its speed. It continued heading west without showing any sense of alarm or the courtesy to recognize it was hooked.

Finally, after the tension of the line was sensed, the shark turned east, heading back to the opening. Ray got a good look at the eight-foot monster as he furiously retrieved as much line as possible. Cutting his line before the fish made it's next run, Ray stepped back a few feet. As he watched the shark swim into deeper water, he felt invigorated and victorious.

I have a story about a blitz. At the time we were fishing at our favorite spot, Stonewall Beach. I got hold of my brother Ken one night and I said, "Well, what do you say we give it a try?" Another group of guys had been fishing up there and hadn't caught anything in a while. Not much had been going on for a couple of weeks. The fish had moved out to another spot. So I said to my brother Ken, "Let's give it a try up at Stonewall, tomorrow morning." So he said, "Okay."

So we go up to Stonewall. It was half past three in the morning. We go down over the cliff, and we've each got a flashlight on and our fishing gear. Ken put his light down near the water, and there on the edge of the shore were big menhaden just piled up a foot high all along this shore. And we said, "Holy cow! There must've been some fish in here." And Ken looked a little farther, and there's half a bass laying in the undertow. The half that was there must've weighed thirty pounds. Evidently, the sharks had been in there; a shark had taken half the bass and the other half had come ashore.

I said, "They've been in here. I wonder if they're still here?" So we each made a cast. We're both using wooden Atom swimmers. They were the best. In fact, I had a famous one rigged up—my red plug; I had it for a good many months. I never had one quite like it. The back of it was up out of the water a little bit and the front of it would be down, but it would still stay on the surface. And it had beautiful action to it. Oh, I caught a lot of fish with that one plug. Finally, I lost it.

We never ran into any sharks that night, so they evidently weren't in there when we were fishing. But a different night I was fishing all by myself up at Stonewall. It was a very dark night. I heard a noise—rocks rolling around. So I got my flashlight and went down to check. I found a shark that must've been fifteen feet long. He'd been going right along the undertow into the bait, and a sudden wave had thrown him onto the beach. He was on the beach thrashing his tail around, knocking rocks all over the place—a huge shark! Its teeth were huge, too. It scared the hell out of me! Because it was a dark night, and then to go up and see this thing. A wave came up and he finally worked his way back into the water again.

Years before, there were a lot of sharks in there. I caught one that must have weighed about two hundred pounds. I took it with a swimming plug, on twenty-pound-test line. In fact, down at the Tisbury Pond one night we were catching so many sharks that we got the hell out of there. And there was an old man who used to fish with us named Pop Blaisdell. Percy West, Pop, and I would go up there a lot. Pop Blaisdell loved to fish, but the best part of fishing for him was having his daughter, Mrs. Gouldey, bake a pie. So every night we'd have to go in and have pie and coffee. He got more kicks out of serving up pie and coffee than he did fishing. One of his sayings was, "There's only one trouble about fishing, there's some fool that always wants to fish."

One night, Pop Blaisdell comes out of the house and he's got a big hunk of meat in a bag. He's got a great big shark hook with about a three-inch bend and it's a quarter-inch thick. They used them sometimes for a gaff hook. He's got that rigged up with about forty feet of this small dog chain.

We said, "What are you going to do with that?" He said, "I'm going to get one of them. I'm going to tie this chain around the bumper of the Jeep. I'm going to heave this out there, and I'm going to catch one of them damn sharks." He never did.

Some people don't think sharks will take a swimming plug. But they will; at times they'll take a plug. One night, at dusk, I was plugging at Stonewall Beach with Percy West, Tony Gaspar, Buddy Oliver, and Bob West. I could see fish breaking offshore. I hooked onto this fish that I thought was the world's largest bass because he took almost all my line off the reel. I had him on so long that the rest of the guys got sick of hanging around waiting for me to land it. They figured I had a big fish, and they wanted to see it.

So they walked down the beach a ways and started fishing themselves. Well, it took me about fifteen more minutes before I got the fish in close enough to gaff. He was a shark that weighed more than two hundred pounds. He was more than two feet in diameter across his belly. I got him up on the beach. Now I'm wondering,

"How am I going to get my plug out of him." He had plenty of teeth. I'm not about to put my hand in his mouth to get the plug. Tony Gaspar and the rest of the guys are standing real close to him. Bob West said, "I know how to get the plug out of that son-of-a-gun," he says. Well, there was a big piece of driftwood laying up on the shore. Tony Gaspar's standing there and Bob gets this big piece of driftwood. He's going to belt that shark on the nose, to stun him. So he hauls off, but misses the shark's nose. He hits Tony Gaspar across the toes with that big hunk of driftwood. Tony goes dancing around. I guess it pretty near took his toes off. Finally, we jammed a stick in his mouth, so he couldn't bite us. Then we worked on it with a knife and got the plug. He had clamped down on the stick, but it was big enough so you could get your hand in to get the plug out.

About a half hour afterward, Percy West got a shark that was almost as big. This one was so big that Buddy Oliver was straddling him. Tony ended up getting whacked on the toes again. I think they were blue or sand sharks. These were real big, with two or three rows of teeth. He was so big, up on the rocks thrashing his tail he could throw rocks around that were a foot in diameter. So that's a damn big shark.

The Mattakesett Creek Company had the right years ago to seine anything in Katama Bay from a herring to a narwhal. My father, when he was in the trucking business in 1935, used to rent his truck to the Herring Creek Company to haul the herring that they caught down at the end of Herring Creek. The fishing boats would use the herring to bait up for their trawl. And the herring came up in the bay so thick, the bass would be after them. So they not only caught herring, but they caught all these beautiful striped bass. They did this right in Katama Bay. They had the right to do it. I've seen bass caught there that would go sixty or seventy pounds. Their tails would be out of a barrel.

They used to seine and catch all these beautiful bass. Steve Gentle knows about this. They'd leave their seine on the shore; they'd seine the herring and keep the bass. So some guys got together to do something about the seiners catching all these big bass. They went down and poured acid all over their seine. So the next time they went to seine, their seine fell all apart.

Francis Bernard wanted to go fishing with me. I took him up to the west side of Tisbury Great Pond. He'd never done much fishing before. Well, we really slayed the fish. We landed right into a school of bass. The only problem was that I caught all the big ones and he caught all the little ones. We caught about a dozen between us. There weren't many bluefish around; this being the late 1940s. The bluefish, for some reason or other, hadn't come back in their cycle. It was very different in 1984 up at Lobsterville. That was the best bluefishing ever.

No one told me about it. I happened to be up at Menemsha Basin one day working on an asphalt job. I noticed down in the bend at Lobsterville flocks of small herring gulls and the big gulls. I said, "There's something going on over there." My brother-in-law happened to be here from California, so I said, "Carl, I think there's something going on up there." He says, "I'll go up tomorrow and see." I didn't bother going up, but he went up with his wife, my sister. And boy, they landed big bluefish!

I never saw anything like that before. The fish were huge. Carl had one weighing around eighteen pounds. It went on day after day. It was almost twenty-four hours a day fishing for six weeks. I saw a kid there with a blue that went at least twenty pounds.

Bluefish stories can be very unusual. I caught a bluefish once without a hook in it. This is a fish story if you ever heard one! I was casting down at Wasque. There were plenty of good-size blues there. They were running 10 to 12 pounds each. All of a sudden I got this fish on the beach. I looked and it hasn't got any plug in it. It opened its mouth and the plug went in the mouth out through the gill. The blue was caught without a plug in it. It was caught by the wire of the leader on my plug. The plug was still on the leader, but there wasn't a hook in the fish at all.

Steve Gentle had an outing of about five guys in a fishing party. They were just fishing away. One guy got a fish on and the other four grabbed their rods. They were casting away. One of the other guys caught the guy with the fish on right in the mouth with his plug. So the guy's standing there with the plug caught in his lip and his friends are worried about him. When they went over to help him, he yelled, "Get out of here." He doesn't want those guys bothering him at all. He brought that fish in before they tried to get the plug out of his lip. He landed the fish!

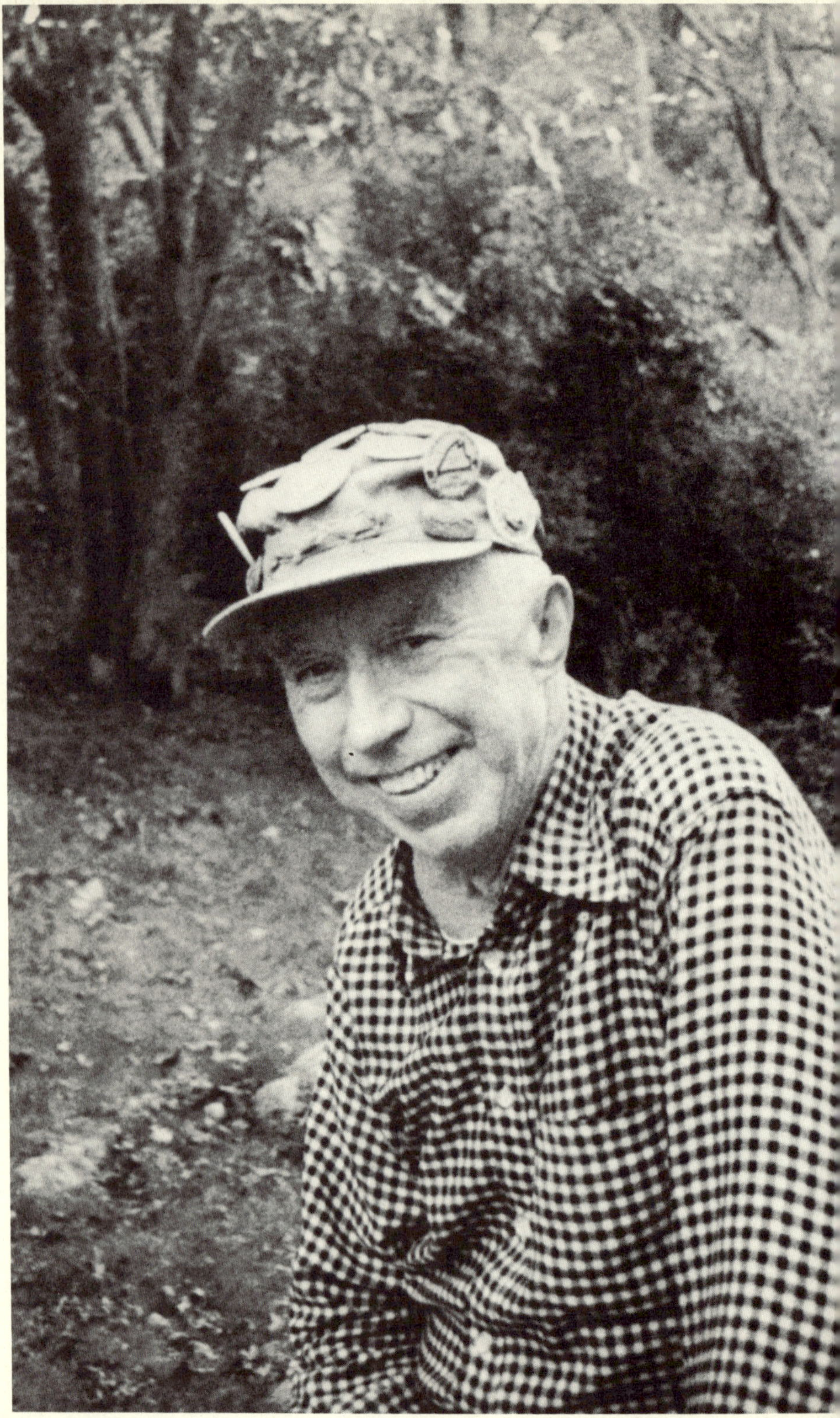

10

Jerry Jansen

The hats worn by fishermen can be colorful, strange looking, both or neither, but they are always practical. The hats are usually some variation on a baseball cap with the logo of a brewery or tackle company above the brim.

The most interesting fishing cap I ever saw sits on the head of Jerry Jansen. The first time I saw Jerry fishing the south side of Gay Head, at a spot he's fished for forty years, I was mesmerized by his hat. Buttons and pins tracing the history of modern surf fishing on the East Coast covered every available space. Derby buttons and fish and club pins decorate the plain brown, short-brimmed cap. His headgear looks like a pin cushion designed by a sadist to torture fishermen with sensitive scalps. Jerry Jansen's fishing hat is embedded with so many pins and buttons, I expect his head to flop down under its weight. Yet, defying gravity, Jerry holds his head high, proudly displaying his fishing heritage.

I first got interested in surf fishing when I saw these old German guys from Ridgewood, Queens, and places like that fishing the

JERRY JANSEN

Rockaways on the western end of Long Island, New York. They would take the awning off the delicatessen store, bring it down to the beach, then set it up and have a big party. They would bring watermelons, a bunch of hams and all kinds of stuff. They would spend the whole day at the beach, speaking German and fishing. That's why I got interested in surf fishing. I saw these people having such a good time.

In the late 1930s, I used to fish Montauk Point on the eastern tip of Long Island. I was living in New York City at the time. The drive to Montauk took four hours each way. We used to go out Friday night and sleep in the car over the weekend and come home Sunday afternoon exhausted. The roads were not what they are now, but the people out there were a little bit more amenable to having fishermen around. It's a big tourist area now; it's gone downhill.

In those days surf fishermen could get a room for $2 a night. People would take the fishermen into their homes. They'd give you a room, charge you two bucks and give you breakfast, then send you on your way in the morning.

If you couldn't drive to Montauk the Long Island Railroad ran the Montauk Fishermen Special. The train would leave New York City about two Saturday morning. It would drop you off at Montauk station. I took it myself once in a while. I had a tough time getting from the Montauk station up to the point. Guys would be there with a limousine service. They used to charge $10 to take you up to the point and come back and get you. That was the way we used to do it. It was a hard way to get out there.

Before the war mostly old-timers were fishing Montauk. These old geezers were fishing there for years. They'd fish mostly at night. You could walk up to them, talk to them, and fish with them. If you got a fish on, you could expect that they would leave you alone until you got your fish ashore.

After the war, a bunch of meat fishermen came out to Montauk. Somehow or other, it seemed to change. I don't know where they came from—whether they were converted Jersey meat fishermen or what the heck they were. But, when you were fishing at Montauk there would be a mob of guys if the word was out: "The bass are in"—the newspapers would carry it—Dick Cornish of the *Daily*

JERRY JANSEN

News and Frank Keating from the *Long Island Press*. You'd stand there casting in a crowd.

Say you got a hit—you had a fish on, your rod was bent the first minute or two of the fight, there would be twelve guys casting over your ears to get there because they'd think that's where the fish were. As soon as you got the fish in and put it on your stringer, you had to look for another place to fish because everybody and his brother was there. They would hit you over the head if you tried to fish in your old spot. The fact that the fish might be twenty or thirty yards up the beach didn't make a difference to these guys.

I remember last year I was fishing Gay Head on the Vineyard. We had a guy up here with a big red dog, and the son of a gun would come in and throw a plug right over your ears. The dog's name was Rusty. He would holler at the dog, "Rusty, stay! Rusty, stay!" Rusty wasn't going to stay; Rusty wanted to have fun, too. This guy ruined the whole fishing scene. Some of the guys would say, "That's a Montauk fisherman!"

The second Derby in 1947 was the first Derby Jerry Jansen entered. The prizes included a $4,200 Steelcraft cabin cruiser, a new Plymouth, a couple of small bass boats with motors, and cash prizes.

George Marshall, a Vineyard resident, caught the grand prize winner, a forty-five-pound thirteen-ounce striper. Jerry called George "Landlocked Marshall" because he never took the boat out of the harbor.

The prizes were modest in the first Derby. In the second Derby, 1947, they gave away a brand new Plymouth automobile.

That first Derby the off-Island fishermen didn't have a prayer. The people running things wouldn't tell you where anything was. You didn't even get a chart of the Island to show where the fishing spots were. Every good spot was posted with "No fishing allowed!" When you came up here then, you were "Joe Blow" looking to go fishing. They didn't make it interesting or easy for you. The Martha's Vineyard Rod and Gun Club wanted to run the contest. When the chamber of commerce started getting complaints from fishermen who came here, they wanted to get more involved.

JERRY JANSEN

Fluctuations in baitfish availability, natural cyclic changes in sportfish populations, and changes in the ocean floor, can turn a once-productive fishing spot into a barren hole. The spots that Jerry Jansen fished in the 1940s and 1950s, including the Mussel Bed at Squibnocket, the opening to the Tisbury Great Pond, the south side of Gay Head, Lobsterville, and Rum Runner's Rocks in Chilmark, have been less productive in recent years, reflecting the steady decline in striped bass populations.

The early years Jerry fished on the Vineyard provide insight into fish populations and their effect on various fishing spots around the Island. But the early years were also the beginning of life-long friendships that grew in strength with the shared experiences of fishing at the edge of the surf. When recalling the highlights of a forty-five-year-long surf fishing career, the memories of meeting and fishing with Ralph Grant, Bud Oliver, Sergei de Somov, Abner B. McCutcheon, John Hokansen, and Mort Urosky share importance with the number of fish caught.

I had read in *Salt Water Sportsman* that Martha's Vineyard was the place to be. In my early days of fishing on the Vineyard—the late 1940s—the first thing I looked for was Squibnocket Point. Squibnocket Point was where the old bass club used to be located. It was a tough place to find.

The road going into Squibnocket Beach in those days was so narrow that guys with new automobiles wouldn't drive in because it would scratch all the paint off the car. I had an old car at the time. I used to park outside and walk in first to make sure it was the right place. I had to go park in two or three places before I finally found it. I took the car in. And the car got all scratched up, but it was an old beat-up '39 Dodge, so I didn't mind too much.

In those days at Squibnocket, the Mussel Bed was a good place to go. You had to get out there at low water.

When you used to go in there, to the right of the parking lot was the gate to the Hornblower place. About a quarter-mile down the road there used to be a little hooded stand with a book on it. And there was a light there. It was similar to a lectern stand. And they wanted you to sign your name and where you came from and what time you came in. They wanted you to log-in to come on the beach. That was the Hornblowers' idea of security at the time. That's all they wanted you to do. You could park your car in the parking lot and fish the bowl and the Mussel Bed, or you could drive all the way up to the point. You could fish all the way along that beach if you wanted to walk it. But you could drive up there in those days. And Mrs. Hornblower got interested. She used to come down there and fish with the guys once in a while. She was a tin fisherman. All she ever used was the block tin squid.

If you didn't want to go all the way up to the point, the bowl on the up-Island side of the Mussel Bed was a good spot. You'd have a whole string of guys standing along the beach there casting into the bowl. If the tide was down and you were careful you could walk out onto the Mussel Bed. The mussels would all be alive. If you liked mussels, you could pick up a peck of them if you wanted them. That's what attracted the bass. You could hear the bass crunching away. At night, you'd hear this noise because the bass would be ripping them off the bottom.

That's where George Marshall caught his Derby-winning bass in 1947. He came in with a big load of seaweed on his line, and he had a bass in the midst of it. Everybody said the bass was on by the time George caught the seaweed. But in any case, he got quite a big fish.

I used to fish out on the bar with my good friend John Hokansen, who has since died. John and I used to wade out on the bar at low water. You had to watch yourself and know what time the tide was coming up. You would have four feet of water over the bar at high water, and it would be coming fast! So you had to be careful about how you got out there. We would stay out there a certain length of time and wade back in along the edge of the bowl on the up-Island or west end of it. You'd come in sometimes with water up to your chest, and it was kind of dangerous. Sometimes you came in with two or three fish on a stringer. You had your hands full getting back in to the beach.

One night in the early 1950s John and I stayed out on the Mussel Bed from four-thirty in the afternoon to five the next morning! Even though we stayed out there for about thirteen hours, we didn't get one hit the whole night long! That was some night. Boy, you talk about getting tired! I was sound asleep on my feet.

John was older that I am. He was a Scandinavian. His family was from Norway. John was a tough old bird. I was about to fall in the water and let myself drown. It would've been a relief. I went to John and said, "John I want to drown myself. I could use the rest!" "Oh, Jerry," he said, "let's go over here and give 'em two more shots just to keep 'em honest." He waded over to the corner of the bowl by the big Shoe Rock, and made a couple of casts there. I said, "Forget it. There are no fish out there." There were none out there that night. We fished hard that night!

In the early days I used to fish Gay Head and Lobsterville. We would climb down the cliffs by Devil's Nest in front of the old Coast Guard windmill, which pumped freshwater up to the Coast Guard station at the Gay Head Light. The twisted remains of the windmill are still sticking out of the cliffs. The Coast Guard station has since been moved to Menemsha. That climb down was the son-of-a-bitch of a run. It was very steep, very high, and when it rained it used to be slippery because of the clay.

If we felt it was too dangerous, we would go in on the south side of the cliffs, just before they started to rise. The spot was marked by the old Coca Cola stand near the last row of telephone poles going in toward the water. There was an Indian who had a house there. We used to walk past his house and follow this old beat-up path. He used to sell Coca Cola and cigarettes and candy in a little shed.

You could bring your car in if you wanted to. There was room for about six cars on the beach. That was a great fishing spot. Some nights I would walk from the south side of the cliffs all the way around to Lobsterville. That was a tough walk. I fished the whole beach all night long. I would fish every inch of that beach, including Pilots Landing and Dogfish Bar.

This is the story of the "Death March." I was fishing with my wife Lilly, John Hokansen and his wife Tessie, and Abner B. McCutcheon and his wife Hilda. McCutcheon and Hilda were both artists. They met in art school in Italy many years ago. She was a descendant of the Lipton Tea family. She was evidently very wealthy. She met Mac in Italy. She had a definite British accent. She was a funny dame; she had a good sense of humor. Mac was kind of dull but he was a good fisherman.

The Lobsterville Road back then stopped about two miles short of the Menemsha jetties. John figured that with the wind out of the northwest we should walk to the jetties. The beach was a long way from the road and full of pebbles which made it hard to walk on. "We'll take the car down to the end of the road and walk across the dunes," John suggested, "It's not a bad night."

So we all decided to take the walk and go over to the Menemsha jetties. We loaded up our gear and started the walk. We got halfway across and McCutcheon started to complain. "It's a death march," he kept saying. It took about four hours. John got mixed up on his directions.

The dunes were full of brambles and poison ivy. We all had waders on, so we didn't get any poison ivy. But what a hike! We got out there, made a couple of casts, then we had to walk back. Mac was worried about getting back. His wife Hilda said, "What, come back? You may not come back. Don't worry about it." He said, "I'm beginning to believe you. This is a real death march. Now you've got me convinced." Now, of course, they have a road built right up behind that place and it's easy to get there. In those days, it was hard to get anywhere on the Island.

There was a guy I met named Mort Urosky. He changed his name to Morty Ross. It was easier for him. He was a writer. He wrote articles for a guy that used to put out local bulletin books on fishing: fishing in Cape Cod, fishing in New England, fishing here, fishing all the way down the East and West coasts. He would write about the whole country. He used to get information from guys like me, and he used to publish it.

One year, Morty came to the Vineyard with a friend and stayed in a cottage near where I was staying with Lilly in Menemsha. They went out fishing with me and John Hokansen. Morty was a hard fisherman. He used to like climbing on rocks. So John and I took him out to Squib one night. And it was kind of a quiet night where the water was rolling in very heavy. There was not much wind but there seemed to be a very strong tide running. Evidently there was a storm offshore, ground swell conditions being what they were. And every three or four waves that came in, there'd be a big seven-footer.

So we're going out on the bar. Morty had never been out on the Mussel Bed. This was not a good night to go out there with the surf coming in as hard as it was. I said, "Morty, it's a tough night because there's a lot of hard water coming in." "Well," he said, "I'll stand on a rock. I'll be okay. I've got my creepers on, you know." He was all set to go out. We were all using standard gear. I said, "John, we'd better go out with this guy because he's liable to get knocked on his can and get hurt." John said, "We'll go out with him."

We go out on the bar. We pick a spot, kick a couple of rocks out of the way and stand in there. Morty goes way over to the right by Shoe Rock and climbs up on a stone. He looked like a sea gull standing up there, all bent over, casting away. Suddenly, this huge wave comes roaring in. John yells, "Look at this one, Jerry. Look out!" We could see it coming. We could see it gathering about two hundred yards out. It really wasn't a wave. It's what you would call a sea. And it's coming in. It came across where we were. We were standing on the Mussel Bed. It came up about four feet high, so John and I both had to jump in the air and land on the water behind it because it just lifted us up. We both took it in the armpits, then landed on our feet. John says to me, "Where's Morty?" We turn around and there's Morty shaking himself off. He was still on top of the rock. I don't know how he did it but he held on. The water came right over him. How he stayed on, I don't know.

Morty decided to come in off the rock after that close call. But when he started to come in he was walking kind of funny. "John," I said, "look at Morty." John said, "I bet he's full of water." And John says to him, "Hey, Morty"—John can keep a straight face; I can't— "did you see that big breaker coming in?" Morty said, "Did I see it! I was in it! My waders are full of water!" He took his waders off. He was wet from top to bottom. He must have had twelve gallons of water in his waders. Morty never came back here. We never saw him again.

JERRY JANSEN

Jerry Jansen remembers fishing with Buddy Oliver. When Bud died in July, 1986, Kib Bramhall was inspired to write the following letter to the Vineyard Gazette, *August 8, 1986:*

A FISHING LEGEND
Editors, Vineyard Gazette:

It should be noted on the occasion of Jess J. (Bud) Oliver III's untimely death that he was one of the Island's legendary surf fishermen of the late 1940s and 1950s when the Vineyard was becoming a mecca for striped bass anglers. His fame was such that Life magazine published a photo and short article about him in which the editors said he could cast 150 yards, a claim that he never made himself. On the contrary, he was a believer in the short cast because he knew that stripers feed close to the beach at night when he did most of his fishing. In its September 1956 issue, Salt Water Sportsman *magazine published a feature article by Frank Woolner titled "Bud Oliver—Vineyard Surfman," in which some of his angling achievements were noted. Perhaps the most astounding was the time he beached 56 and 52-pound stripers on successive casts just after the annual derby had ended.*

Kib Bramhall
West Tisbury

Another fisherman I used to meet up at Squibnocket was the former police chief Buddy Oliver. He used to love fishing Squibnocket. He used to walk up and go around the point. And he liked a southwest wind; that's what he used to tell us, "The wind blows southwest," he said, "get down to Squib and walk up toward Zacks Cliffs. That's where the fishing is." He never wore a hat. It would rain and blow like mad, and the guy never wore a hat. I remember that. He used to go out and fish, and never would even put his hood up.

I can remember fishing with Ralph Grant and Buddy Oliver at the Tisbury Pond opening. During the Derby in the late 1940s we had a difficult time finding the fish. They were supposedly being caught all over the Island. John and I knew, though, that the fish were not coming from the places where they were being reported because we were covering those places. I'm talking about Makonikey and Split Rock. We did a lot of deducting and decided that they had to be coming out of Tisbury Pond. In those days they used to open Tisbury Pond halfway through the Derby. Ralph Grant and his brothers used to do the opening. They used to go down there with bulldozers and fishing rods. After two turns of the tide, the water was alive with bass. The fish would come from all over to get in on the feed. The idea, of course, was to keep the off-Islanders from getting any fish. That was the name of the game.

We didn't know the roads down to the beach area of the Pond. We weren't familiar with the access and certainly didn't have permission to cross anyone's land. We knew what Ralph's car looked like. We also could recognize the cars of a few of the other guys.

Finally, Ben Morton told me, "Go down South Road, make a right across from the yellow house. Go in on the dirt road there and go all the way down. Go as far as you can. The gate to Quansoo will probably be open. You'll come to Black Point Brook. Don't try to cross the bridge with your car. Just park by the bridge. When you get onto the beach there, walk to the left until you come to the opening."

So John, Tessie, and Lilly came along. Lilly came along for the walk. She'll go anywhere for a walk. When we got to the bridge, all the fishermen's cars were there. We saw Ralph Grant's car there and a few others that we recognized. I said, "This is where they are!"

We walked over the bridge and down the beach. There was Ralph Grant. "Hello, Ralph." "Hello, Jerry. How are you?" "Fine, Ralph. How are you?" "Fine." He was looking as guilty as he could. We had asked him where they were getting the fish, but I can't really blame him for not telling us. This place was wild with surf fishermen—all natives. We were the only off-Islanders down there.

They were all standing around talking. Most surf fishermen spend ninety percent of their time talking and ten percent fishing. John said, "The tide is flowing right. That bait's going to be coming out. The way the water's running, there's got to be a bar out there. There's got to be a place to wade out to get a shot at these fish." So he asked Ralph Grant and Buddy Oliver, "When does the bar clear, and when can we get out to the point?" "Oh!" the guys said, "You can't walk out there. That water runs strong and the sand is soft. You'll just slide right in. It'll take you right in with it. You'll never be able to walk out there! You can't get out there!"

John and I walked down the beach to discuss our plans. I said, "John, those guys say you can't get out there." He said, "Well, we're going to stick around because that's where they're going. That's a bunch of lying men." So we stayed back. We went up the beach; we walked away from them in the direction of Rum Runners Rocks. Then we came back about an hour later. There's the whole bunch of them standing out there on the bar catching fish. So I said to Ralph, "I don't see anybody falling in the water." "Oh no," he said. "They will. It'll come in pretty hard." He had to cover himself. But we caught him with the "goods" as it were. It was a fun thing, of course. And we did get some fish.

I met Jerry in fall, 1977, after first light at Gay Head. The striped bass were hitting the beaches on the south side of the cliffs like clockwork. Any fisherman who wasn't plugging by five-thirty in the morning usually missed catching one. I can remember three mornings in a row where the bass hit between five-fifteen and five-thirty alongside the same rock.

After the fish passed through, giving the baitfish a chance to calm down and prepare for future attacks, the surf fishermen grouped together to discuss the events of the morning. The opinionated stranger from New York City with the bull neck and strong shoulders introduced himself as Jerry Jansen. I have met many colorful fishermen at six in the morning at Gay Head, including Hank Schauer, but none had the pin-laden hat or exaggerated stories of Jerry.

Although I had never met him before, his name was familiar. So, I said, "Jerry, did you write a fishing book back in the 1950s?" "I sure did," he said. "Where did you get a copy of that? I haven't seen any around in twenty years." "I bought it at a yard sale on the Vineyard," I told him. "If I bring it to the beach one morning could you sign my copy?" "Sure! Sure!" said Jerry.

I rode around with Successful Surf Fishing *in the glove compartment of my Jeep until fall, 1978. Finding Jerry on the beach at*

JERRY JANSEN

Gay Head again, I ran back to the car for the book. Six in the morning on the beach, with the surf roaring, the gulls diving and the sun brightening the clay strata of the cliffs, Jerry autographed my copy of his book, "Tight lines—Jerry Jansen."

    I used to teach people how to take and pass Civil Service examinations in my field—painting. This was back in 1952. The fellow who ran the school happened to be a disabled war veteran. He was a good friend of mine. His name was Lenny Miller. I worked with him in Civil Service. He set the school up. He couldn't go back to his job in the welfare department because he got badly wounded during the war. He developed the idea of teaching people real estate and civil service topics. Painting was one of the things he asked me to get in on. I did a good job for him, and for myself. I made a lot of money doing it.

    One day he said, "Jerry, I want to set up a sports institute. I want you to teach fishing. I have a guy who's going to teach golf and I have a girl who's going to teach archery. So we'll have a three-way school." Archery was coming along at that time; golf was getting popular; and surf fishing was coming along. Well, I developed a curriculum in surf fishing. Turned out the dame that was going to teach archery got pregnant and the guy who was going to teach golf got a job as a pro at some golf club, so I was left alone at this sports institute. I was the guy teaching the surf fishing. I did this for three or four years.

    We used to charge $25.00 for five classroom lessons and two field trips. We took them down to the beach and showed them practical aspects of casting. I used to bring half a dozen rods and reels, for people to use, so they'd get an idea of what they could do themselves.

    Anyway, one year, this guy shows up at class. He sits through the whole course, doesn't open his mouth once—not a peep out of him, until the last session. He said, "I work for the *Wall Street Journal;* I'm a reporter. The *Wall Street Journal* is trying to broaden its purview—expand its readership, provide other items of interest to its readership. We'd like to do an article on you because you teach fishing in a classroom on Second Avenue and Eighth Street in New York City."

So he took me out for a bite to eat. He told me he wouldn't do the article without my permission. I gave him my permission and cooperated any way I could.

The following week the *Wall Street Journal* came out with the article about my fishing course. Mike Hunt, one of the vice presidents of E.P. Dutton, saw the article. The guy calls me up at my job. I was working for the New York City Housing Authority at the time. And sure enough, he said, "You've got to write a book on surf fishing. This subject is becoming a big thing in sports. We see it in all the sports pages. You're mentioned in all the fish and game editorials." I said, "Well, I don't want to write a book. I've got no time for this stuff." He wouldn't take no for an answer. Finally, I agreed to do the book. He gave me a $500 retainer. The book was called *Successful Surf Fishing*.

The use of lobster tail as bait was common practice from the bass stands of the old Squibnocket Club during the years 1869 to 1888. In the book American Game Fish, *published in 1897, Francis Endicott tells of bass fishing with lobster tail at Gay Head:*

> When fishing at Gay Head, Martha's Vineyard, I paid but one dollar and fifty cents per hundred for young lobsters. Mr. Tillinghast of New Bedford stood by me where I was fishing, and kept me supplied with bait. The tail was cut off and the shell peeled from it—that made one bait; the rest of the lobster he cut up fine and threw into the water as 'chum,' to attract the fish. . . . In less than an hour I had two, one of twenty-five pounds and one of fifteen pounds.

When Sergei de Somov revealed to Jerry Jansen that lobster tail was the bait responsible for many of his prize catches, Sergei was continuing a tradition started before the turn of the century. It is not surprising that the elegant and sophisticated Sergei fished with lobster tail, while most fishermen used bunker and mackerel chunks, which were more available and less expensive. Jerry hates baitfishing so he was probably casting tin.

Sergei liked Zacks Cliffs. I got to know something about his techniques because we belonged to the same fishing club on Long Island, the East End Surf Fishing Club. I don't think it's around anymore. We also belonged to the Long Island Beach Buggy Association.

He would go up to Zacks and take his little red Jeep out on the beach. When the water receded, he would scoot around the point with his buggy and get close up to the rocks behind it. He would work his way down Zacks Cliffs this way.

He used lobster tails for bait. Instead of cooking the whole lobster, he would break off the tail and cook the rest. He would put a big hook through the tail with a six-ounce sinker and heave it out into a heavy surf. And he would take bass. That's where he got his bass. That's how he won the Derbies: with lobster.

When I started fishing in the mid-1930s, there were no striped bass around. They had disappeared. The historians will tell you that the Squibnocket Bass Club and the other bass clubs all died out because the stripers were gone. There were no significant numbers of stripers from the late 1890s until the late 1930s. Then the striped bass started to show up. The idea, the challenge, of catching a striped bass became an obsession.

When Lillian and I first came to the Vineyard, we went down to the old bass club. There was a guy who had a striped bass in the trunk of his car. He opened the trunk and showed it to all the fishermen. Lillian said to me, "The way those friends stood around and looked at that fish, I understood what surf fishing was all about."

The idea of coming to the Vineyard to fish for bass and blues gives me something to look forward to all year. I can completely relax up here. And now my life is coming to an end; I'm getting old. And the bass are going away, too. So maybe I'll come and go with the bass. I don't know.

I've done a lot of fishing. I've spent a lot of time on beaches all over the East Coast. There's a Babylonian proverb that says "The gods do not deduct from man's allotted span those hours spent in fishing." I hope I get those hours back. I would spend them with Lilly and go fishing. There's nothing in the world like surf fishing. To go out, to look for the fish, to meet the guys, to see the fish, to

JERRY JANSEN

catch them or not catch them, to put my skill against the fish, to analyze, to think, to plan, to scheme, to buy, to walk, to get sunburned, to get wet, to get back home brokenhearted without a fish when everyone else caught one.

There are things you do in your everyday life—the work you do, the jobs you do, the things you produce, the houses you build, the books you write, the clothes you sew, the pies you make, the children you bring up—that are challenges all the way along the line. I think, though, surf fishing epitomizes all the things that a man will do in his life. It gives him a chance to live his life every time he goes fishing. Maybe the Babylonian proverb is true, I don't know.

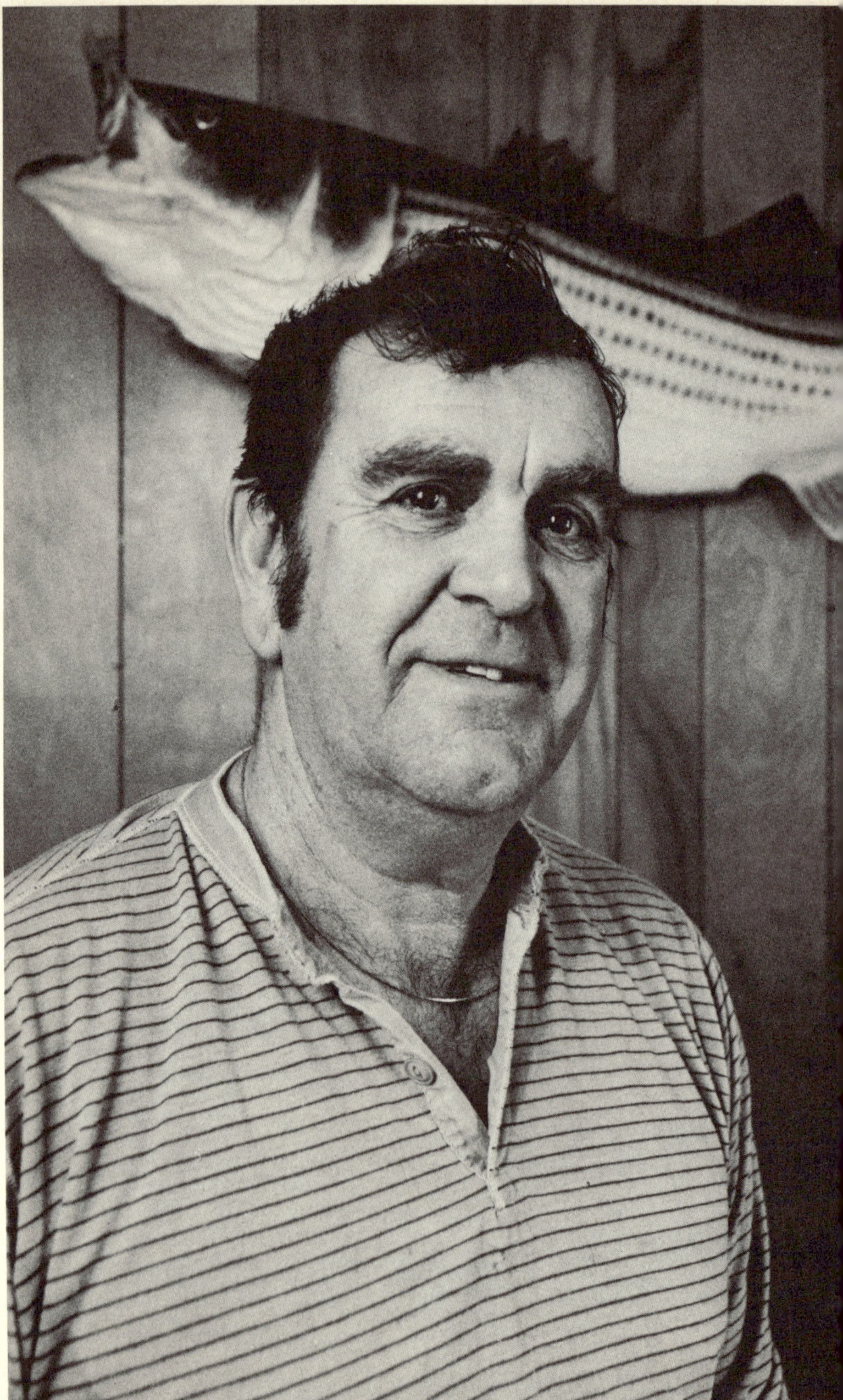

11

Francis Bernard

During the Martha's Vineyard Striped Bass and Bluefish Derby, I am often tense from lack of sleep and worrying. I worry about other fishermen finding me at my favorite fishing hole; I get territorial when I fish the Derby. I stand on a rocky outcropping on the North Shore ready to ward off intruders with glazed dark eyes and a menacing manner. If evil spells had been within my power, there were many mornings when I would have paralyzed the arms of intruding fishermen or broken their rods into sharp splinters of graphite and Fiberglas.

To relieve the tension of the regular Derby, four fishing friends and I established the West Tisbury Fishing Club and Derby. The five participants freely share information. The West Tisbury Derby runs until the Sunday after Thanksgiving. These late fall fishing excursions can be so cold that my teeth chatter and my finger tips turn a horrid dark purple with numbness. The fellowship and challenge of catching large migratory bass and blues make the discomfort of those cold nights fade.

Francis Bernard enjoyed the friendship and excitement provided by fishing clubs. He belonged to the Valley Falls Striper Club in Valley Falls, Rhode Island, the Vineyard Surfmasters and the Martha's Vineyard Fishing Club. Francis was awarded numerous trophies and patches for fish entered in the R. J. Schaefer Fishing Contest. These fish were weighed in during membership in the Vineyard Surfmasters. The 50 on his 1973 R. J. Schaefer patch represents his fifty-pounder. The 60 on his 1975 R. J. Schaefer patch represents his sixty-four-pounder. The sixty-four pounder is mounted and hangs over his living-room couch, casting an icy stare at all who pass by.

About seventy-five fishermen formed the Martha's Vineyard Fishing Club in 1969. The club was organized to compete against other clubs in New England. Its primary goal was to retire the R. J. Schaefer Trophy. In 1970, the Martha's Vineyard Fishing Club won the twenty-fourth annual R. J. Schaefer Salt Water Fishing Contest. They won again, as Grand Winners, in 1972, 1973, and 1974. Having won three years in a row, they retired the trophy to the Vineyard. Club members also competed against each other. The points that were awarded for total poundage went into the Schaefer Contest and the Fishing Club Contest. Trying to determine the best Vineyard fisherman, which was based on a point system for big fish, led to fierce competition. Soon after the trophy was retired in 1974, the club broke up.

At times the fierce competition led to distrust and jealousy. Not all the fishermen in the Martha's Vineyard Fishing Club wanted to belong to such a large club, where politics could stand in the way of friendships. So, in 1971, a group of ten fishermen, including Fred Keiner, Roger Andrews, Bernie Arruda, Tommy Taylor, and Francis Bernard, formed the Vineyard Surfmasters. This was a private club, unlike the Martha's Vineyard Fishing Club, which was open to the public. In 1975, the Vineyard Surfmasters, with Fred Keiner and Francis Bernard leading the way, won the R. J. Schaefer Salt Water Fishing Contest for stripers from the surf. The club came in third in total points for the East Coast.

Small private derbies and clubs are a Vineyard tradition. Large fishing derbies, open to the public, were numerous and popular after World War II. Francis Bernard enjoyed fishing in the large derbies and the small fishing clubs. Most of all, though, Francis enjoys fishing alone.

I started fishing in 1947 when I was fourteen years old. I used to fish with Al Doyle, Tony Gaspar, and Bernie Arruda. We used to fish for fluke near the Tisbury Great Pond, using mummichogs as bait.

During the 1950s, I started fishing with Ralph Grant. I would park my '52 Chevy at the airport and Ralph would pick me up in his Jeep. On the night of a championship boxing match, Ralph wanted to go fishing. Ralph said, "We're going to go fishing, but I want to get home at ten to watch the fight." We went to the Tisbury Great Pond opening with our conventional tackle. We weren't using spinning gear yet.

So we got down there and Ralph caught three or four fish before I got anything. I couldn't catch a fish. I said, "What's going on?" Ralph said, "There's plenty of fish here; what are you doing?" He came over and watched me fish. I could cast well. I was using a Penn Squidder with forty-five-pound-test line. I was excited and nervous, so to impress Ralph I made these long casts. He said, "Those fish aren't out there, they're close to the beach." That's how I learned to never take my plug out of the water until it's on the beach. The fish were right in the waves.

I met Jerry Sylvester and he taught me some things about fishing a plug. He never believed in using hardware on any lure. He used a wire leader and tied it directly to the plug. I had snaps and swivels on my rig. One night at Stonewall Beach, he said, "Take all that garbage off your plug. The less hardware, the better. The snaps and swivels take action away from the plug." Now, all I use is a barrel swivel at the top of the leader. If I want to change a plug, I cut it off and tie directly onto another one.

I was fishing at Long Beach with my brother Edmund. The week before I had noticed some deep water between the beach and a sand bar. It wasn't there the previous year, but a winter storm had changed the beach. I told him, "About a half-mile down the beach is a shoal spot. Let's go down there." He said, "All right." We caught about ten bass between us. There were a lot of fish in there that night.

I think half the fishermen fishing today would give up if they had to use conventional reels again, especially if they had to pick out a backlash at night. The backlashes always seemed to occur when the fish were coming in. You get nervous and excited because you know the fish are there and you can't seem to get the thing out.

I remember buying my first rod. I went to Leonard's Service Station in Oak Bluffs, right where Ben David's is today. It was run by old man Leonard and his son Howie. They used to sell Calcutta poles, so I bought a Calcutta pole. I remember it curved to the left about three inches. I put my own rod tip and guides on. I used regular nylon line to wrap the guides. My first reel was a push-button Pflueger. We just clamped the reels onto the rods with stainless steel clamps. I used the wooden Atom plugs. The plastic ones weren't out yet.

I've heard fishermen say they can "smell the fish." I don't think they smell fish. I've never smelled a fish in the water. I do think it's possible to smell the baitfish getting chopped up and devoured by bass and blues.

I was with Albert Fischer III near the bass stand at Squibnocket and I detected a faint smell of fish. I've heard people say it smells like melon, but I think it just smells like fish. It's just a baitfish smell. If the wind conditions are right and there are stripers feeding on a school of menhaden, and they're smashing it around, then it was possible to get a fishy smell in the air.

There were many times fifteen, twenty years ago when I would get up in the middle of the night to go fishing. In those days there weren't many cars around. I'd leave home, get halfway to the airport, heading out to the Tisbury Great Pond, and I'd notice a car following me. Somebody was following me to find my fishing spot. They'd even hide out near my house to watch.

FRANCIS BERNARD

I was fishing with Donald Ben David one night at the Chilmark Pond opening. I caught a bass there that won the Resident Shore Bass category for the Derby. The fish was more than forty-seven pounds. They had the weigh-in station at the old furniture store in Oak Bluffs, which has since burnt down. When people at the weigh-in station asked me where I caught it, I said, "Chilmark Pond opening." Well, no one believed me. The other fishermen never showed up there. They went everywhere I didn't tell them. I fished for a whole week at the Chilmark Pond opening and caught fish. I had the place to myself.

When I had a Jeep, if I caught a fish I would throw it in the back and cover it up. Before I had my Jeep, I had my old '52 Chevrolet. I couldn't take this on the beach, so hiding my fish was more difficult. I used to park the Chevy at Quansoo, cross the Black Point foot bridge and walk down to the opening of the Tisbury Great Pond. It was about one mile to the opening, and as I would work my way down to it, I'd stop and cast. I started to catch fish as I was walking along. This was about one in the morning. I kept catching fish all the way down to the opening. I would bury them and kept burying them as I went along. I had fish buried at different intervals for the whole mile.

Eels are a versatile bait. Steve Bryant bottom fishes them, Kevin Hearn casts and retrieves them, and Hank Schauer rigs them with a lead head and two hooks. In addition to fishing the whole eel, fishermen have devised ways of using eel skin. Eel-skin trolling rigs with hollow metal heads, Cuttyhunk rigs with a light metal sleeve in the head, and eel bobs with two ounces of lead replacing the meat in the head of the eel are all effective in different conditions.

Another productive use of eel skin is to place it over a wooden swimming plug. Effective for catching both striped bass and bluefish, this is the method favored by Francis Bernard.

One evening I was fishing with Albert Fischer III, and his father Albert, Jr. We were fishing near the Squibnocket parking lot. I had my truck and Albert had his. Not much was happening, so I drove down to Long Beach. I looked down the beach with my binoculars and saw four or five big gulls sitting on a stranded lobster pot. I looked at the waves and saw baitfish. Just as I looked again, I saw bass slicing through the waves chasing sand eels. I caught two fish right away using plugs, and then they wouldn't touch a thing. So I called Albert III on my CB. I said, "There's a bunch of fish down here, but they stopped hitting plugs." Albert drove down to fish with me. We didn't get any hits so we decided to change our tactics.

In the back of my truck I had some eel-skin plugs wrapped in foil. I had them all salted down, so I put one on, and I caught three more fish. I gave Albert a skin plug and he caught a couple of bass. The eel skins were pulled over Danny plugs. As I was landing a large striper in the surf, a bluefish hit the Danny plug. The bluefish almost hit the striper right in the face. Now I had two different kinds of fish hooked on one plug. They started to thrash around, so I just brought both of them onto the beach. Albert couldn't believe it. The bass weighed thirty-three pounds and the bluefish was around nine pounds.

I use eel-skin plugs for serious striper fishing. Many fishermen don't use them because they involve a lot of work. I usually set my own eel traps so I can trap eels that are the same diameter as the plug.

I put the eels in a pail and throw salt on them. The salt gets in their skin and kills them quickly. I grab the eel by the head and cut across the skin and muscle behind the head until I feel the backbone. Then I make a slit down to the stomach cavity. I run the knife carefully between the skin and the meat. You have to be careful not to cut the skin. Finally, I just grab it and peel the whole skin off. The skin will be inside-out and a bluish color. There still may be some meat on the skin, if so, I remove it. I fish with the skin's natural side out.

After the eel is skinned, the skin is pulled over a Danny plug. I've already removed the plug's hooks and I cut a one-eighth-inch groove in the wood near its head. A stainless-steel wire is tied in the groove, holding the eel skin in place. About three inches of eel skin should extend from the back of the plug to give it a more natural look in the water. I make two small slits in the skin where the hooks go through. I replace the two belly hooks, but I leave the tail hook off.

FRANCIS BERNARD

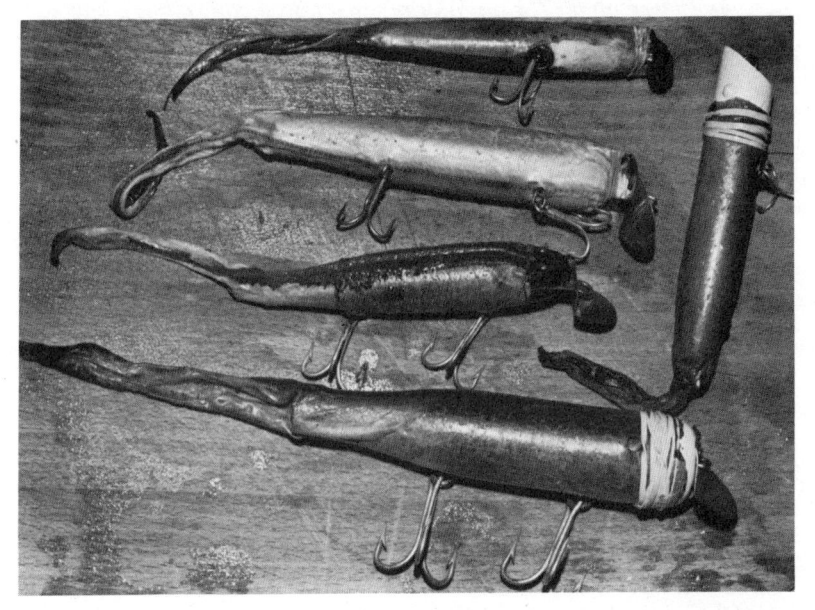

These eel-skin plugs were made in accordance with the technique used by Francis Bernard.

The fanatical drive to catch fish in the surf provokes some fishermen to leave their safe perch on the beach. These fishermen may venture into the ocean to cross swift currents at pond openings and to seek out large flat boulders in deeper water. Although migrating stripers, blues, and weakfish feed close to shore, sometimes beaching themselves in their savage pursuit of bait, they can also stay beyond casting range. A frustrated beach fisherman, whose plug falls consistently short, will try dangerous maneuvers to reach, and hopefully catch, fish.

In his book, Atlantic Surf Fishing: Maine to Maryland, Lester Boyd described the terror he felt when his inexperienced companion knocked him into the surf:

> The wash from the breaking wave, waist deep, toppled and buried him. His body hurtled into mine, at which point I

joined him in that gritty, cold, green-and-white turbulence. We were under for not more than a few seconds, but a few seconds spent with your face pressed into the sand while the backwash is trying to suck you out to where the next wave can finish the job is very unpleasant.... A man doesn't need many experiences like that to teach him the power of the surf. I have seen half a dozen men go in over the course of years. All of them came out, but not everybody who goes in is that lucky. Some are still in there.

Francis Bernard and Barry Hobby experienced the dangers of careless ventures off the beach. The temptation to cast a little bit farther taught both fishermen that currents lurking offshore can pull without mercy.

In 1965, I was fishing at Cape Higgon on the North Shore when I ran into the two Maciel brothers and Barry Hobby. Barry had this little plastic boat with him. He got in it wearing his waders. He took along some eels and one paddle. There was a flat rock to the right of me, about twenty to thirty yards out. He wanted to get to that flat rock. But as he headed out there, a strong northeast wind was blowing. With only one paddle, he had difficulty controlling the boat. The wind caused him to miss the rock and he headed out into the sound.

He still had his waders on. The boat was so dinky that he couldn't possibly stand up to remove them or he'd fall in. So I hollered to him that I would try to cast a line out to him. So I just threw the eel over his shoulder and he grabbed my line. I yelled, "Wrap it around your arm, so it doesn't cut into you." I pumped him in easy. You could hear the wind going through the line. I said, "If this line breaks, you're gone!" Finally, I pulled him into knee-deep water. And when he got near the beach, he just threw the rod on the beach. I just thought, "Thank God, he's all right." I think he was hysterical when he got to the beach, though. He probably saw death stare him in the face.

I almost lost my life three or four times when I was fishing. I remember a close call at the Tisbury Great Pond opening. I started the night fishing off the Coast Guard Station at Menemsha. There was a bunch of small bass breaking near the ramp. I was standing on the boat launch ramp in the back of the building. I could see bass chasing bait around. I kept plugging but I couldn't get them to touch anything. Finally, I put on an old wooden Atom plug and cast near the pier. I tried retrieving the plug at different speeds. I cranked it as fast as I could and caught four or five bass. They were small fish, around six or seven pounds. Then I left Menemsha at two in the morning and went to the opening. I'd been catching fish there at daybreak.

I parked my car and walked down to the opening. I was on the west side, but I wanted to be on the east side. I thought I could wade over to the other side even though the tide was running out fast. Now it's about three in the morning and I'm wading across, and I step into this hole. I went right under; the water rushed into my waders. I flipped around and started getting pulled out of the opening into the ocean. So, I stuck my rod in the sand to slow me down. I hit a sand bank, and I grabbed it and just laid there. It's a good thing there was a little spit of sand that built up off the opening.

I got up and dumped the water out of my waders. Then I fished and caught bass right until daylight. I didn't dare return to the other side until I could see my way. I went way up inside the pond and made it back all right.

Another time, a similar event happened at the Edgartown Great Pond opening. But that was during the daytime. There was a guy on the east side. I was on the west side. He was hollering to me, talking to me, like we're old friends. I thought I would cross the opening so we could fish together and talk, only I couldn't make it. I was stuck in the middle of the opening and felt myself going down. He came out near the water to meet me and I handed him my rod. With him pulling on the rod, I finally made it across. My car was on the west side, so I had to get back across the opening. Before it got dark, I went way up inside the pond and made it back.

I learned. I'm not crazy like that anymore. I have more respect now for the water. I don't take any chances!

The world above the fisherman, like the world below, is a source of beauty and curiosity. Spectacular shooting stars and the Northern Lights increase the enjoyment of a late-night fishing trip. The moon, with its immense mass sucking at the oceans and shaping the tides, has often risen above the eastern horizon in startling colors of orange and red that rival any sunset. The constellations, with their twinkling stars, provide dim light on moonless nights. The flickering red, green, and white lights of aircraft head for unknown destinations with their white exhaust tails crisscrossing against the black sky in a childlike game of tic-tac-toe.

One morning at daybreak, as Francis Bernard was leaving the Tisbury Great Pond, he was admiring the cloud formations and flocks of gulls. Suddenly, the intrusive sound of a giant eggbeater and the blurring sight of rotor blades flailing at the peaceful sky broke his concentration.

I was fishing all night at the Tisbury Great Pond opening. There were a lot of fishermen because it was spring and it had just been opened. Most guys left early to get ready for work. I was on vacation, so I could stay later. Bernie Arruda also stayed, figuring he'd start work late. Around eight-thirty we got into some bass. We caught six or seven stripers apiece. We washed them off and threw them in the back of the truck and prepared to leave.

I noticed one of those big Coast Guard helicopters flying up the shoreline. I've seen them before out looking for things and never thought twice about it. They went by a couple of times, swang out and came around again. I got in the Jeep and headed out on the inside of the pond, which was low, because the pond was open. As I drove from the ocean side of the pond to the inside, I noticed the helicopter coming over the bridge near Black Point at Quansoo. It landed right on the sand flats next to the pond.

So I thought they were looking for somebody. Maybe there was a missing boat or a drowning. I saw this guy get out wearing his orange suit and helmet, so I stopped the car and got out. He came running over to me; he wanted to know if I would sell the fish. I started to laugh. I said, "I'm not going to sell you any fish, but I'll give you one." He said, "We want to have a big party—a big feed of striped bass." They were going to have a party at Otis Air Force Base, so I gave him a fish that weighed around twenty pounds. He wanted to pay me. But I said, "I don't want the money. I might need you guys someday." He was satisfied with that. I watched the helicopter take off and that was it. They were waving good-by. They were happy because I gave them a fish. That's exactly the way it happened. Bernie saw it. He was driving behind me.

Herring runs have been a food source for generations of New England Indians. Although documentation is sparse, some archaeologists believe herring were used as fertilizer in mounded dirt piles where corn and beans were planted. These fish were trapped during their spawning run in weirs or nets. The fish weirs were barriers of brush or stone set at right angles to the shore, ending in a circular enclosure with an opening on one side.

Herring are also a food for striped bass which congregate near runs waiting for an easy meal. Francis Bernard, taking advantage of the struggles within this natural food chain, uses live herring to catch big bass.

I like to fish live herring at the Gay Head herring run. The herring really start running in April and May, but I have caught herring in February at Katama. Herring are more lively before they spawn. A spent herring has lost a lot of its strength. I use a herring net to catch them, and I have a wire keeper to put them in. I prefer the small herring. I make a wire keeper out of regular lobster-pot wire. The keeper box stays in the water so the herring stay lively.

Big bass off the mouth of the herring run love to feed on the smaller fish. I usually hook the herring with a No. 2/0 hook through the dorsal fin, then cast it out where it can swim around. When the tide goes down the herring may go down in the grass and stay there, so I have to put bobbers on the line to keep them up. I run a wire through the bobber and connect it to the barrel swivel above my leader with a link. The leader is about three feet long.

I was fishing with Donald Ben David at the Gay Head herring run using bobbers. We decided to hollow out the center of the bobber and drop in a flashlight. The flashlight was a small one-battery light. The top turns to control the on–off. We taped up the bottom of the bobber so the light wouldn't pull out. I rigged a herring, then before I cast, I turned the light on. We could see by the light which way the herring was going. When a bass grabs the bait you can see that light tear across the water and get pulled down. I used to catch a lot of fish that way.

You can also snag live herring with a treble hook cast into a thick school. Cast the treble hook, let it sink a little, and then jerk back on the rod. At least four times I've been snagging herring and I've hooked bass. The bass were so thick feeding on the herring, that I hooked them in the tail and in the side of the face. I caught one forty-one pounder like that. I never forgot it. I hooked him so close to the beach it startled me. He took off to the left and shot right up the beach. I ran fast to keep up with him. When he got in the shallow water, he started to thrash. I hauled him in. He tried to get back out, but he couldn't. I had him hooked just in back of the gill.

In 1975, I caught a sixty-four-pound striper by bottom fishing an eel at the Tisbury Great Pond opening about eight days after the Derby had ended. Alan Cordts had been fishing with me, but he left before I caught the sixty-four-pounder. People always tell me, "You catch plenty of big fish," as if there's nothing to it. I say, "You don't know the time and research that I do prior to catching those fish." If I caught a fish for every hour that I went fishing, I'd have fifty-thousand times more fish than I've caught. I'm lucky if I catch a fish during every five hours I spend fishing.

I like the challenge of fishing so much that if I could catch fish every night, I wouldn't go fishing that much. If I know I'm going to catch two or three bass every night, I may not want to go. I'll skip a night. If I go two nights and I don't get any fish, then I feel challenged. I say, "I'll get you. I'll outsmart you. I'll find you."

Striped bass are unpredictable. One night they're at one spot, and then the next night they're not. You never know; the bait moves. I get a kick out of fishermen who tell me, "We caught fish last night at eleven, so they'll be there at twelve tonight." I have to laugh at that.

When I was in my twenties I could go fishing on two to three hours of sleep a night for a week. I don't think I could do that now. I would need four to six hours of sleep a night. I love to go bass fishing. I'd rather catch striped bass than bluefish. Even though bluefish give a scrappier fight, they're much easier to catch than bass. There's no challenge. You could throw anything out there and catch bluefish. Bass are more difficult to catch. They're more challenging. You can feel the brute strength of a thirty- or forty-pound bass.

I would've given up a night with Marilyn Monroe to go catch bass, if that was the choice I had. And that is the real truth.

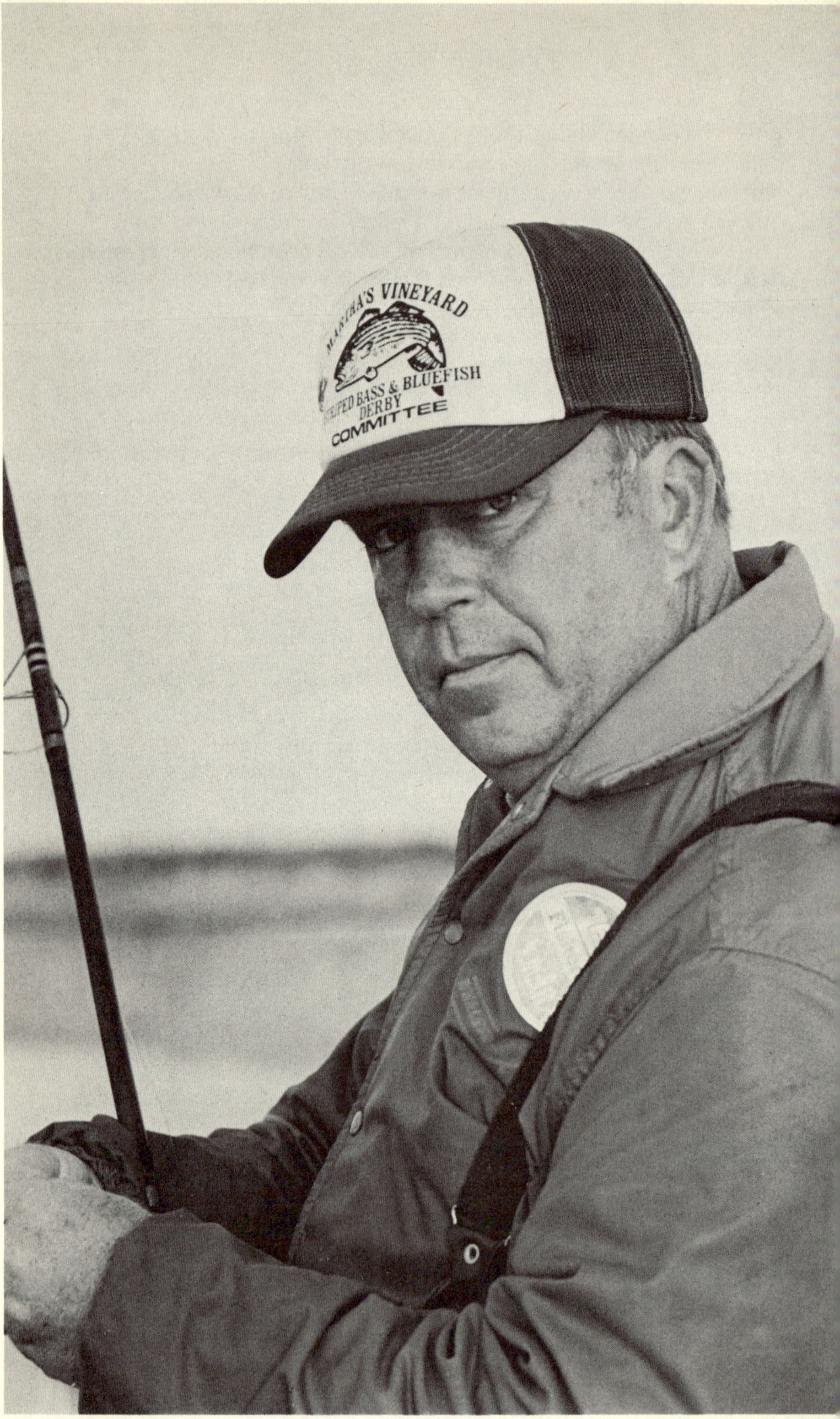
MARTHA'S VINEYARD
STRIPED BASS & BLUEFISH
DERBY
COMMITTEE

12

Cooper Gilkes III

I have often had the feeling that there must be a better means of transportation to the fishing grounds I love, than the four-wheel-drive vehicles that—on more than one occasion—I have buried to the axles in the soft sand at East Beach and Katama. And, it was during one of these unintentional excavations, with sand thrown high into the air by the useless spinning of the deflated tires, that I first met Cooper Gilkes III. Like me, he was on his way to the Edgartown Pond opening, where spring bass gathered to feed on herring. When he saw me in my vehicle he stopped to help.

Before that day, I was only familiar with the name Cooper Gilkes III because of the frequency it appeared on the Derby chalkboard recording the daily winners and overall leaders. His powers of attracting fish to his plug or bait have placed him at the top of the Vineyard modern-day surf-fishing community. Although he is often called for advice or comments on some unusual fishing story, Cooper is not interested in being a living legend. He would rather read about the response of Island children to one of the fishing tournaments he helps organize with his friends from the Martha's Vine-

COOPER GILKES III

yard Rod and Gun Club. Cooper thinks when kids have a fishing rod in their hands, they're not going to stand on a street corner, they're not getting in trouble, and they not only have a purpose, they have a good purpose.

One of the big highlights of my youth happened when I was fishing with Timmy Baird and an off-Island kid, Doug Severino. We were going down to Wasque in July. About thirty years ago, there was an opening from Katama Bay to the ocean. We used to take the ferry across and walk from the cliffs all the way down to the opening, which was back to the right toward Edgartown, about where Metcalf's Hole would be. My uncle John O. Sylvia was fishing down there.

I had a Clayt Hoyle rod, and I think Timmy had one, too. We were using fifteen-pound test, bottom fishing with sea clams. We couldn't hold bottom. The lines just kept going slack. I couldn't understand it. I said, "You don't suppose that's fish doing that, do you?" He said, "No. No. It can't be." He was wrong. I held the rod. The line went slack and I reeled like crazy. When I set the hook, all hell broke loose. The rod bent over, the line screamed out and parted. That kept happening all night long. We went through all our sinkers and hooks. We ran out of everything.

As we were leaving in the morning, we ran into my uncle who was fishing about a quarter-mile down the beach from us. He had two nice bass on the beach. They were real nice and weighed somewhere around thirty-five or forty pounds. When he showed us the fish, we couldn't believe it. We'd never seen bass that big. That was our first experience with really super big bass.

We decided to return that night, so we went to Brickman's to get more gear. I got some long-shank gut hooks—the plastic leader hook, which I wouldn't even think of fishing with today. I told Timmy that I was not going to go back there with fifteen-pound test. I was going to change over to twenty-pound test. Timmy stayed with fifteen-pound line. Doug came with us again and he decided to use twenty-pound test.

When we got down there that night, we weren't that excited. We had convinced ourselves that the fish that had parted our lines were sharks. We had totally convinced ourselves of that. We set up knowing that if the lines went slack, we'd had a hit.

Generally a bass will hit three different ways on the bottom; you're either going to get two bumps, as if it was hitting a plug, or you're going to get a pickup with the fish heading directly away from you, or it will do the reverse and come right at you. As soon as it comes toward you, the line goes completely slack. Many people miss a hit right there. They don't recognize it. If you're bottom fishing and suddenly your rod tip comes up and the line goes slack, ninety-five percent of the time if there's no tide running, that's a fish.

Timmy took the first hit and had a nice run; and it parted off. Then I took a hit. Doug took a hit at the same time. My fish took me down the beach about twenty to thirty yards before I could land it. There was a really heavy tide running. When I came back up the beach, I was very excited. I caught my first twenty-five-pound bass. I said, "Timmy, they're not sharks. They're bass. We're in heaven!" Then we all got excited. We didn't even put the rods back in the sand spikes. We stood right there and held them all night long. We caught a lot of fish.

About three that morning I had a hit. The fish kept going and going. I couldn't stop it. I remember saying to Timmy, "I've got a shark. I know this one is a shark." It went almost to the end of the line. I brought it back in, and it went back out again. All the time I'm walking down the beach toward my uncle, who was about a quarter-mile below us. Believe it or not, that fish took me past him. He had two rods out. He reeled them both in. Timmy had put his rod down, and was walking down the beach with me. The whole time we're talking about this shark that's on the end of the line. We just wanted to see it. We didn't care if we landed it or not. We had about twelve bass on the beach already.

I finally got the fish in the surf. Timmy went down, and put his light on it. He looked at it, and the fish came up and went down again. Tim said, "It's a *huge* shark." Deep down inside I really was hoping it was a monstrous bass. So I tightened on the drag, and I backed up on the fish. Now no fisherman is supposed to do that. But I was tired, and I wanted to catch bass. I didn't want to play around with a shark. Then the fish came up on its side in a wave. I didn't see it clearly because I was on top of the dune. Timmy was down on the water's edge. He turned around and screamed at me, "Coop, it's the biggest bass I've ever seen in *my life!*"

I was tightening up on the drag, so I came running over the top of the dune, tripped, got up and, in the process, got the reel full of sand. With the next wave, the fish came right up on the beach. Timmy couldn't pick it up because the fish would not open its gills, so he just fell on the fish and pinned it. When it finally opened its gills, he picked it up. That was my first fifty-pound bass. I walked back to my uncle, and my uncle looked at me and said, "I don't believe it. You got your first fifty-pound bass." I was sixteen years old. That fish weighed about fifty-four pounds.

We were pretty well tired out by eight that morning. We had fished all night, and kept thirty-two bass. We were completely out of it.

Before we left, I went over to the bait basket. There was one sea clam left—a little one. I asked, "Anybody want this?" Nobody wanted to fish. I said, "Well, I'm going to throw the thing out there." So I hooked up the sea clam and threw it out. There was a big white wash in front of us and the water was *very* shallow. The sinker landed right in the wash. I swear to this day there probably wasn't four inches of water in there.

Timmy and I were sitting together talking, and I got a hit. I set the hook—down the beach I go again. I went by my uncle again. He said, "Cooper, don't tell me you've got another big one?" I said, "I swear. I'm telling you, I think I got another real big fish." That fish was fifty-one pounds.

Now we've got thirty-three fish. We've got to get them up to the parking lot on the cliff, about a mile away. Well, we start lugging them toward the car. We had been up for two nights straight, so we were completely exhausted. We filled up the trunk of my old Dodge. We took the back seat out. We're putting fish in the back of the car. I didn't think I'd be able to get this car out of the road. Finally, on about our fourth trip to the Dodge, a lady came along in an old square-back Jeep. She stopped, loaded up the Jeep twice and took them up for us. Otherwise, I don't think we would've got them there.

COOPER GILKES III

As we head home, we're going over the Big Bridge. My brother Bobby was on the bridge. He was all excited. He waved to us and said, "Stop, stop, stop. I've got a big fish." Doug got out and walked around the car and said, "What do you mean 'a big fish?'" Bobby holds up a bass about ten pounds. Doug says, "Let me show you something." He opens the trunk of the car. We had one of the fifty-pounders on top of the pile. He grabs the fish, opens its mouth, and takes the ten-pounder and sticks it in the bigger fish's mouth. That devastated my brother! He's never forgotten. I didn't know what was going on. I was sound asleep in the car.

During the 1985 Derby, I had a chance meeting with Michael Dietz at the West Tisbury landfill. The gulls working the festering food scraps did not induce me to cast a plug. I quickly told Michael that I caught a thirteen-and-a-half-pound bluefish that morning at Makonikey bottom fishing fresh butterfish. Then I left hoping to find gulls swooping and gliding in a less noxious environment.

That evening Michael went to Makonikey with butterfish. He caught a thirteen-pound, ten-ounce bluefish that won the third daily prize, knocking me off the board. This, I thought to myself, is why fishermen lie.

Cooper, like most surf fishermen, won't easily reveal where he most recently caught fish. Although when intimidated by an elder, his resolve will sometimes weaken. He has learned that telling the truth may not be enough to maintain a fragile trust. Fishermen lie so often that a true answer is often ignored by the one who asked the question.

I've had nights that would probably shock people. I had several of those nights with my fishing buddy George King.

George and I had set some eel pots. We figured we'd take the eels and try Makonikey. The tide was right. George put on an eel; put it out. On his first cast he hooks a fish that weighs around thirty-two or thirty-three pounds. Some guy came over and said, "Ha, fifteen pounds." Georgie got in a heck of an argument over the weight of the fish. He got so mad he said, "Hey, I'm not even going to fish here. I don't want to fish with these guys." It was crowded. It's a tight spot to fish. "So," he said, "we'll go down to Goff's."

So we drove down to Goff's. Somebody was on the end of the jetty. We said, "Ah, geeze! Here we go again!" It turned out to be Matt Perry. He saw us and decided to leave. So we're walking out on the jetty, and I said, "You know what the chance is of fish being out there?" Only George said, "Let's go out and try it."

So we went down and threw out an eel. Just as the eel hit the water we had a run. I said, "I got one on," and he said, "So do I." The rip was there and so were the fish. I can't tell you how many fish we caught. I know it took us two-and-a-half hours to lug them all out of there. We levelled Georgie's Chevy pickup truck. Looking back on it I'm not too proud, but it was done.

At the time, we were fishing and driving a truck for Ralph Grant. We would go into work, get through work, run the eel pots, get home, grab a couple of hours of sleep and go fishing.

The fourth night we were there, the word's around we were into the fish. We're really hitting them big. Everybody's looking for us; nobody can find us. We're hiding the truck in the garage at Mink Meadows. Cars were pulling into the parking lot, turning around, looking for us and driving out. We had one guy crawl under my car in my own driveway. He was looking at the tires to check the tread. This is the honest to God truth.

The night before, somebody tried to tail us. We noticed, and lost them. So this particular night, we are coming back and decide, "Well, the best thing to do is let somebody find us, and then we'll be squared away." So at three in the morning we drive all the way to the West Tisbury opening. We've got fifteen fish in the back, and we are sleeping at the West Tisbury Great Pond. We just wanted to get caught at West Tisbury and they'd say, "Ah ha, we know where you're fishing; you're at West Tisbury." This is to show you how crazy fishermen are.

Finally, down the beach comes a Jeep—it's Kib Bramhall. He came up to the truck. "How's it going?" he says. "Oh, a good night, a real good night," we said. We had taken fish out of the truck and dragged them up and down the beach. Kib doesn't even look at the drag marks. He doesn't look at the back of the truck. Any normal fisherman would walk over, look in your truck and say, "You had a good night!" So he starts to go down; then he comes back and looks in the truck, and says, "Oh, you really did have a good night." So he walks down to the opening, flips out a plug, and he's on. We're absolutely freaked out. We never even thought about trying to fish, we're so tired. The bass were in there solid.

The afternoon before, Al Doyle had stopped me on the street. He said, "I don't want you to lie to me. I want to know where you're fishing." Now, I've always respected my elders; I really have. Al has been real close to the family. So I said, "Al, I'll tell you what. We haven't told a soul where we were fishing, and I'm not going to lie to you—get over to Goff's." He said, "Okay, fine."

After we left the West Tisbury Pond opening, we went to sell the fish we caught at Goff's. I think we were down by the Seafood Shanty or the Harborside Restaurant. As we're unloading the fish, Al pulls up. And is he angry! "You lied to me, boy!" I said, "What are you talking about?" He said, "You got those fish at West Tisbury."

Beach Road, on the northeast shore of the Island, separates Joseph Sylvia State Beach from Sengekontacket Pond. Two openings, one at Little Bridge, the other at Anthiers or Big Bridge, allow the waters of Nantucket Sound to mix with the waters of the pond. Schools of baitfish moving through the openings attract bluefish, bonito, and striped bass.

While fishing at Anthiers Bridge, Cooper displayed the talent and determination that contribute to his legendary status. Some fishermen would resign themselves to losing a fish that didn't ideally match the tackle they were using. Cooper, inventing new techniques as necessary, did not want to experience the bitter disappointment that can lead to sleepless nights and exaggerated stories about "the one that got away."

Zane Grey, after losing a big fish, wrote he felt a "failing spark within my breast. . . . I watched him swim slowly away with my bright leader dragging beside him. Is it not the loss of things which makes life bitter? What we have gained is ours; what is lost is gone, whether fish, or use, or love, or name, or fame."

I'll never forget this story. My wife and I were setting the seine for some bait to use in the eel traps. It was high noon in July about ten years ago. We set the net at the bend in Beach Road near Edgartown. This is a hundred-and-fifty-foot-long net. Lela's on one end;

I'm on the other, and we're pulling it in. We got some bait we expected, but we also got four small bunker. So, I said to Lela, "You know, I'll bet if we take these bunker in a bucket of water and run them down to Anthiers Bridge, we can catch a bass." She said, "Let's go."

In the car was a seven-foot rod with a little freshwater 940 Penn reel that had six-pound test on it. I also had a nine-foot Eagle Claw bass rod with 704 Penn reel.

I rigged up a bunker on the nine-foot rod for Lela. She went down and fished it off the bridge. About this time Arthur Winter pulls up to watch. I was just standing by the truck talking to Arthur. Because the tide was coming in, Lela let the bunker go up inside the pond. The bunker didn't get twenty-five yards up inside that pond and there was an explosion! A striper had nailed the bunker. She let it run, then set the hook. I said, "Okay, bring him down to the beach, and I'll give you a hand when you get to the beach." So she walked down off the bridge and we landed the fish. I picked the fish up and took it to the car.

I put on another bunker for her. She goes out on the bridge again. Arthur is starting to kid me about letting her catch all the fish. So I said, "You want to see something? Watch this."

I took out the fresh-water gear and tied on a No. 8 Golden Eagle Claw trout hook. I hook the bunker in the back and walk down to the water letting the rig go out. Just then Lela hooks up with another bass. There was a guy standing next to me watching all this with Arthur. I said, "Here. Hang on. Just keep your thumb on the spool, and I'll be back in a minute." So I went down; helped Lela bring in her second bass. Same size as the first—twenties or thirties, somewhere in that area.

I went back up on the bridge and Arthur says, "That's two bass!" I said, "Yeah, yeah." I reached over. I took my rod from the other guy. Right then—*boom!* A big one hit mine. Arthur hooks on the last bunker for Lela. She hooks up with another bass that starts running up the pond on the Edgartown side. My bass made a run up into the pond, too, so I head down on the Oak Bluffs side.

I went as far as I could go to the drop off. I fought the fish there for a few minutes. The fish ran all the way to the end of the line. I was on the knot. The rod went straight down. I was leaning into the water thinking "It's going to break; it's going to break." Then it just eased up, and it came back again.

In the meantime, Lela had beached her fish. Arthur had come down and was standing beside me. I said, "I've got two choices. I can get my line back and force another run, or I let him go under the bridge and lose him." I decided to stop him before he comes too close to the bridge.

I was putting no pressure on the fish at all, and he was swimming back toward the bridge. I refilled my spool up about three-quarters. We're talking almost two-hundred yards of line. I put almost three-quarters of it back on. I reel like crazy. I got him up tight again. And that son of a gun took me right down to the knot a second time. Only this time when he hit the knot, I knew I was in serious trouble. I mean this was six-pound test.

"Arthur," I said, "I think this is a real fish." He's got too much power, he's too strong, and he's running too long. So now I'm in the water up to my neck. I'm on the knot, and we're playing back and forth. Then the fish came up and rolled in the middle of the channel way up inside the pond. The tail was enormous. You could see it. The tail just came right out of the water and turned over and flopped. I could tell he was tired. I said, "Arthur! Did you see it?" He said, "I saw it. I saw it. Unbelievable!"

That's when I decided I might have to start swimming to keep from losing it, so I kicked my boots off. I had a lot of heavy tension on the rod. I'm wading out to keep the line from breaking. Each time I reached a point when I thought the line might break, I'd go out a little deeper. That fish just kept leading me off into the channel. Pretty soon I was swimming a little bit.

Then he suddenly started coming at me again. I came back to the beach. This time I really let him come in himself. He came in tight and I said to Arthur, "I think he's tired enough so that when he gets in close, I'll be able to handle him right in here."

The fish came right up. For some reason it didn't go to the bridge. It came up the channel I was in on the Oak Bluffs side. When I did finally start to put pressure on him, he turned on his side. I saw him and freaked out! I thought I had a fifty-six-pound bass. Arthur couldn't believe it. And that son of a gun took off again, and dumped three-quarters of that spool.

COOPER GILKES III

The tide was rising all this time. The flats are now completely covered. The fish is no longer staying in the channel. He's coming up on the flats on the other side. He was straight across from me. About a quarter-mile down to the right, Ed Bugbee had a sign stuck out there that read "No Shellfishing!" Eventually the fish worked its way down to the sign and went around it. I said, "That's it, Arthur. Forget it. It's all over. Before I can even swim out there, he's going to part that line." The fish, believe it or not, turned right around and swam exactly the opposite way, undid itself from the sign and kept right on swimming. We finally got the fish to the side of the beach where we could see it over the drop off. We were now down past the boat ramp. All this time, I was in the water playing the fish.

Now the fish is right in front of us, so we can see it as plain as day. We now have a crowd of about sixty people watching. All kinds of people came over to see what's going on. People are stopping in the road. I am a total mess. This thing has worn me to a frazzle.

About forty-five minutes have gone by. I know time is important because there is no leader and things have got to be wearing out. We had the fish up twice. Arthur tried to pick it up but couldn't. It didn't open its gills. Arthur couldn't pounce on it because it was still in the water, and its back was up. Finally we got it close. It turned on its side. Arthur picked up the fish, and the hook fell out of its mouth.

Later, I went into the coffee shop. And it's all over town. Arthur had been back in the coffee shop telling everyone, "Cooper caught a fifty-six-pound bass on six-pound test."

Actually, it was forty-nine pounds fifteen ounces.

The Columbus Day Blitz, as previously mentioned by Whit Manter, involved two large schools of frenzied striped bass feeding on two pods of terrified helpless bunker. As Whit worked the school moving east, Cooper and his friends moved with the school heading west until both fish and fishermen met. Cooper remembers many details about the Blitz, including his failure to leave the beach to pick up his wife so she could share the day with him.

The night before the Columbus Day Blitz I was fishing with Ed Medeiros, Eddie Jerome and the wives. We had fished all night.

COOPER GILKES III

Two of us fished Metcalf's Hole, and one of the parties had gone down to the Cape Poge Light. We all met back at Metcalf's Hole at dawn. The wives were going home, but we decided to take a ride to West Tisbury Great Pond because we had heard a rumor that the day before some bunker were on the beach. We were all supposed to be at work that morning.

Then Bernie Arruda arrived at Metcalf's Hole. We told Bernie about the story we had heard. Bernie said he was going to go on up. We told the wives we were just going to take a quick run, and we'd be back.

The weather was quiet. The sun was up nice. We proceeded up the beach, past the Edgartown Great Pond, past Oyster Pond, past Hadley's. We pulled up on top of a dune in Eddie Medeiros' truck. Looking down the beach you couldn't see a thing. It was mirror calm. There was no sign of fish, and somebody in the truck said, "Let's go back; let's turn around and go home."

After some discussion we decided to keep going. We went around the next point, about a hundred yards down. And there was Bernie, on the beach, dragging a forty-pound bass out of the surf. This is on the other side of Hadley's—just below where Whit was fishing. Bernie said, "Forget it. The Derby's already won. It's in the back of my truck." Everybody jumped out. We ran over to his Jeep; and I'll tell you, the fish in there had to weigh fifty pounds. We couldn't believe it! Then I looked out at the water. The bunker were right inside the cove, and the bass were outside the bunker. They were just going back and forth, back and forth. They wouldn't let the bunker out of the cove. It was an awesome sight. Twenty to thirty bass at a time were putting a rush on the outside of these fish.

Ed, Eddie, and Bernie started fishing with Danny plugs. I put on a two-ounce sinker with a treble hook up the line on an eighty-pound-test leader. I snagged a bunker. As I was reeling in I got a hit almost immediately. I landed a bass that went thirty pounds. While I was landing the fish the other guys had the hooks straightened on their Danny plugs. Ed Jerome decided to rig up for snagging bunker. We went to one point of the cove, while Bernie and Eddie fished the other point. One of us always had a fish. This was not normal. It was nine in the morning. We're seeing everything happen. If there was any way for bass to hit a plug or live bait, we saw it happen that day.

When we first started, the plugs did as well as the bunker. But as the day wore on the bunker were taking over the whole show.

At midday the four of us took a break. We went up to the truck. There was a steep twelve-foot embankment from the truck to the water. We climbed up and watched this blitz. It's still building momentum. We're sitting there watching *huge* fish just rolling into the bunker. It was too much and we started fishing again.

While Eddie Medeiros was reeling his line in, he said, "Look at this." He showed me a frayed spot. I said, "Boy, you'd better change that. That's asking for trouble." Eddie got on to a big fish. He sweated that fish out—every single second of it! That fish weighed fifty-six pounds. He won the resident shore bass part of the Derby with that fish.

After that, he was done in and went up to the truck. Bernie quit; Ed Jerome quit. They're all up at the truck. The truck is levelled. We had to put air back into the tires because the tires were down to the rim. But I kept fishing. These fish are still going back and forth in front of us. I could not conceive of leaving that beach. I knew that big one was out there!

At about four that afternoon Whit Manter, Jackie Coutinho, and some of the other guys worked their way down to us as they fished another huge school of bass. Their fish worked toward us and eventually the two schools merged. Then we all ended up fishing together for another two hours.

I'll probably never, ever have another day like the Columbus Day Blitz, although I've come close. I saw fish caught every which way. I don't think I've ever hammered bass for such a long time. That was the longest I've ever had them right in front of me.

Hook-ups with sharks are not common for most Vineyard surf fishermen. When they occur in Vineyard waters, the fisherman is usually seeking a smaller, less threatening species. Frank Stick in The Call of the Surf *describes successful shark fishing as an extremely rewarding surf-fishing feat. "Like the blow of a sledge he had smashed into the bait and, irresistible as a six-cylinder car, he was tearing out to sea. I put all my weight and strength against the rod, and bore down upon the brake with both thumbs, but this fellow minded it not in the slightest. I have hooked good fish in my time, of a hundred species, but never before nor since have I felt greater power than was in this creature."*

Cooper was prepared for the shark battle at East Beach. He had the proper gear. His guests for the day were several members of the Boston Bruins. Out of uniform, without protective padding, the hockey players felt vulnerable in ways they did not feel when on the ice.

This is a story about scaring some Boston Bruins. Some of the Bruins were down in 1980, and through Paul Schultz I met them at a clam boil. They wanted to go fishing, so Ralph Case and I took about five or six of them down to East Beach. We were going bluefishing. There weren't many bluefish around. They weren't really interested in that. One of them asked what the big rod and reel were doing in the back of Ralph's truck. We said, "Oh, we catch sharks with it." They wanted to know where. "They're right here, right now," I told them. "And they're big ones!"

Ralph caught a twelve-pound bluefish on regular spinning gear. We put the shark hook through it and live-lined it from the beach. We used the special gear we made up for shark fishing; a fourteen-foot-long rod with one hundred-thirty-pound-test line with a one-thousand-pound-test leader. The reel was a 10/0 conventional.

The bluefish was out there for about two minutes before it started going freaky. I can always tell when I'm going to get a hit. The bluefish immediately comes to the top, and starts jumping and swimming erratically. Then it headed down the beach on an angle away from us. Right behind it was a two-foot fin. Nobody could believe it. Ralph and I knew it was coming. We were ready for it. When I do this, I go on star drag because it feeds the line off steadily. I don't put the free spool on because when the shark hits the bluefish it just tangles the line on the reel. The shark hit the bluefish. We set the hook, and after a twenty-five-minute fight we had the shark on the beach.

It looked like either a tiger, brown shark, or porbeagle. It weighed about three hundred pounds. We didn't kill the fish. We cut the leader and let it go. After seeing all this, I guarantee you these Boston Bruins will never swim on East Beach again.

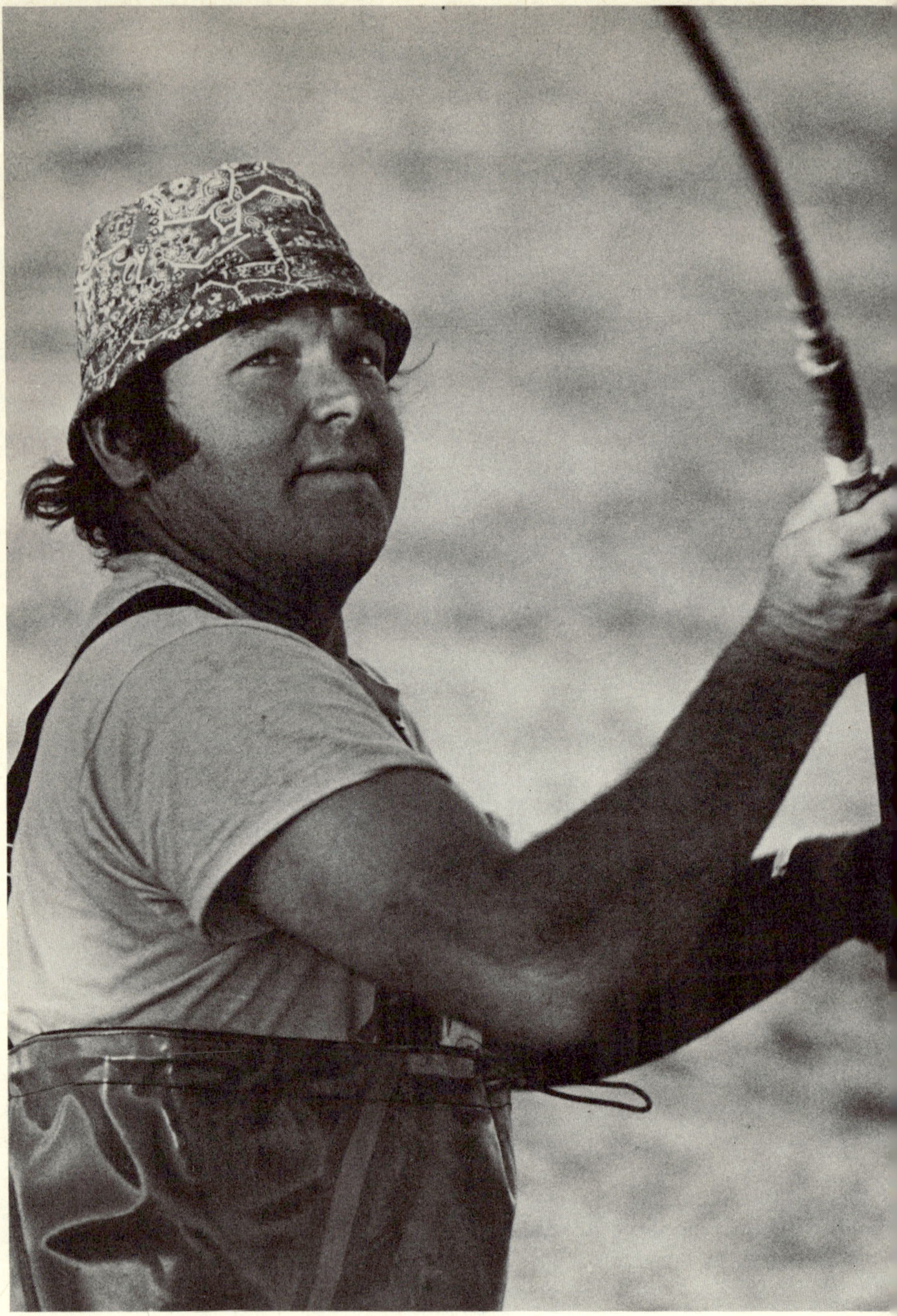

13

Paul Schultz

The Vineyard surf-fishing season begins in March when snowstorms are still rumbling up the coast from Cape Hatteras and the air is still cold enough to freeze wet fishing line, turning it into a taut guitar string. Past experience has taught fishermen the herring will arrive soon along the South Shore, looking for the same pond openings that generations have sought for thousands of years. Primitive instincts direct the fish to migrate and spawn. And, although it is only March, the fishermen know the squid are beginning to stir and fill themselves with eggs and ink. Most important, the fishermen know that following the herring and squid will be the bass and blues during May. These fish chase the bait north along well-marked routes flowing through the massive ocean—water within water, marking the path to the Vineyard surf and the hooks of Vineyard surf fishermen.

During those stark winter days, Paul Schultz is preparing his tackle. While northeast winds push snow against his house, he is changing hooks and greasing reels. His fishing diary stands ready. It *will help pinpoint the best locations when tides and winds coincide with the available baitfish.*

My father owned a cottage at North Pond in the Belgrade Lake area of Maine. The day school got out, we would leave North Vassalboro, go to the camp and stay there until school started in the fall. I used to sit on the dock with a little handline and fish for seven to nine hours a day without stopping. I'd come off the dock for a sandwich and go right back out with my handline. When I got to be about five, my parents let me take the little boat and row out a hundred feet off the beach and fish along the lily pads. When I was eight I was allowed to go anywhere on the pond. That's how I started fishing.

I moved to the Vineyard in 1962. I was sixteen and a sophomore in high school. I met Sam Jackson and his brother Wayne, who later became my brother-in-law. We used to fish Menemsha, Cape Poge Gut, Wasque, the Big Bridge, the Little Bridge, Makonikey. We got a lot of bass, but not too many blues. There weren't too many blues then. Eventually, I got my own four-wheel-drive vehicle and started fishing on my own.

I remember my first striper. I was fishing with Sam and his crowd. We used to leave on Friday night and return Sunday night. We fished day and night. My first bass was down by the East Beach jetties. We were bottom fishing. We had about eight rods out. We were using sea clams, mackerel, and squid. I had a piece of squid on my rod. Around ten at night I reeled in a bass of fifteen pounds. I was using thirty-pound test and a big surf rod, so it wasn't that much of a fight. That was my first bass.

My first bluefish was caught at East Beach, about four-hundred yards down from Wasque. That was when the opening was there. I was plugging, and I hooked up with a small one, five or six pounds.

I saw my first weakfish when I was fishing with Ralph Case down on South Beach. We were bottom fishing during September, maybe the first week of the Derby. Ralph hooked a fish, and we brought it ashore. Neither one of us could recognize it. We're looking at it, and a guy came by and we asked him what it was, and the guy said, "Oh, that's a sea trout." Then another guy came by and said, "You caught a squeteague." A third guy came by and said, "You caught a weakfish." So we had three opinions from three different guys. We took it home and looked in a fish book. We found out it was called all three names.

When I first started fishing in the 1960s there weren't many bluefish around. If you caught a bluefish, it was really something great. You would catch more bass than bluefish. I remember being out striper fishing and seeing a guy catch bluefish. The guy thought he caught a special fish, where, nowadays, it's reversed.

I didn't catch a bluefish the first year I fished. I concentrated on bass the first year I fished and I caught them instead. It was the second or third year that I fished before I caught a bluefish.

The first bonito I caught was in 1965, the year I graduated from high school. I didn't catch it from shore. I was boat fishing with a few friends. We were using Kastmasters, and I hooked up with one. I fish for bonito from the shore now, but I would rather catch stripers.

The striped bass is still the status fish for me. I love to catch stripers, even though I tag and release ninety-eight percent of them. I keep maybe two or three fish a year.

I probably became a fishing fanatic when I came back from the service in 1970. I had spent fifteen months in Vietnam. I was out in the boonies, right on the Cambodian, Laotian, and Vietnamese borders. Every month we got a check. I kept $25 a month, and the rest I put in the bank. I arrived home April 16, 1970. I had enough money saved so I didn't have to work until March 1971. I could fish any tide any time and anyplace I wanted.

That's when I first started keeping a fishing diary. Every time I catch a fish, I go home and log it in my book. I log the place, the time I caught it, what the wind was doing, what the tide was doing and what I was using.

I don't record each fish, but the group of fish I caught at a particular spot. I may write "twelve bluefish at Wasque." If I went down to Cape Poge Lighthouse and caught three more, I'd list that group separately. I still keep the diary. I can look at it before the season starts and review what has happened in the past.

During the first couple of years that I kept a diary, I noticed that during June, July, and August in '70, '71, and '72, I was able to catch bass all summer. For many years after that period I could catch them in May, June, September, October, and November, but not during July and August. During the past two to three years I've noticed more bass around, and I started to catch them in the summer months again.

I've noted changing patterns in the bait available. In '86, it seemed like most of the bunker were in Edgartown, and the year before I remember they were up in Vineyard Haven. The butterfish slacked off in 1986 along with the false albacore. Only two or three were caught all summer, and then for the first two weeks of the Derby they weren't around at all.

The beach changes daily. Each wave deposits or removes sand. Beaches that were once easily accessible by foot or car can change dramatically in hours, as the force of strong winds and the incessant pounding of the surf cause major shifts of sand.

Along with the changes in beach contour, the debris at the tide line changes. A bleached tern skull, or a shiny piece of driftwood may disappear overnight. Arriving unexpectedly in the same place, a jellyfish or sea clam shell may sit with sand-rimmed edges. Sand eels, bunker, silversides, and herring are often washed up in pieces after an attack by bass or bluefish. A drowned deer that had been chased by a dog pack into the sea washed up on the North Shore.

On a raw day in mid-November, 1977, I came across a dead tuna fish resting on the beach between Katama and Wasque. A large chunk of flesh was torn from its back, the result of an unhappy encounter with a predator. After close inspection, and not without some consideration of taking a steak home for dinner, I continued my journey to Wasque. I returned home along a different route, so I did not see the tuna again. I wasn't the only fisherman out that day, however. Paul Schultz was exploring the beach looking for pods of bait and diving gulls when he discovered the tuna. His encounter with the tuna turned into a tiring adventure that legitimizes the saw: "Leave well enough alone."

After the Derby, in 1977, I still had a batch of eels left. I believe it was November 12. I gathered the eels and headed to Wasque. Three-quarters of the way there, I noticed a fish lying in the edge of the surf line. So I stopped to see what it was, and it was a big tuna fish. I thought my father would like to see something like this. He's seen bass, blues, and other fish I've brought home, but he's never seen anything this big. I went back into town to get my father. While I was at his house, I called Cooper Gilkes. Cooper arrived with Ralph Case. We all went down and checked it out. We were looking it over, when Cooper took a knife and cut the tail. He said, "It's bleeding; it's fairly fresh. Maybe we ought to see what we can do with it." So with that, we decided we were going to take it home.

We unsuccessfully tried to lift the head up onto the back of Ralph's truck. So we got a tow rope and put it through the fish's gills and hooked it to the trailer hitch of my Ford Bronco. We put Ralph's truck behind the small sand dune with the tailgate open, and had my father tow it right up the sand dune so the head was starting to go onto the tailgate of Ralph's truck. After about an hour-and-a-half we got it into the back of the truck. We tied it down and went into town. The tail of the fish stuck out the back of the truck because the fish was ten feet long. In the meantime we got on the CB and started talking to people. By the time we got down to Lawry's Seafood Restaurant, where we weighed the fish in, we had fifteen, twenty cars waiting for us. Harold Lawry said, "Well, if you want me to get rid of it for you, it has to be cleaned. I can't take it whole."

None of us had ever cleaned anything this size, so we asked around. Finally Ted Henley helped us. He showed us how to gut it and take the head and tail off. Well, we cleaned it. We tried to put it back in the truck, and we couldn't get it up. With the head off, we couldn't use the come-along or the tow rope because there were no gills. So we found an old dolly and tied it onto the dolly. We got hold of the police, and they had a cruiser lead us the wrong way up Main Street in Edgartown, around two-thirty in the morning. We got it back to Lawry's and threw it on a scale. It tipped the scale at 630 pounds—gutted, no tail and no head. Then it went into Lawry's freezer.

A few days later Harold Lawry took the tuna off-Island to sell. We didn't know that at the time there was a quota on certain tuna. You were supposed to have tuna tags to sell tuna. The people who tuna fish had to have a license and tags. Once the quota for each variety of fish was used up, you couldn't sell any more.

Harold ended up at the Freshwater Fish Company. They knew about the quota and said they would have to check with the fish and game department before they could buy it. Someone from fish and game checked out the fish, but he wouldn't release it until they sent someone to the Vineyard to make sure the tuna wasn't caught from a boat. I think Freshwater Fish Company tried to pass it off as a yellowfin tuna but this was a bluefin. That's why all the commotion was raised.

So the state guys came down to investigate. They wanted to make sure they weren't on the trail of some tuna poachers. We showed them the pictures of the fish lying on the beach. They interviewed Cooper and everybody. They found out we were legit, but they wouldn't release the money until almost four years later—the summer 1981. Mike Wild was at the Martha's Vineyard Commission, so I talked to him about it. He made a phone call to somebody and I received a check in the mail. The state paid me and then I split it up with Ralph and Cooper. We don't know what happened to the fish. We don't know if it was used to feed people or if it just got thrown out.

If I had to do it again, I'd write a note that said, "This was caught by famous angler Paul Schultz." I would stick it in the mouth of the tuna and leave. Maybe we should've steaked it up, so we each could have had fresh tuna steaks for the next five years. There was no way of knowing there was a quota because we don't fish for bluefin. We go out for bass and bluefish. But it really turned into an all-night adventure.

An explanation for the demise of the bluefin near Metcalf's Hole is found in the National Geographic Society's The Book of Fishes: *"The tunas themselves are preyed upon by killer whales, which are said to seize them by the nape, cut the spinal cord, and thus kill them instantly. The fish sometimes become stranded, presumably either while pursuing prey or perhaps while fleeing from enemies."*

You never know what you'll run into washed up on the beach. In 1977, it was the bluefin tuna. November 4, 1981, I found a tarpon. My friend Jerry Gonsiewski was visiting from Tarpon Springs,

PAUL SCHULTZ

Paul Schultz (left) and Ralph Case stand alongside the washed up "troublesome tuna." Fishing can be an adventure without even putting a line in the water.

Florida. He comes up every year. He usually arrives during the last week of October and stays for two weeks.

We went down to Cape Poge to see if we could catch any bass or bluefish. We had a favorite spot called the Duck Blind, because that's where everybody duck hunts. When we got there, Jerry said, "I'll work to the right. You go to the left." I said, "Okay."

I was working my way to the left and I worked myself down about a half-mile from Jerry. It was a moonlit night. I looked off in the distance and I saw this fish lying on its side, right in the edge of the surf line. And, at that distance, it looked like a striper. I went over to look at it. I knew it wasn't a striper. I picked it up and took it back to Jerry. He said, "What did you get?" I said, "I'm not sure. I think it's a tarpon. But I'm not sure." We put it in my fish box and went down the beach where we ran into Kib Bramhall. I said, "Kib, what's this? Is this a tarpon?" He rotated it and looked it over carefully. He said, "Yeah, it's a tarpon. Where did you find him?" I said, "It was up the beach two hundred yards." So we looked at it and I said, "Maybe I'll throw it back in the water." He said, "Why don't you take it to Gus Ben David up at Felix Neck. He'll probably be interested in it." So, we took it to Gus Ben David, and I believe he sent it to the Woods Hole Oceanographic Institute. I never found out why it was up here.

That same summer I heard a story that some guy in Hyannis hooked a tarpon on a Ballistic Missile, while he was out bluefishing. So there were two that year—one live one and one that didn't make it.

The striped bass uses its senses of smell, hearing and sight to close in on bait or lures. The striper's sense of smell is the most sensitive of the three. The fish has two sets of nostrils, unlike many species which have just one.

To compensate for the darkness of night, the striper has also developed an acute auditory system. It must be able to differentiate between the sounds of bait and predator to survive. Artificial lures that remind the striper of a favorite food are beneficial to fishermen.

The bass uses its senses of smell and hearing to find the food and its sense of sight to close in on it. The striper has an almost humanlike eye, with an iris that adjusts to light, and a retina with rods and cones. The cone cells are color sensitive and helpful for daytime feeding. At night, the rods rise up to the surface of the retina to replace the cone cells. The rods are more sensitive to light than color, which makes them more practical for night feeding.

The topic of lure color came up during a fishing excursion to the Tisbury Great Pond opening, where I met Paul Schultz and Dick Barbini. I had parked at Long Point Reservation and walked a mile to the beach in a heavy fog late in the afternoon. Schoolie stripers were in the surf hitting small Rebels and Needlefish. Paul and Dick both were using yellow Rebels, a lure color I had not previously seen, and were having great success. Paul said the yellow Rebel seemed to excite the fish more than the black-back, blue-back, and other color designs.

Recently, I ran into Paul late one night at Mink Meadows and the Edgartown Pond opening. Again, he was using the small yellow Rebel. This is a lure he prefers to use day or night. His uncanny success may have more to do with his presentation and retrieve than color, because the bass cannot detect color at night.

I met Bill Smith at a sportsman's show in Boston. He had bass and bluefish pins from the Derby. I mentioned to him, "Oh, you fish from where I come from." And he said, "Where's that?" I said, "The Vineyard. I see your Derby pins." He said, "Yap."

He had a booth for his tackle shop, Adams Bait and Tackle, on Route 139 in Pembroke, Massachusetts. We chatted for a while. I talked to him about fishing on the Vineyard. He said, "I come fishing there a lot, but I don't have much luck catching bass or weakfish." So I said, "When you come down, give me a call." I gave him my phone number.

A couple of years later, right after some gentleman caught a seventy-three-pound bass on the Cape, he came down with a few of his friends. He didn't call me, but I met him at Wasque.

The previous night we had caught about eighteen bass, all in the twenties to forties. The night he came down, there were two fish caught. I caught one thirty-eight pounds and a guy down the beach caught a thirty-five-pounder.

Bill and I were talking about fishing, and I gave him a ride to his car. He said, "Well, the next time I come, I'll give you a call."

PAUL SCHULTZ

I met Bill in 1982. In 1984, Bill made plans to come down for the last weekend of the Derby. He asked me what to bring for fishing tackle. I told him, "Bring your yellow Rebels." He thought that was the funniest thing he ever heard. He said, "Nobody ever uses yellow Rebels." I said, "You bring them down, and we'll show you what we use them for down here."

We went fishing down at Cape Poge. He put on the yellow Rebel, and he got the biggest weakfish of the Derby. He won the weakfish division—13.55 pounds. That was his first indication that a yellow Rebel was something to use.

The night he caught the big weakfish we ran out of yellow Rebels. The next day, instead of sleeping, the two of us were painting Rebels with a yellow-back. We painted both broken-back and solid Rebels. And that's the way Bill Smith ended up using yellow Rebels. Now he kids me because he uses them over on Nauset and catches fish there, too.

When I first started surf fishing in the 1960s, there were quite a few yellow Rebels being used. I had saved some. When I returned from Vietnam, I kept using them. People started to see me using yellow Rebels and they'd start asking for them. I think the yellow-back makes it look more like a bunker or a shad. I think the color makes it stand out a little more. To determine which size I should use, I look to see what kind of bait the fish are chasing. If it's a small bait, I'll go with the small broken-back; if it's a larger bait, I'll go with a bigger one. I think live bait is best. Next best are yellow Rebels.

In the fall, I usually fish four spots: the Cape Poge Gut, the west end of Squibnocket (along Long Beach), Mink Meadows and Pilots Landing. During the last part of October and the first part of November—if you want to find me—I'll be in one of those four spots. Very seldom will I fish other spots unless somebody calls me and says they got fish at Makonikey or the Big Bridge or places like that.

I worked on the Edgartown ambulance as a volunteer EMT. I had been on a few runs during the summer and I met this gentleman at the Martha's Vineyard Hospital named Dave Preston, who is now a doctor up near Boston. He had been fishing and he had caught a lot of bluefish, but nothing else. So, I said, "Give me a call one of these days and I'll see what we can do about catching you a striper." He called me up and said, "I'm off next Monday." So we met at Alley's store. He left his car there. Dick Barbini was with me. I said, "We're going to go up and try Lobsterville." We got up to Lobsterville and I said to him, "This is the area. If you go up toward the house here to the left, it's a good area for bluefish." We all walked up there and sure enough, we got four or five bluefish apiece.

Then I said, "We'll go back down here by this last telephone pole. I like it right by the last telephone pole on the road." We walked back down there, and I said, "It's a good spot for bass." On Dave Preston's first cast he caught a bass—the first bass of his life. It was only fifteen pounds, but he was really excited.

He came down from Boston a few years later. And, in two nights, we caught seventy-eight bass and sixty bluefish, including my first bass on a fly rod and my first couple of bluefish on a fly rod. Dave caught his first bass on a fly rod. We were also using surf rods. My fly rod bass was eight pounds and I think his was ten. We caught bass up to thirty-five pounds using regular tackle. That was the third time I went flyfishing, but the first time I caught anything. I've invested in some fly equipment now. I carry it in the back of my truck. If the fish are in close enough, I'll get the fly rod out and start flyfishing.

Fishing is relaxation for me. Some people like to go play golf or go hunting. I prefer to go fishing from the surf. This year is the first year that I tried marlin fishing out in the dumping grounds during the Boston Big Game Fishing Association tournament. It was interesting, but it was also very different from surf fishing. I like surf fishing best.

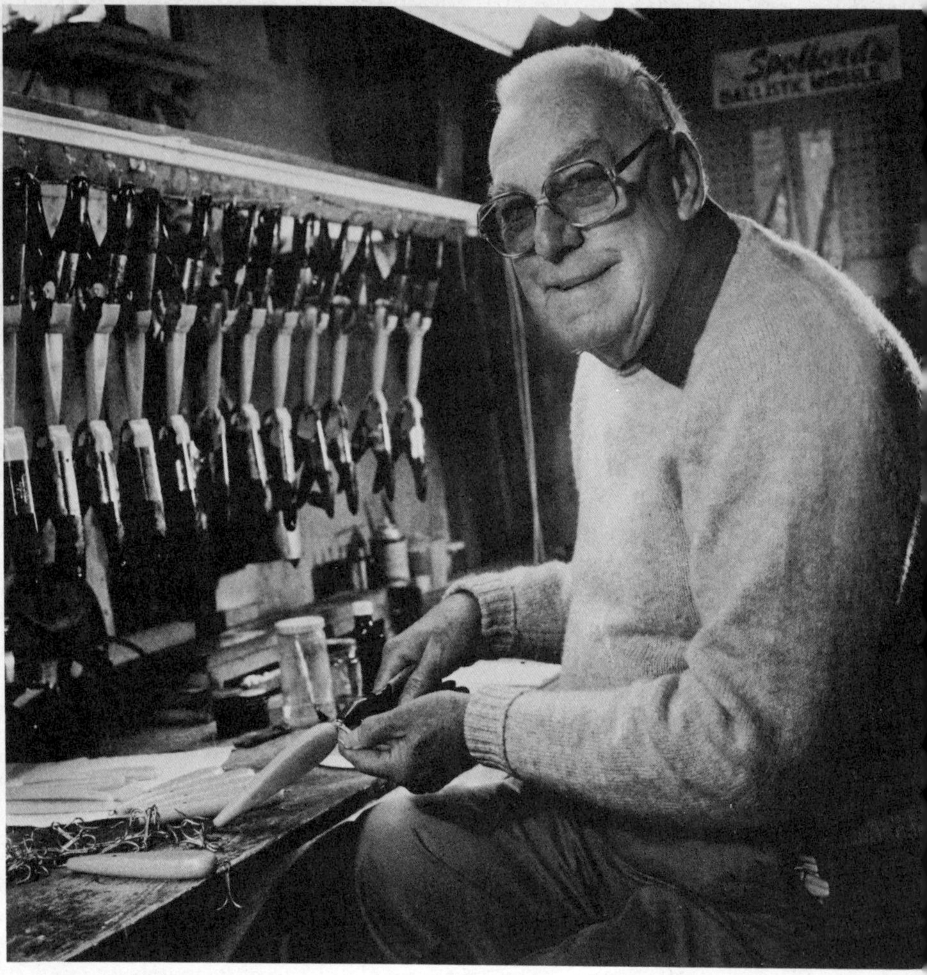

14

Arnold Spofford

At Zacks Cliffs one fall evening, hundreds of small bluefish were silhouetted in the curls of the onrushing breakers. The sun's setting rays, passing through the waves, clearly highlighted the fish as they sliced through the water feeding on sand eels. The commotion caused by the screeching, diving gulls filled the air. A grand challenge was created not only in catching the fish, but in avoiding the gulls as my line sailed through the air cutting into a strong southwest wind. I was successful in catching the fish, but I had to release two startled gulls that fouled my line.

Bluefishing has provided me with some of my most memorable fishing. The variety of conditions and locations where these fish can be caught around the Vineyard is almost limitless.

Arnold Spofford seeks out bluefish with a variety of tackle at a variety of Vineyard fishing spots. Unlike some surf-fishing fanatics, who concentrate on hunting for striped bass, Spofford will fish just as hard for the grand bluefish. He roams the beaches in his Jeep looking for bait slicks, gulls, and swirls.

ARNOLD SPOFFORD

I did a little bit of surf fishing in New Jersey before 1943. In New Jersey, I was primarily a freshwater fisherman. In 1943, I moved to New England with my family. We settled in Merrimac, Massachusetts, right near the Merrimac River. I continued freshwater fishing for a short period of time. Then someone took me fishing for stripers at Plum Island near Newburyport. Like so many of these things, if you catch one the first time out, you're hooked for life. That trip started my addiction. I really became seriously interested in surf fishing in the spring of '44. In those days—it was still during the war—we fished with conventional reels. You couldn't get good linen line. During the war, they came out with some substitute materials. Monofilament was not on the market yet, but soon to come. Spinning reels were just beginning.

In 1944, I started to fish at Plum Island, with my buddy Leo Holt, who was a mechanical engineer. He and I got our heads together and we designed a spinning reel for surf fishing that he built on his lathe. We first used it with a terrible line that was available, in the spring of '45. We had all kinds of trouble because the line was not braided. As we retrieved the lure or bait we put more twist into the line. That made an unbelievable mess most of the time. We did catch some bass in the twenty-five-pound class at Plum Island.

Getting into '45 and '46 we felt the need for large, good plugs. We'd made a couple of rough ones. One night we were fishing near the mouth of the Merrimac River and we were having bass knock our plugs all over the place without being hooked. Leo was a very impatient guy; he still is. He came from Minnesota, and his brother is still out there. After we had these plugs batted around without hooking a fish, Leo called his brother and said, "Send me some muskie and largemouth plugs right away. The biggest ones you can find, a dozen or more; tomorrow morning put them on a plane." We got the plugs and took them down to the river mouth that night. One of them, I remember, was a South Bend Bass-Oreno. We began to take bass on the plugs.

The muskie lures were about six or seven inches long. They weren't as large as the first wooden Atoms which were about eight or eight-and-a-half inches long. There was another plug on the market that was designed, partly at least, by a fellow named Dick Harding. I can't remember the name of his plug, but we used it, too. It was a large wooden plug with a metal lip on the front; it had good action. From that time on, that was the type of thing we used.

So along about 1946 we were getting good bass at Plum Island. Then, though, we had no bluefish at Plum Island at all. Today they do.

Even here on the Vineyard the bluefish were at the low end of a cycle in the mid 1940s. They got very few bluefish during that period. In the early days of the Derby, as the records show, a five-pound bluefish was a good bluefish!

I started fishing the Derby in 1951. I had an old beat-up Jeep, and I came down here all by myself for a long weekend. I didn't know the first thing about fishing the Vineyard, and stumbled, more than found my way, to Wasque. I did get a couple of small bluefish that weekend, but nothing that I entered. I have fished in the Derby every year since 1951.

I started fishing on Cape Cod. I fished Nauset Beach. Most of the bluefishing that I did, though, was right here on the Island from 1951 'til now. I retired in the fall of '73. My wife and I moved down here permanently about a year later. And, of course, I've fished the Vineyard hard ever since. Very hard, I guess.

About four years ago, during the Derby, I got up very early. I went out past the lighthouse at Cape Poge. I went the back road, along the back of the pond all the way past the lighthouse, then turned right to come back toward it. On that bar, before I got back to the lighthouse, I saw about a dozen big bass, right in close, sticking their tails out of the water. The wind was blowing right in my face, and it was fairly rough. The fish were out only thirty feet, and I could reach them with a fly rod. In fact, I was almost standing among them. But I couldn't get a hit. I tried nearly everything. They'd move back and forth along that bar.

It was the first week in October. It was absolutely beautiful because the sun was coming up a little to the right. I could see those big wide tails sticking out of the water. I never figured out what the bass were feeding on. I suspect they were feeding on those little tiny brown crabs because there were some of those around. It was rocky, so I don't think they were eating worms.

The next morning I said to my wife, "Why don't you get up with me and we'll go out there. I think those bass will be back in the same spot again." She agreed, so out we went. It was another beautiful day. The sun was just making first light. The sky was getting pink. We got around that bend, looked at that bar, and there they were again. Once again, I couldn't get a hit. She tried; she couldn't get a hit.

The next day I went back there alone. My wife didn't come with me. I used everything. In sheer frustration, when I couldn't get the bass to hit a Herter's Popper, I started to retrieve it real fast just so I could throw it out again. As I was doing that, one of them came up and belted it! He wasn't one of the biggest ones, but he did weigh thirty pounds. I won the Senior Division of the Derby with that fish.

It wasn't their backs that were out; their tails were out. So they were grubbing. I saw the same thing one year down near Oyster Pond. There was a bar there that year. Some of the guys found some bass there and told me about it. They were big fish with their tails sticking out of the water. I caught one that weighed about twenty pounds on a jig, of all things, figuring they were on the bottom. I noticed at that time these little crabs that apparently just hatched. They're brown crabs, and only as big as a quarter or half dollar. I suspect that's what the stripers were after.

In 1965 there was a sand spit that formed off the opening of Katama Bay near Wasque. During the Derby, everyday on the incoming tide, two hours before it peaked, big bluefish would arrive. You could set your watch by them. Now in 1965, the fish weren't quite as big as they have been recently. But, they were bigger than they had been in previous years.

So the fellows would come down. Chappaquiddick was truly an island then, because Katama Bay was open to the Atlantic. In those days you were permitted to stay in a camper over there, which my wife and I did during the Derby for a couple of weeks. This particular day, after these fish had been running for a week, or so, Dick

ARNOLD SPOFFORD

Hathaway came down to fish. We came over on the Chappy ferry and drove down to the east side of the opening.

Some of the local people had to go home by seven-thirty in the evening when the ferry stopped running. But some people stayed along with Hathaway. So I fished with Hathaway. We would cast, both using Atom poppers, both casting roughly the same distance. The Atom popper with the white body and blue head was a very popular plug in those days. As we would cast, we would step away from each other a little bit; then, as we were retrieving, we'd take a step toward each other so we could still hear each other talk. Every once in a while we'd catch a six- or eight-pound bluefish.

Then we both cast, and the plugs landed almost in the same position, the same distance. We started popping them in and started moving toward each other. We took just a step when we had simultaneous hits. I knew I had a good fish. He knew he had a good fish. He had to come over me, and I had to go under him, because his fish started to run with the tide up into what would be Katama Bay. Mine stayed, more or less, where it was.

My fish weighed twelve-and-a-half pounds, which, in those days, was a good fish. His weighed fifteen pounds ten ounces and won the Derby that year. I remember it just as if it were stamped in my mind.

Fooling fish with baits made of wood, metal, plastic, or feathers is an ongoing challenge to surf fishermen. Although most fishermen are satisfied with the selection of colors and shapes cluttering the wall at their local tackle shop, a small group experiment with lures of their own design. These lures are lovingly shaped, molded and painted in some musty work space. This type of dedicated tinkering can often lead from personal satisfaction to surprising commercial success.

Arnold Spofford, closely observing the slashing frenzied feeding of bluefish, worked to develop his popular Ballistic Missile. To fill a void left by the Boone Company's cutback in production of its wooden Needlefish lure, Spofford developed a variation made from plastic and weighted differently. Unlike many lures which don't stand up to the test of time, Spofford's lures perennially attract fish. Mark Sosin and John Clark, in Through The Fish's Eye, *com-*

ment on the temporary effectiveness of so-called "Killer" lures: "Anglers frequently wonder why last year's 'Killer' lure has lost its effectiveness, while other artificial lures are successful year after year. For one thing, the lure in question can represent a particular type of bait that is no longer present in an area for one reason or another. Or, it may have been so effective on the vulnerable portion of the stock as to take nearly all of them. The lures that do endure and continue to produce fish possess what scientists call a 'releaser.' There is something about them that causes the fish to attack."

    I always enjoyed making lures. I made them out of broomsticks, and just about anything you can imagine, on a wood-turning lathe I've had since I was a very young man. I'd turn down a piece of broomstick four or five inches long, put screw eyes in it, or drill through it and paint it. I gave them to some of my friends who used to fish the Derby with me.

    One of the lures we called the Nantucket Bomber because it was heavily leaded and you could cast it a mile. That was more or less a conventional popper with a cupped lip up front. That was the type of plug I generally used in those days. The Pencil Popper came on the market about the same time. I knew Stan Gibbs who made the Pencil Popper. I used to stop at Stan's place over in Sagamore when I was on my way back from Nauset Beach.

    So the popping plug with the cupped lip that I was making for myself and the Pencil Popper, which really doesn't pop but slides more on the surface, led to a development that supposedly came out of Nantucket called the Rabbit plug. It was leaded, so it would cast well. In fact, it was heavily leaded.

    There was an article in *Salt Water Sportsman* about the Rabbit plug. They said, because of the way it was leaded and everything, it was not commercially feasible to manufacture. Well, I'd been thinking along those lines, not exactly that way, but thinking of the cupped shape and the Pencil Popper shape and trying to find a medium ground. At the same time, a fellow down on Long Island made such a lure and had a drawing of it in *Salt Water Sportsman;* and I saw that drawing. This guy's design looked more like a teardrop. The Rabbit had the heavy end in front, but it was weighted in the back for casting purposes, and it was faceted. I liked his general idea, so I set about to make one on the lathe, which I did. That's how I developed the Ballistic Missile.

I think bluefish like my lure because bluefish are like young men; they enjoy the chase. I think they just like to chase something that's moving fast on the surface. Many times when you see a baitfish skimming along the top, there's a bluefish after him. Sometimes I don't think they're hungry in the first place, but they're savage eaters.

Many people make a mistake in thinking that bluefish will hit anything because the fish are so abundant. They think that you don't have to cast a specific lure or worry about presentation; if the bluefish are there, they'll hit anything. That is not true.

When I first put my Needlefish lure on the market, there were other Needlefish lures available but they were made of wood. I thought it would be a good idea to make one out of plastic, because I already had my Ballistic Missile plastic bluefish plug. The Needlefish seemed to be a very effective style of lure. I think, primarily, because it imitates a sand eel. So I designed a Needlefish in a wooden pattern, and worked with a plastic mold. I went to the same molder who was doing my Ballistic Missile and we came up with my first Needlefish lure—five-eighths of an ounce. I got the first moldings when the bluefish were already here because it was probably around the first of June. I don't remember the exact date, but they hadn't been here very long. Sometimes when bluefish first arrive and settle in for a bit, they get fussy.

One day I rode past Wasque to East Beach. The tide was wrong at Wasque, so I didn't stop there. I saw two buggies farther up. In the first buggy was Al Prada from Edgartown; I don't remember who was with him. They were just sitting in the car and looking at the water. I looked, and I could see bluefish fins. They would fin against the tide for a bit, then swing around and go with the tide for a short distance.

I went past them because there was another vehicle up there. It was a car with Connecticut plates. I knew the people only by sight, and I still know them only by sight. There was a school in front of them and they were just watching, too. Now, these are small schools, about the size of a living room. Maybe twenty-five or fifty fish that I could see. So I figured they were probably lined up all the way up the beach. But nobody was fishing. One of the fellows just looked at me and threw his hands up as if to say, "They won't hit anything!" So I went up another few hundred yards, and there was another pod of blues. So I stopped and decided, "I'll try my new Needlefish," which is really what I was out there for anyway. And on the first cast, *wham*, I had a fish. I landed him. Second cast, I had another one. No problem at all.

I was using the light green color, which is still the best seller. I just stumbled on that color. I was looking for a light green color chart sample I could send to the molder and tell him, "Make it in this color." I went down to Manter's Paint Store. They have a chart up there and a bunch of sample colors. I picked the one I liked from the bedroom colors, and sent it to the molder. That's how we selected the color. It's Bedroom Green.

Anyway, I continued to catch bluefish. Other buggies moved up. They had watched me with binoculars. There were five fellows and myself—two on one side of me, three on the other. I got fourteen fish and they got one. That started it. Some of them apparently went to Ruth Meyer at Larry's Tackle Shop, and wanted to know if I was going to sell Needlefish, so she called me. Anyway, that started the Needlefish business.

I think that the greatest strength of the Needlefish is that they will take bonito and false albacore when few other plugs will. In 1985, a nineteen-and-a-half-pound false albacore was caught on one of my Needlefish. It set a new Derby record.

The most successful lures work because of their profile. It's more important than color or body. Action of the lure is important, too, though. You really have to move it right for bonito and false albacore. When you turn your reel fast enough to bring that lure in at the right speed, wiggle your rod tip to give some action to the lure. Use the smallest size Needlefish because bonito like small baits. Bonito have excellent eyesight. You can't use a leader if you're fishing for bonito. They shy away from a leader. Generally they like small lures and no leaders.

On a cold Wednesday in November, 1984, a north wind was blowing a stinging cold gale as I set out for Lobsterville for a final attempt at catching the monster bluefish that had been roaming the shore between the Menemsha jetties and Dogfish Bar. Gorging themselves on sand eels for the fall migration, abundant bait and warm water held them close to the beach.

The Jeep vibrated and swayed under the force of the wind when I parked at the bend in the road near the old Weaver houses. After selecting a three-and-a-half-ounce Hopkins hammered metal lure, I cast fruitlessly into the wind, my line bowing out in a graceful arch. Stimulated by the salty spray that covered me from my head to my waders, I decided to change over to a three-and-a-half-ounce metal Krocodile. Success was instantaneous as I foul-hooked a seventeen-pound bluefish behind its dorsal fin. The ensuing battle, with the fish almost at full strength, made my heart race. It fought as if it was a bonito on light tackle. I caught four more fish, which weighed between twelve and fifteen pounds.

Spofford spent many days at Lobsterville during the same fall. He always found the fish feeding, and easily fooled by plugs, metal squids, and flies. Old-timers say it was the best bluefishing they ever had on the Vineyard.

I'll never forget it. I've never seen anything like it, and maybe I never will again. It was after the Derby, and I heard that these big bluefish, in the fifteen-pound class and bigger, were in close, all the way from Menemsha Inlet past Dogfish Bar. The first time I went up there, after I heard the story, I found them right at Lobsterville Beach, where the paved road comes closest to the beach. I stopped, took a couple of casts with a Needlefish, and was on. This was right in the middle of the day.

So the next day I came back with my fly rod. I went a little farther down toward Dogfish Bar. Down there I met Roberto Germani. We would cast flies out there. A big bluefish would swirl and come up on a fly. Either you had him or you didn't. Some days you'd miss five or six fish in a row. I don't know why. These fish were almost all more than twelve pounds. The biggest one I landed weighed seventeen-and-a-half. I was releasing all of them; so was Roberto.

I quickly learned that a fly rod fatigues the fish more quickly than a stiffer rod. But you still don't bring one of those big fish in with an eight- or twelve-pound tippet, the weakest part of the line, in less than fifteen minutes. I suppose if you wanted to try horsing them and risk breaking them off, you might be able to beat that time. But you're there for the fun of it anyway, so you might as well play the fish out. I found that after I hooked, landed and released six fish, my arm was sore. All six were at least twelve pounds. I got home one night, and my muscles were jumping in my upper arm. So I set limits. I would catch six and go home. That would usually take about two hours. Roberto and I would be hooting and hollering at each other 'cause his fish would run east and my fish would run west, and our lines would cross. We had a great time.

The fish were there every day from after the Derby to almost Thanksgiving. I think my last blue was the Sunday before Thanksgiving. About that time a northeast wind came up and the water dirtied.

Soon after the bluefish left, the mackerel arrived in Menemsha. Running back and forth in the channel, they provided early winter, light-tackle fishing into January. Mackerel often arrive late at Menemsha. But along with the bluefish, few old-timers could remember catching mackerel everyday from late November into early January.

I've had some of the old-timers tell me the mackerel sometimes arrive very late in the fall. When they came in the fall of 1984, I fished for them every day pretty nearly from right after Thanksgiving until just before Christmas. They were caught after that, though. Jack Coutinho caught a bucketful January 1; then it got wicked cold.

It was cold enough for me just before Christmas. I was fishing along with a husband–wife team. They had a big fish box; a one hundred-twenty-five-pound commercial fish box. They were filling it with mackerel. I had a regular bucket. We both gave up at about the same time because the wind was so cold that my nose was running. My wife takes a dim view of my coming home with my handkerchief full of mackerel scales. Those other people are walking off the jetty ahead of me. Each one was carrying a rod. With their other hand they carried the fish box two-thirds full of fish. They're wiping their noses, too. So I got the idea that if you cut leg warmers in half, then slid them over your wrists and forearms, you'd have something on which to wipe your nose. Spofford's Nose Wipers! But my wife Ellen didn't think that was such a great idea.

When I was mackerel fishing from the Coast Guard pier,

where I had to lift the fish, I used twenty-pound monofilament line, a short rod and, usually, a half-ounce diamond jig. Other lures that worked well were the half-ounce Shorty Hopkins and the half-ounce white ball leadhead jig with a wiggle tail on the back. Mackerel love that; so do bass, by the way. It's a great lure. Of all the standard lures, it's the most underutilized on the Island. Kib Bramhall uses it a lot in the spring. I use it year-round.

If you're trying to get mackerel on a fly rod, I recommend a miniature version of the same fly that we use for bonito—white with a little lime-green top, and a No. 4 hook. I love flyfishing for mackerel. Some fellows climb part way down on the jetty rocks, leaving themselves enough room for a back cast. I don't like to get down on the rocks, though. Over on the other side of Menemsha Inlet, right across from the Coast Guard pier, there's a little stretch of beach. The year they were in all summer, I was catching them over there on a fly rod.

Striped bass stocks have declined dramatically in recent years. Pollution of the species' spawning estuaries in the Chesapeake Bay, overfishing by commercial gill netters, haul seiners, and recreational anglers, combined with the natural down cycle of a fish, whose population has historically fluctuated, has put unusual pressure on the species.

In the late 1800s elite bass clubs were established on Pasque, Cuttyhunk, and Martha's Vineyard. Then, for undetermined reasons, there was a precipitous drop in the bass population, around the turn of the century. The bass clubs disappeared along with the fish that justified their existence. After making another comeback in the 1920s, stripers declined from 1932 to 1936. Theories for the population drop included blaming commercial bunker fishermen for depleting the food fish.

Pressure on the fish in 1941 precipitated the development of the Maryland Fish Management Plan to put some controls on the sport and commercial anglers. Any decline that coincided with the popular bass derbies of the 1940s was sure to create some controversy.

The June, 1948, issue of Hunting and Fishing *magazine, made the following claims: "Many experts believe that the bass population* is declining; a dilemma which they trace to three sources: 1, too many striped bass fishing derbies; 2, illegal seining of stripers; and 3, lack of consistent laws along the Atlantic Coast. We're not citing the Martha's Vineyard Derby in particular; merely using it as an example, since it more or less started the current trend toward these angling affairs."

The cycle of controversy, along with the cycle of the fish, continued in 1984 when the thirty-ninth annual Derby was criticized for including striped bass. Petitioners collected signatures, friendships were tested, and editorials were written. Although reasons for the decline of the bass are numerous and complex, the Derby served as a symbolic target for many who were concerned with the survival of the species.

O. H. P. Rodman, in his book Striped Bass, gave this advice in 1944, which still holds true today: "It is up to both parties to be reasonable in their differences. Calling names does no good. Factual evidence and friendly discussion of the matter is more to the point. Since the greatest and most important production of stripers for the entire Atlantic Coast is in the Chesapeake Bay states, corrective measures here are paramount. You can't get a good crop of apples next year if, to harvest this year's crop, you cut off the most productive branches. With the right laws there can be plenty of stripers—more than ever before—for both sport and commercial interests alike."

During fall, 1985, there were more bass around this Island than I've seen in a long time. They weren't all big, although there were plenty of big ones.

I was fishing near Squibnocket with Don Mohr and Clark Akers, in the middle of the day, using little white jigs and black Pencil Poppers. Every day we were getting bass in good numbers. One day, we had about ten each. We released almost all the fish. Don and Clark each kept one to eat. These were all eight- to twelve-pound fish. I caught more bass last fall than I've caught in a long time. I had a twenty-five-pounder on my fly rod!

The bass are declining again. The reasons are complex. Not everyone agrees that pollution and overfishing are the cause of the decline. Some people believe the decline is just another natural cycle of the bass. I think more knowledgeable people would be taking the position of natural cycle if it were not going against the tide to do so. But, how can you not be against pollution? How can you not be against overfishing? And those things are a factor. There's no question about it! They probably were factors in past declines.

If you're going to have state regulations, they should be common regulations, because it's a migrating fish. They ought to be up and down the coast. If you let the fish go by Long Island without being netted and then it gets netted in Rhode Island, it's counterproductive.

I'd like to see a moratorium on the sale of bass for three years, until we get a grip on the thing. But I think, with or without a moratorium, the bass are probably going to come back. I think last year was unusual. We probably won't get a big population of bass around the Vineyard again this year.

I think fishing is good for a marriage. My wife would agree with that, too. But I will tell you this. When I told my family Ellen and I were going to get married, my mother took her aside. She said, "There's only one thing I'm going to tell you. He's been fishing since he was eight years old, and I don't think he'll ever stop."

I enjoy the challenge, trying new things and, most importantly, the fellowship. I get more out of that than anything. I enjoy people coming from off-Island who remember me. They come up to me and shake hands. Usually I remember them, but sometimes I don't. I'm just another fisherman.

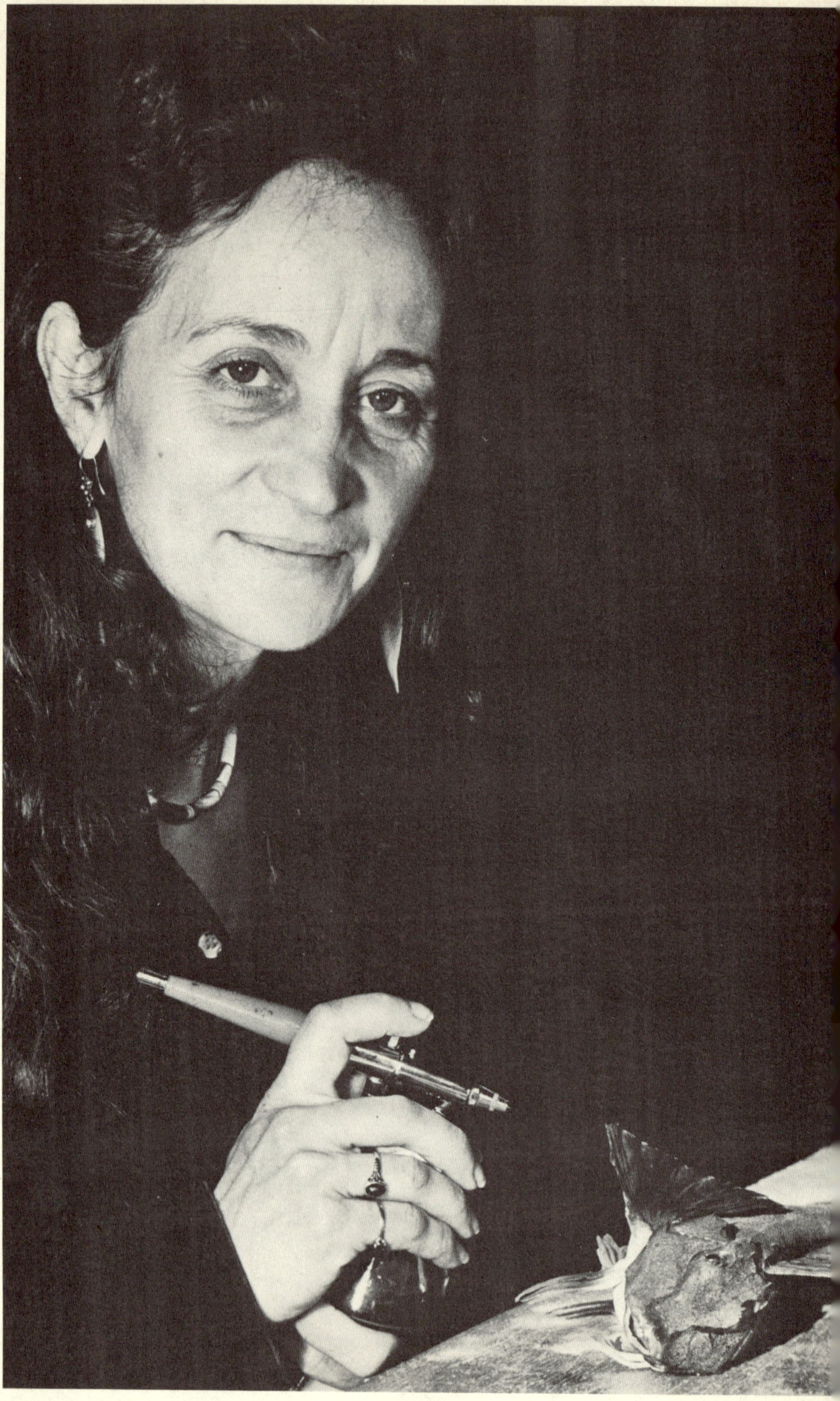

15

Janet Messineo

During the Derby I like to use fresh butterfish or bunker to catch big bluefish. Dedicated surf fishermen often jig and snag baitfish during the day, and then fish all night. Sleeping is an intrusion. Vanity is lost along with most social graces.

Recently, I saw Janet Messineo at Wasque. A northeast wind had flattened the rip. The bluefish weren't hitting, but Janet fished on and off for five hours, a sparkle in her eyes and a smile on her face. Bone-and-silver fish-shaped earrings, reflecting the light of a late spring sun, were swaying from her ears.

At Derby time, jigging for tinker mackerel at Menemsha she looked startlingly different. Janet looked so tired she appeared to be walking horizontally, defying gravity, straining against a strong wind. Her hair, tangled and matted with salt spray from previous encounters in the surf, was pleading for a comb. Squid ink, bunker oil, mackerel scales and butterfish slime caked her hands and clothing. Bandages and adhesive tape covered the line cuts and hook punctures that created a bizarre pattern of dots and lines on her fingers. It was Derby time on the Vineyard and Janet had fishing fever.

After watching other people surf fish over the years, I started to get interested. The idea of the sport excited me. I would ask guys who knew how to fish to take me along. I'd say, "I won't cry. I promise. I'm not afraid of the dark. If I get wet, I won't say a word." I was twenty-eight years old and I was begging people to take me fishing. They'd say, "Oh, you're a girl. You won't be able to take it out there."

Finally, one night, Tim White said, "All right. You want to go fishing? I'll take you." So we went to the Vineyard Haven–Oak Bluffs bridge. Tim grabbed some butterfish and I grabbed my little two-piece rod. About five minutes later, he said, "This isn't a good spot. Let's move. Bring that in." I started to bring in my butterfish. I suddenly had a tremendous hit. I said, "Tim, I'm stuck on a lobster pot." He said, "No, that's a fish!" It was a fifteen-pound bluefish. That was my first bluefish.

I remember my knees were knocking. It was unbelievable. After that, I kept dreaming about fishing. I had a dream that I hooked a large fish that was pulling me into the ocean because I didn't understand my drag system.

I fished with Tim White some more. He taught me all about fishing with butterfish. He was a real North Shore fisherman—no four-wheel-drive, no waders, just hip boots and wandering out at night. For a long time I didn't understand my equipment. I didn't understand the drag. So he helped me a lot with that. And, when I got a tangle, he'd make me fix it myself. He let me make all my own mistakes. He didn't keep coming over and saying, "Okay, this is what you do." He didn't teach me much about time and tides. We would just go, and he would hardly talk to me. He'd just be there with me, and let me struggle along. It wasn't until I met Jack Coutinho that I learned about time, tides and the winds.

I didn't get my driver's license until I was thirty, which was two years after I started fishing. I finally had to get my license because I would wake up at three in the morning from some fish dream and feel like I had to get to the beach. I once had a friend drop me off at the Edgartown bridge at four in the morning with my big old flashlight and my primitive equipment. The night was pitch black and rats were running across the bridge. I ended up huddled in the corner of the bridge just scared to death and thinking if I had a fish on I wouldn't know what to do with it anyway. I'd be afraid it was going to pull me over the bridge. I was just terrified.

At seven in the morning, my friend came back for me and found me huddled in the corner of the bridge. I said, "Don't ever listen to me. Don't ever do that anymore. When I ask you at three in the morning to take me out fishing, tell me no."

Also, before I got my license, Cathy Weiss would pick me up at four in the morning and we'd go out to Katama and park her car. At five in the morning we'd be hitchhiking to the Edgartown Pond opening. One morning I remember seeing Steve Amaral and a whole bunch of guys out there. We'd be casting our plugs two feet in the air and they would land near the guys. We were just a nuisance, but it was still fun.

I couldn't figure out how these guys had more than two plugs. I'd go out and buy two plugs, go fishing and lose one. I used to look in guys' buckets and some of them had forty plugs. I thought they must be rich to have that many plugs.

Jackie and I have been fishing together about eight years. When I met Jackie I still hadn't caught a striped bass. Tim was basically a North Shore bluefisherman. I wanted to learn about fishing the South Shore. I bought my four-wheel-drive vehicle at that point. I could catch bluefish like crazy, but I knew there was something more happening out there. I wouldn't go out at night by myself in my four-wheel-drive looking for bass. I didn't have enough nerve.

Jackie took me under his wing. He taught me how to fish with eels. We fished the winds and the tides. We fished late at night. My equipment got a little bit more sophisticated.

Once I met up with Jackie he taught me about cutting back my line. I learned from him that your equipment is important. I lost fish every way possible: my drag was too tight, my drag was too loose, my line was frayed, my leader was bent, or the hook was rusty. So I learned that when I'm fishing I have to have the right equipment and I have to maintain it.

I strip off old line. You can lose the fish of a lifetime because you didn't want to cut back a couple hundred feet of line. I try to replace old hooks, but I still get careless. Recently, I was out at Tashmoo opening, and I was catching snapper blues. I had a little old Swedish Pimple on with an old hook, and a bonito showed up. All of a sudden *wacko*, and I lost it because I had an old rusty hook. You always have to be prepared for the unexpected.

I caught my first bass with Jackie. He took me to Gay Head one morning. He said, "You stand here. I'm going to go over there." I wouldn't argue with him, even if I thought he was totally wrong. I listened to him because I figured he knew more than I did.

Roger Andrews and a bunch of other guys were also fishing. We were there most of the night. I'm standing at that spot fishing, just like Jackie told me to. I was thinking there aren't any fish in Gay Head. A short time later I got a fish on and landed a twenty-six-pound striper. I was the only one to catch a fish that morning. Jackie said he couldn't believe it; he turned around and saw me coming up the beach, dragging this fish behind me. Catching that striped bass ignited a fishing fever in me.

A three-species fish blitz is rare in Vineyard waters. Population fluctuations of stripers, blues, and weakfish make it unlikely that all three will be present and feeding at the same time. Yet, there have been a few of these blitzes reported by Vineyard fishermen.

I experienced the excitement of this fishing buffet, on the west side of Gay Head cliffs between the old Coast Guard windmill and the bowl, while fishing with Hank Schauer. I didn't catch a bass that morning although other fishermen had some success. I did, however, land several bluefish and a weakfish.

Janet, fishing with Jack Coutinho, also took part in a three-species blitz.

I like to call this story "The Biggest Blitz of My Life." The blitz took place during six nights from October 19 to October 23, 1979, on the South Shore near the Tisbury Pond. Fishing on the beach, during those nights, were Bernie Arruda, Whit Manter, Steve Amaral, Jack Coutinho, and myself. Jackie and I were fishing together. We caught hundreds of pounds of fish a night. Most of the nights we caught a combination of striped bass, bluefish, and weakfish. The stripers ranged between twenty-five and thirty-five pounds.

We were using white, medium-size Stan Gibbs swimmers. The big ones didn't seem to work as well. Before we went out fishing one night, Jackie asked me to buy some extra plugs at the tackle store. So I went to the store and, instead of picking out the medium-size ones, I picked out these little tiny Stan Gibbs swimmers. Jackie got angry because he was worried he wouldn't have the right plug. The fishing started off slowly that night. We were all casting, but nothing was happening. I had spent my money on those little plugs, so I thought, "Well, I have a smaller rod; I think I'll put one of these little ones on." So I went down the beach and caught five fish before anyone else had a hit. Bernie, Whit, Steve, and Jack were all there. They couldn't figure out what I was doing. Finally I said to Jackie, "I'm using the little plug that you were mad at me for buying."

We used to get to the beach right after dark so nobody could see us. And we would clean up and leave just as it was barely getting light. We were sneaking and hiding. We would hide behind the dunes if we saw any cars coming. One night we got there a little bit early; it was still a little light. As the five of us started fishing, we got bluefish after bluefish. Shortly after the bluefish disappeared, the weakfish came in; and we caught weakfish after weakfish. These were the first weakfish I ever caught. I remember putting my light on them. They were so beautiful. We caught weakfish for about an hour or two. There was a little bit of a lull and then the bass came in.

The bass blitz wasn't like the typical bluefish blitz, where you'd have a fish every cast. There was a long period between fish. So if I caught nine stripers all night, that was a lot of bass! Jackie may have caught ten or eleven. That would be our catch for the night; we always put our catch together.

The morning after the biggest blitz there were piles of bluefish, weakfish, and stripers everywhere. The sun was just starting to provide light. The five of us looked around in amazement. I wished I had a photograph of the sun coming up and the five of us and our fish. Five fishermen take up a pretty good area of the beach. We don't all fish on top of each other. The sight was one I won't soon forget.

When Steve Bryant invited me to fish the Tisbury Great Pond opening in spring, 1987, my heart raced with anticipation. I imag-

ined my rod bent in a graceful parabola as a big fish stripped line from the reel.

The road to the opening is blocked by a locked gate. This evening Steve had the key. There are gates at Scrubby Neck, Hornblowers and The Fence at Zacks Cliffs. A few select fishermen have access to these fishing grounds. Over the years, I have often thought that the secret to catching big fish was having a key.

Steve's uncle, Danny, and his father, Nelson, were already fishing when we arrived. The previous night Danny had caught some nice bass and was back for more. Bluefish, feeding on a school of bunker, were being caught sporadically. The bunker were bunched at the mouth of the opening where sand had formed a shoal. The bluefish, attacking from below and the rear, were forcing the bunker close to the beach. Many bunker beached themselves in their desperate attempt to escape.

Three years ago Janet Messineo was at the opening when a school of bunker rippled the surface of the water as if a thousand pebbles had fallen from the sky. Derby winning bass were taken by Janet and Jack Coutinho that morning. Bernie Arruda, after six consecutive nights of fishing the opening, had decided to catch up on some sleep and missed this blitz.

This is the story of the biggest striped bass I ever caught during the Derby. It took second place in the Resident Shore Division and also won the Women's Division. I was fishing with Jackie Coutinho, who won the Grand Prize.

It was October 10, 1984. We were fishing down by the Tisbury Great Pond opening. We'd been fishing for three weeks and hadn't weighed in a fish. We were fishing every night, every rainy day, whenever the tides and winds were right. After another fishless night, we decided to stay a little later into the morning. Normally we would leave about five, five-thirty when the sun started coming up. Bernie Arruda wasn't there that night but Phil Tucker was there. So, there were just the three of us. Phil Tucker was a little bit closer to the opening than we were.

About eight-thirty in the morning we saw little splashes in the water. We just looked at each other, and we knew it was bunker.

We ran up to the car. We took our plugs off and rigged our bunker snaggers. We ran back down to the water. Jackie snagged a bunker first; it took me a little bit longer to snag one.

Soon after Jackie snagged his bunker I saw his rod go right over, and I knew he was on to a fish. I knew that there was a big school of bass. The bunker were moving fast through the waves. I don't think I saw any bass, but I knew they were around. I knew something incredible was chasing the bait.

It wasn't until Jackie had his fish on the beach that I even had a hit. So I had my bass on. My knees were knocking and my adrenalin was pumping. Before the fish hit, I could feel the bunker on the end of my line swim faster, as if something was pursuing it. I had my bail open after I snagged the bunker, so it was swimming freely. After the bass hit, the line was just zinging off the reel. I waited no more than fifteen seconds before I flipped the bail and set the hook.

When I had the fish on, I thought about what Tim White had once told me: "Use your head when you have a fish. Don't get excited, and don't think about anything else. Don't analyze the whole thing. Just concentrate and feel where the fish is. Keep your line taut." I know that I always concentrate a lot on my footing, because you have to kind of crab walk down the beach sideways. I think it takes concentration to keep your line taut, your rod tip up and your footing secure. I try to project where the fish is and make sure that I'm doing everything right technically.

I'm glad Jackie wanted to fish more that morning. It had been so long since I had caught a striped bass that I had just about given up hope that I would ever catch another one.

Once I got my fish on the shore, I just wanted to look at it and enjoy it. I knelt down beside the fish and admired it. When I catch fish and I take them off the hook and throw them under the car, I'm not appreciating the moment of landing the fish and being thankful for the gift of catching it. So I spent a little time with my fish, and then I finally decided that I'd better get up and fish again.

I went back to cast, and the bunker had just disappeared. They were gone within half an hour. All of a sudden everything went right back to the way it had been.

Jackie wanted to stay and fish some more, but I just wanted to get my fish on the scale before it lost any weight. We finally decided to go to the Derby weigh-in, and come back to fish later that day, which we did.

I remember the feeling of these two fish in the back of the car. The weigh-in was in Oak Bluffs. When we were coming around the corner, near the Flying Horses, all of a sudden it just struck me. I remember feeling sick from the excitement. I thought I was going to walk into Derby headquarters and faint. But I acted like a strong-willed fisherman. I pretended to be tough and grabbed my fish and dragged it into the Derby headquarters and threw it on the scale. Actually, I was a little disappointed when it only went to forty-five pounds, and Jackie's was 48.75.

I always thought that if you went out during the first day of the Derby or the first week and you had caught a fifty-pounder that took the lead, then you wouldn't even have to fish the Derby. You could just play around and see what other people are doing. But after I weighed in that forty-five pounder, I became even more obsessed. Jackie was the same way. We put in more hours—if that was humanly possible. We figured that if anybody was going to beat us, it was going to be ourselves. And so, from October 10 to 16 we fished twice as hard.

When Chisie Farrington published Women Can Fish *in 1951, she held seven world fishing records.*

Chisie was primarily a boat fisherman, seeking big-game fish all over the world. During World War II, however, boats and gasoline were not available for sportfishing, so Chisie tried surf fishing. She wrote: "I grew to love this sport but again I was slow at learning to cast. At first the line would land in a bunch at my feet, then it would go out a few yards but never out straight and never where I wanted to put it . . . you cast for hours in one place because you heard the bass were there the night before, only to find out the following morning that while you caught nothing, they were being taken a few miles distant from you."

About the appeal of surf fishing and stripers she wrote: "These early hours seemed a bit strenuous to me just to catch striped bass. I don't think they put up a particularly hard fight after they are hooked and I would rather play a bluefish. My choice of hours for this sport is in the evening, when I can see what I am doing and can enjoy my surroundings. I like to walk along the beach, feel the spray in my face, and watch the setting sun. I like to see the birds, especially in the fall when the migration of ducks and geese is traveling south."

Surf fishing, especially for striped bass, is demanding and invigorating. Janet Messineo doesn't hesitate to put in her time. Alone, or with Jack Coutinho, she carries on a tradition of surf fishing that started with Louise de Somov, Bernadette Metcalf, and Joan Arruda.

The year after striped bass were removed from the Derby, Janet pursued the bonito and false albacore with the same intensity she once pursued the bass.

The 1985 Derby was the first Derby without striped bass. Bluefish, weakfish, bonito, and false albacore could still be entered. I was a bluefisherman before I was a bass fisherman, so I felt comfortable. I have more confidence catching bluefish than I do striped bass.

The first day of the Derby, I was fishing Lobsterville Beach with Jack Coutinho. We were bottom fishing with butterfish. I caught a 14.35-pound bluefish. We started fishing at midnight, as soon as the Derby started. For some reason I wanted to be the first one walking into Derby headquarters to weigh a fish. The fish turned out to be the biggest bluefish of the day.

The second night I went out and caught a 15.35-pound blue. I think that was the biggest fish for that day. Something special was happening. I was having a good start. It seems like when I fish with Jackie, he always catches the bigger bass and I always seem to get the bigger bluefish. I just fished a really good Derby. Before the Derby, I spent a lot of time fishing for bait. While the Derby was on, I didn't want to take time out to go baitfishing. And that worked out to my advantage. I'm trying to do that this year, but there doesn't seem to be any bait around.

I hadn't caught a bonito for a couple of years. I usually fish off the Oak Bluffs ferry dock for bonito, but recently they've been running the boat later and into the fall, which interferes with daytime fishing. Usually by that time I'm bass fishing so hard that I don't have any time for bonito fishing. But this year I had a little more time on my hand, so I decided to start fishing the ferry dock. After all that, my first bonito of the 1985 Derby wasn't caught at the ferry dock. I took it at Lobsterville Beach while bottom fishing with butterfish early in the morning. I was using a No. 7/0 hook, and wire leader and a four-ounce pyramid weight. I was using big gear for bluefish. Along comes an 8.55-pound bonito.

One thing I've learned about surf fishing is that the "rules" don't always hold true. People say you can't catch bonito with a leader, then somebody will take one on a popping plug with a leader. They say don't ever use metal at night; and somebody will do something with metal at night. The exceptions to the rules help me when the conditions are not right. You have to keep your line in the water because you never know what might happen! So, here it was during the Derby, and I caught a prize-winning bonito while fishing for bluefish.

I caught the winning albacore off the ferry dock in Oak Bluffs. I was fishing for bonito with a white Needlefish when I hooked up with the albacore. It was my first false albacore and it weighed 11.7 pounds.

It's really difficult fishing on the dock. You have to be careful of the pilings; the fish run up and down the dock and sometimes they go underneath it. One fisherman told me that if you open your bail, the fish feel like they're free and they'll swim out. This happened once for me. Most of the time, you lose them. I wanted that albacore badly. I had enough time to get real nervous about it. My heart was pounding, and my knees were knocking. When I got it close to the dock, a guy gaffed it for me.

Taxidermy is an art form that enables the fisherman to display his catch. These fish often hang in shrinelike settings surrounded by trophies, plaques, and photographs.

Taxidermy has an ill-defined and hard-to-trace history. The embalming done by ancient Egyptians was a means of preservation that did not try to reproduce the lifelike appearance of the subjects. Well-conceived taxidermy tries to duplicate the shape, attitudes and facial expression of fish or animals as they appeared in life.

During the history of fish taxidermy, two techniques evolved— skin mounting and plaster casts. Both methods can provide realistic results. I prefer the skin mount because I like the idea of the real

JANET MESSINEO

fish being part of the mount. The plaster method is entirely reproduction. Janet Messineo went back to school to learn skin mounting. She has added a new dimension to her surf fishing and her life.

In 1978, Jack Coutinho caught a fifty-three-pound striper that took third place in the Derby, Tim White took second with a fifty-six pounder, and Dick Hathaway won with a sixty-pounder. After I saw Jackie's fifty-three-pounder, I wanted to catch a striped bass weighing more than fifty pounds and have it mounted. I thought it would be nice to sit in my living room and look up on the wall and remember all the stories of the past fishing season. I figured that would keep me going through the winter. I didn't intend to mount a striper if it weighed less than fifty pounds. When I weighed in this forty-five-pounder during the Derby, I think we already had an idea that they were trying to get bass out of the Derby. There was talk of a moratorium on bass. They were becoming scarce. So I figured that because this fish won a major prize for me, I'd change my mind and have it mounted.

I sent my fish to Wally Brown in Falmouth, Massachusettes, who does Fiberglas reproduction work of the fish. It took a year-and-a-half for me to get it back. He charged $10 an inch; my fish was forty-seven inches, so it was $470 for the fish.

I went to Arnold Spofford one day and told him I wanted to learn about taxidermy. He gave me addresses from a fishing magazine. I wrote to some of the taxidermy schools for information. I talked to Spider Andresen and Kib Bramhall, and they were really supportive. They thought it was a good field for me to get into. They thought we needed a taxidermist on the Vineyard.

I decided to go to the Pennsylvania Institute of Taxidermy, to learn skin mounting. Skin mounting uses the real skin of the fish. Fiberglas reproduction work doesn't use the fish. I was determined to learn skin mounting and open a small taxidermy business on the Vineyard.

In January 1987, I signed up for the Pennsylvania Institute of Taxidermy. I was scared. It had been more than twenty years since I had gone to school and I was not sure if I would be a good student. My class had fourteen students. Most of the students were between eighteen to twenty-four years old. Two of us were nearing forty and there was one old-timer. The course lasted five weeks. During those five weeks I realized I'm a perfectionist. I always took my time and tried to get the best results possible. The first week we learned how to skin fish.

When Wally Brown first started in taxidermy, he did skin mounts, but now, he only does reproduction. Years ago it was difficult to produce a good skin mount with saltwater fish. The fish weren't degreased, so the oils would keep coming through. These oils would ruin the paint job and break down the skin. Many of these fish would crack and break, possibly from incorrect drying techniques. A taxidermist I know in Texas has been doing saltwater mounts for twenty years, using the old techniques, and has never had a fish come back. Using the new materials and techniques, success should come easier. The guy in Texas believes if it has scales it can be skin mounted. And there are taxidermists who also do sharks. They have to do a different kind of body. They use a fish filler. I haven't tried that yet.

I want to work with the real fish. I don't want to get the fish and throw it in a mold, pour Fiberglas and make a plastic fish painted up real pretty. I want to work with the real skin. That gives me a good feeling I didn't get into taxidermy to do Fiberglas reproduction. I got into it because I love fish and I love working with fish.

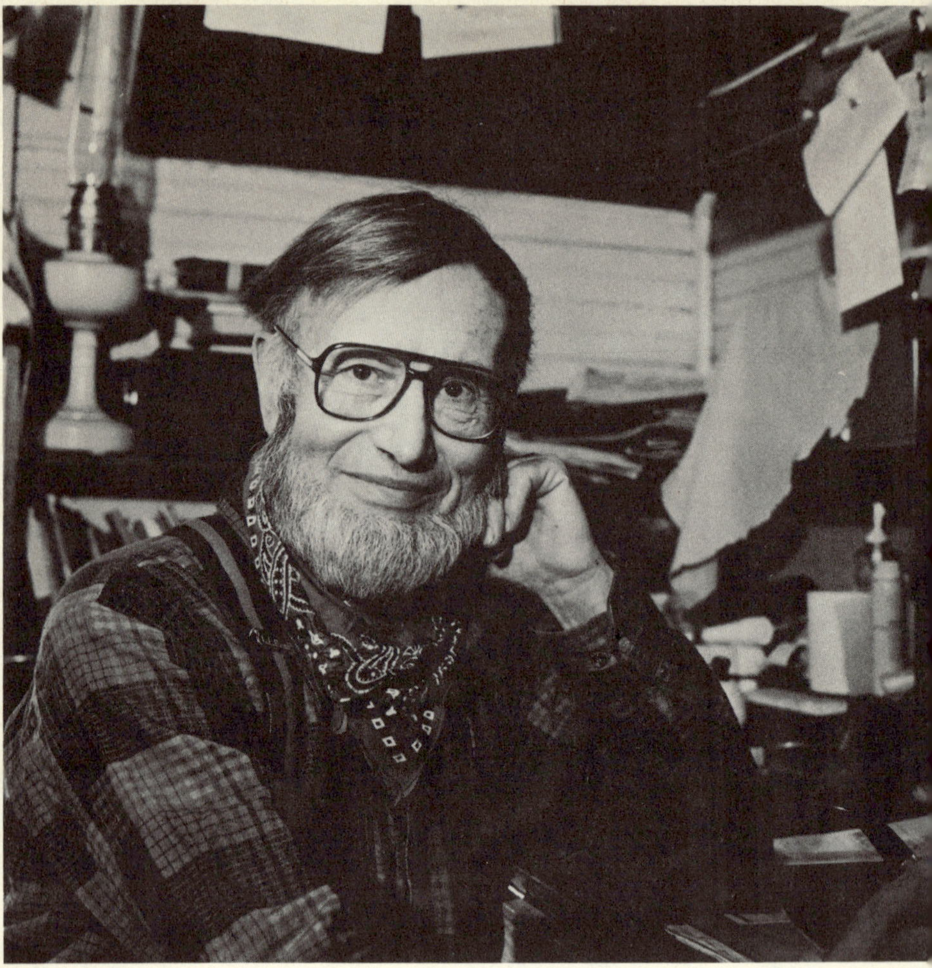

16

Nelson Bryant

While fishing at the Tisbury Great Pond opening, Nelson Bryant caught a striped bass that weighed forty-five pounds. Stripers had been feeding on bunker moving in and out of the pond all week, but no one had caught a bass weighing more than forty pounds.

Conditions at the opening the following night were ideal, except for the presence of an inexperienced stranger who wandered down the beach to fish near Nelson. Tossing his plug with little control he came close to Nelson's line several times.

A short time later Nelson hooked up with a large striper. Using knowledge gained from a half century of striper fishing and remembering the fight and pull of the fish caught the previous night, he estimated the fish's weight to be more than fifty pounds. The fish made several long powerful runs before tiring.

When the fish was exhausted and the expectations of the fisherman great, the stranger unintentionally heaved his plug over Nelson's line, gave a little jerk and cut him off. The line went limp and fluttered in the air. Although Nelson's heart sank, not a word was said. The stranger was unaware that he crossed Nelson's line causing him to lose a big fish. With the fish lost and nothing to be gained by complaining, Nelson quietly walked back to his truck and fiddled with his tackle.

I think most fishermen would have said something. A few would have considered cutting the stranger's line or wrapping the stranger's rod around his sunburned neck. When I asked Nelson why he stayed so calm, he said, "The deed was done. I didn't want to make the guy feel bad. It wouldn't bring the fish back. Sometimes you have to accept these things."

My family moved to West Tisbury on Martha's Vineyard in 1933 when I was ten years old. My father took me fishing for blues in the surf and for trout in some of the small streams. I had a rural, country upbringing in which the outdoors was the most important thing to me. Hunting and fishing became a natural part of my life. I would daydream about being a forest ranger. I used to go into the woods behind our house and build little shelters out of pine boughs. I'd sleep in them rolled up in a blanket thinking I was Davey Crocket.

The first surf fishing I did with my father was at the Tisbury Great Pond opening. At that time most of the gear was heave and haul. I would attach a six-ounce lead Ferron Jig to the end of a heavy line which I would whirl around my head. After attaining the proper speed I would release the line sending the rig into the surf. The lead jigs would tarnish overnight, so I would polish them up with sand to restore their shine. I remember one day my father had rigged up a Calcutta bamboo pole with a vom Hofe revolving-spool reel latched on it. Most of the other men, and I, as well, used nothing but the handline.

Returning from the opening one morning around 1935, we stopped at the general store in West Tisbury with some bluefish. People were crowding around to look at the bluefish. They were only four- to six-pounders, but everyone was excited. They hadn't seen that many blues for a long time.

In the late 1930s, striped bass began a substantial return to the Vineyard. I caught a few on a handline with a Ferron Jig. Some people started to use whole rigged eels. The fishermen would run a chain through the eel with the hook coming out the vent and sew the mouth down around the chain. They just threw it out into the surf.

When I was twenty-one I was in the Eighty-second Airborne. We jumped into Normandy the night before D-Day, June 5, 1944. I didn't last very long on that jump. The third day on combat patrol I was scouting out front with another guy. I saw a machine gun fire. I threw myself to the left, and he threw himself to the right. He took four or five rounds and was killed. I got just one through my chest and lung. I lay in a hedge for three days. We were surrounded. I couldn't get out until the beach forces broke through. I wound up in a hospital in Wales. I was wondering if I was ever going to' have to go back into battle. I remember thinking that I would never be able to hunt and fish again.

One day I asked the nurse if I could go outside and sit in the sun and she said yes. When she allowed me to do that I would sneak off into the woods. The first day I jogged 50 feet, but, within three weeks, I was going a mile or two, getting back in shape and feeling differently about returning to combat.

I heard my outfit was going to jump into Holland. I rushed out of the hospital and got to Nottingham, England, which was our base, with just enough time to put a handful of shells in my pocket and get a carbine before jumping into Holland. I just got touched with a little shrapnel coming down—nothing that hurt.

While I was in Holland I got a V-mail letter from my dad. He wrote that he saw fish breaking at Deep Bottom Cove near the sand spit where it narrows. For three weeks he caught stripers up to five and six pounds on a fly rod. He just had his own little private striper "river" about 40 yards long. It gave me something to look forward to.

After World War II, I returned to Dartmouth and finished graduate school at Brown. When I got out of graduate school I tried various trades on the Vineyard, including cabinetmaking and carpentry and working over at Woods Hole as a cook and deck hand on a schooner. Then I finally became a reporter for a New Hampshire paper and, eventually, I ran the paper. The paper was in Claremont in west-central New Hampshire, which is essentially a rural area. There was fine trout fishing and good hunting around there.

When one works for a small New Hampshire daily, one is generally starving to death, and I was no exception. So after we bought our first home, I found I had to free-lance write to meet the mortgage payments each month. That's when I got into the outdoor-writing genre. I would sell articles to *Outdoor Life, Field and Stream,* and similar publications.

After my fifteenth year of running the paper, and really not making enough money, I told my wife Jean I was going to the paper to ask for an increase of salary or some share in the business. I knew, of course, they couldn't do it. They said, "No." I said, "Well, I'll stay around six months to help whoever you're going to get to do my job."

When we left New Hampshire, we returned to the Vineyard. Jean's brother and I joined in the dock building business, and I built docks for a little more than a year. But docks began to look very much alike. I decided that building them was not a lifetime career. It was at that time that a friend dropped me a line. He wrote, "Had you noticed that Oscar Godbout, the writer of the 'Wood, Field, and Stream' column for *The New York Times,* died? I think that's something you could do, Nelson. Why don't you write the *Times*?" So I wrote them. The sportseditor's name at that time was Jim Roach. I think the letter went something like this: "Have you got any use for a worn-out newsman who has considerable knowledge about the out-of-doors and writes fairly well?" He answered me and said, "Come on down." On the flight down I wondered what pitch I was going to make. And then I said to myself, "You jackass, what kind of a pitch are you going to make at 43?" There isn't any.

So all I did was puff on my pipe and meet the hierarchy. At the end of the day, Jim Roach told me to go home and write three columns as if I were working for the *Times* and to call them in, which I did. After the second column they called me and said, "Come on down. Let's talk salary."

When I inherited the job, I looked at what other writers had done ahead of me. For a while I followed the format they used. I felt that one area where they were weak, though, was in ecological causes. I've written a great deal about acid rain, pollution and dams on wild rivers. So I started to change the format of the columns. Also, perhaps fifteen years ago, there was an urge on the part of many publications to get a lot of "how-to" information into the columns. The column that my predecessors wrote had very little how-to. But it's expected of me. So what I finally settled into is trying to combine mood plus some good practical information. I've published about 3,000 columns since I took the job in 1967.

There is no way to guarantee catching a trophy-size fish from the surf, but a fisherman can increase his chances of doing so by putting in long hours at his favorite spot reading the water.
   Dick Hathaway, a frequent Derby winner, once told me: "I used to sit up in the dunes for hours. If you went with me you'd think I was nuts! But, I'd wait to see where the pods of bait were coming from. I'd watch the waves break and look for the deep water."
   When I caught the largest shore bluefish—18.95 pounds—in the 1986 Derby, friends and strangers wanted to know if I caught a "lucky" fish. Because I had been fishing the particular area for ten years at all times of day and night, in different winds and tides and with different bait, I would have to say luck was not the main ingredient. (Although I might never catch another fish so large in my lifetime.) I would have to agree with the poet Emerson when he wrote: "Shallow men believe in luck, wise and strong men in cause and effect."

I never really cared about catching the most fish or the biggest fish, nor did I ever get particularly fired up over the new techniques. If something worked, I was perfectly satisfied. I was looking for a total experience. I wanted the entire ambience. When I think of striper fishing I think of fishing at night and of fishing alone. I prefer to be alone most of the time. If I could go and bring back a fish or two—I love to eat them—that would suffice.
   Now the only exception to this involved a fishing adventure that took place more than thirty years ago. The late Joe Brooks had a fly-rod record for stripers around twenty-nine pounds. I said, "I'm going to beat that record." I had taken a few small stripers on a fly

Joe Brooks (second from left) displays his world-record striper, taken on a fly rod with a popping bug.

rod down at Deep Bottom Cove on the Tisbury Great Pond fishing at my father's favorite hole. I thought I had the ability to land a big fish.

I started to seek the record in mid-September. I put away all the normal surf gear. I limited myself to fishing the North Shore and places I could reach going through public beaches. I didn't have a four-wheel-drive vehicle, so I couldn't get all the way around Chappy. I would go to Lambert's Cove, where the public beach is now, and walk past James Pond opening and around Paul's Point. That was my area.

And so, every night for three-and-a-half weeks I just flyfished when the wind permitted. For some reason everything was wrong; I didn't get a hit for many nights. And then the final night I'd gone around Paul's Point and was headed toward Menemsha. The moon was just setting. It was around four in the morning, I was flipping out thirty feet of line as I was walking along. All of a sudden I had a strike. It was a ten-pound striper. This was followed by one about twelve pounds and two more in the twelve- to eighteen-pound range.

After a few more casts, a truly heavy fish hit. I could feel the weight. The fish headed straight offshore, and just kept going. I only had about seventy yards of backing. I could feel it was going through that. But there was no way in God's world I could stop it. Then, unexpectedly, the fish changed its mind, and began moving parallel with the shore. I walked up and down the beach with this big fish. During this part of the fight my fly reel came off my rod. I was holding the rod in one hand and the reel in the other. Somehow, I was able to reseat the reel without losing the fish.

I didn't know as much as I do now about playing a big fish on a fly rod, so I probably was too gentle. About twenty minutes had passed and the moon had set. I could see a little motion in front of me. The fish was *right* at the edge of the beach. There was no real surf, just gentle waves coming in. I couldn't resist shining my flashlight on it. The fish had the big streamer fly in its mouth; it just moved its head and the fly fell out of its mouth. I would conservatively estimate the weight of the fish at thirty-five to thirty-eight pounds, so I would have had the world record. That was the last time I ever bothered to fool around going for a record.

In 1947, Joe Brooks caught his unofficial world record fly-rod striper—29 pounds 6 ounces—on a white No. 3/0 popping bug from a boat in Coos Bay, Oregon. He would cast into the shoreline rocks where the water was shallow and the stripers might be lurking. In Salt Water Game Fishing, Joe described the strike:

> That striper couldn't stand that tantalizing action. He swirled under the bug, so close to taking it that I could see the big broad stripes on his side. More because I was paralyzed than from intent, I managed not to strike, but left the bug there, bobbing around on that great upsurge of water. Then before I could catch my breath his big nose came out, mouth wide open, and he grabbed the bug on the go. He came halfway out and I struck as hard as I could, then

watched his long body keep coming out until I thought he must be six feet long."

In the past ten years I have gained more knowledge about landing big fish on a fly rod while tarpon fishing off Key West, Florida. One of the last times I fished for tarpon, I used eleven-weight line with a fourteen-pound-test tippet, which is a heavy tippet. The tarpon I was catching ranged from eighty to one hundred pounds.

What I learned was that with a good rod and a good reel, you can put incredible pressure on a fish. These one hundred-pound tarpon were being landed in twenty-two to twenty-three minutes. It's the same thing with big Atlantic salmon. The longer you fight a fish, the greater the chances of it not surviving. So the idea is to put the whip to these fish, get them in as quickly as possible and then release them alive.

A lot depends on the tippet. If you're fishing a four-pound tippet and you've got a thirty-pound fish, then you've got a different proposition. But if you're using anything more than a ten-pound tippet, you should be able to have the fish at your feet in at least 20 minutes. The rod will bend right around and the tip will be down below your knees. It's amazing how rapidly you can exhaust a big fish.

Like most surf fishermen, I experience dry spells when I either can't catch fish or find them. About six years ago, in response to my complaining, two of my fishing buddies put the following ad in the Vineyard Gazette classified.

Lost Completely

Near the water, my ability to catch fish and the patience to try. If found, call Robert Post before the Derby. Sentimental value.

In an August 17, 1987, New York Times' column, Nelson Bryant wrote of some lean fishing days he shared with Lou Palma:

During the past few years, I had persuaded myself that more than a half century of angling had left me marvelously adapted to the vagaries of the sport—that if fish were not to be had, I would simply smile, recline against a sand dune or tree, sniff the breeze and reflect upon the glories of the natural world.

This self-image faded last week when for substantial chunks of four days, I raced from one end of Martha's Vineyard to the other in a growing fury of frustration at being unable to catch anything. . . ."

Recently, Lou Palma and I fished together on the Vineyard. When I think of Lou Palma, things get a little complicated, because Lou, whom I've known for many years, was a close friend of Al Reinfelder.

Al Reinfelder was a totally passionate fisherman. He would get up at any time of day or night; it didn't make a damn bit of difference. He would stay out on water when he shouldn't. I remember a day on Long Island Sound, in a fourteen-foot-long skiff, when we got into bluefish with light, one-hand tackle. Out in the Sound, the waves were running six feet, and I think they were going to run twelve feet. We must've had forty fish in the boat, and I said, "Al, we've had enough." And he said, "Just one more." And I said, "Al, I don't know how you feel about it, but I have kids at home. I've got to get to shore." Finally, he listened. And the boat swamped as it went up on the beach. We just made it in. Al was that passionate.

Maybe you've had that experience when you can't stop fishing. The last time I fished Lobsterville this fall I was taking a few bluefish. And then it slacked off. And I'd say, "three more casts." And then I'd say, "Well, that wasn't the right number." Then I'd look down the beach and see a stick, and as I walked down to that stick I'd make seven more casts. Now I don't know whether this is just damn stubbornness or whether I'm possessed by the sport. And then after that sort of effort, there's usually a period of several days when I could care less. But the drive always comes back.

Danny, Nelson's brother, enjoys telling fish stories. The following stories, based on his personal experiences, are three of his favorites:

I was fishing the Tisbury Great Pond opening, with my brother-in-law, Jack Lima. I waded out on the bar, and he stayed on the beach, because he didn't have waders. We were casting at right angles to each other, so the casts were overlapping. He said, "I'm on!" At the same instant, I felt I was on. Something didn't feel right. We both had the same damn bass. The bass took both plugs. Mine was in his mouth and Jackie's was on the side of his head. I said, "Jackie, you've got to ease up. We've got the same fish." He said, "My golly!"

I was fishing in Chilmark where Francis Bernard had caught his 50-odd-pounder that won the Derby. I had left early. I left about a half hour before his fish arrived. But I heard about it, so I went back late, and nobody was there. I'm plugging away. Finally, I get a hit, but it doesn't feel right. When I got the bass on the beach, the plug was two feet from its mouth. The bass had swallowed another fisherman's treble hook that was attached to a leader with a swivel at the end. I put one of the hooks on my plug through the swivel. Even I had trouble believing it, but that's what happened.

The day after the Derby was over, back in the 1960s, I lost a big bass at Squibnocket on a pink Atom swimmer when my line parted. A year later I was commercial oystering in the Great Pond. I was using a dredge near Long Cove. Along with some oysters, a pink Atom swimmer came up from the bottom. It was the same plug I lost at Squibnocket which is about eight miles away. I recognized my Ashaway nylon line, swivel, and my special double knot."

Danny's stories made me think of old Gus Amaral. Several years ago he told me, "I was fishing with a friend on Anthiers Bridge and we ran out of sea worms. He said, 'What can I use now?' He used to smoke cigars wrapped in tin foil. So he put a hook in the cigar and dropped it over. Darned if he didn't catch a fish!"

My brother Danny is a very competitive fisherman. He's aggressive and he's good. He's also extremely impatient. And most of the time, quite frankly, he probably catches more fish than I do, unless we're flyfishing.

NELSON BRYANT

I can remember fishing at the Tisbury Great Pond opening when medium-size stripers were being taken in the surf. I had one fish. There were about two or three fish caught by other fishermen. Danny drove up in his Jeep. As he parked, I hooked and landed another one. Well, Danny got out and started casting. He was using the same plug and tackle that I was using. In the next forty minutes I landed another six fish. Danny not only didn't have any, he didn't have a hit. He got impatient. He said, "Forget it! I'm not fishing anymore." He put his rod in his Jeep and left. His wife was with him, and if she hadn't gotten in the Jeep, she would've had to walk home.

The North Shore of the Vineyard, with its rocky outcroppings and steep cliffs, is my favorite place to fish and dawn is my favorite time to be there. The water is often teeming with sand eels and silversides which scatter as gamefish make an early morning run close to shore.

Three years ago I could clearly see a pod of mullet, looking like a large ink spot, swim parallel to the shore, hugging the beach. I tried to snag some with a weighted treble hook but was unsuccessful. This past fall, while bottom fishing in a raging northeaster, I was startled to see a school of bonito pass close to the beach heading east. Their torpedo-shape bodies flew out of the water as sand eels scattered before them. In the fifteen years I've fished that spot I never saw bonito, but one week later when the water was pond calm, they came by again—this time heading west.

The North Shore is also a favorite spot for Nelson Bryant, particularly the area near James Pond. The pond was named for James, Duke of York, the proprietor of Martha's Vineyard until 1671. Its Algonquian name, Onkokemmy, means "beyond the fishing place."

While an undergraduate at Dartmouth, Nelson wrote this short poem about catching a striped bass at night on the North Shore.

> *I brought the lunging thing to me,*
> *Afraid, but caught as deep as he,*
> *And in the moon's light the great fish lay*
> *Clean as wonder burnished with dismay.*

The North Shore is probably my favorite spot. If the night is particularly dark, and let's say you've made a long cast, and at the end of the cast a fish hits, now you just can't see a thing; you can hardly separate—and sometimes you can't—water and sky. When that happens, I sometimes feel I'm hooked to the ocean itself, not just to a fish, and the line is like a thread between me and something mysterious and different. I don't feel frightened; I guess I feel humbled on those occasions.

Then on the other hand, there have been nights fishing the same North Shore area when visibility was excellent. There was a night, for example, about five years after World War II when I took a light spinning rod and small plugs and went to James Pond opening at Lambert's Cove. The moon was full, which meant I probably shouldn't have been fishing, because I sort of go along with that theory that when the moon is full you're going to have trouble. But on that particular night that little James Pond opening was running out. And as I stood there I could see out sixty or seventy yards. In my immediate area, there was no more than sixteen inches of water. So I cast a swimming plug, and I could see the whole event. I could see these big bass fins coming in behind the plug and there was glorious surface action. They were all striped bass between fifteen and twenty-five pounds. I caught four of them and then I stopped fishing. But that was exciting. The fish were visible. You could see them follow the plug all the way in.

About six years ago I went down a little farther past James Pond, tried the same approach, and caught nothing. But then I switched to one of those little Alou Bait Tails, which is like a leadhead jig. There's a channel that runs along the beach and the water was about six feet deep there. Although the fish wouldn't hit the plug, if I let the jig go to the bottom and just drag it, I would get hits on almost every cast. I ended up catching several medium-size bass.

One of the loveliest nights I ever spent was on the North Shore. I caught a ten-pound striper. I'd left so early from home that I hadn't had time to eat and I didn't have any food with me. Around one in the morning, I filleted one side of the fish, skinned it and rolled it in rock weed. I built a little fire on the beach, laid the fish on the coals, covered it with more seaweed, and went off fishing. I came back an hour later, after catching another fish, and ate this marvelous steamed striper. That's the sort of peripheral thing that can have more meaning or provide more enjoyment than actually catching fish. I may be just saying this, though, because I've never caught a record fish of any description.

My fishing on the North Shore has been limited in recent years. When I was a kid I hunted, fished, and trapped. The whole Island was open to me. No one paid any attention to anyone going along the beach. Now, the North Shore, unless you want to ask permission here, there and everywhere, is pretty well off limits. I'm unable to bring myself to ask for tresspass permission because once it was something that I could do without asking. I just don't feel like explaining myself to people who might say, "What are you doing here? This is private property." To me that spoils the whole fishing trip.

A common sight in the workshops and storage areas of experienced surfcasters are old lures hanging on peg boards; old rods stacked in corners, their guides grooved by the constant play of line; and reels, both conventional and spinning, usually missing an arm or a bail spring.

My barn is full of old equipment, much of it in a useless state of disrepair. In one corner is an Ocean City bamboo tuna rod and reel I picked up at an antique auction. Reels with frozen drags and corroded gears are piled in boxes on a shelf. Lures minus hooks or paint, or those that are simply broken in half hang all over the wall. Looking like a tackle store that went out of business for selling shoddy goods, my work area is a constant reminder of the enjoyment and adventure provided by fifteen years of surf fishing.

After World War II, the spinning reel started to compete with the conventional revolving-spool reels. Some fishermen stayed with conventional, others switched to spinning, while many fishermen used both types of reels.

I can cast a heavy lure farther with a conventional revolving spool than I can with a spinning. It's a lot easier on your finger. It's a much more natural motion. As far as playing the fish is concerned you're way ahead of the game. The drag is almost always better, and somehow or other it seems easier with the reel on top of the rod instead of underneath. When I go to the beach I bring both types, though. And when full darkness comes, if there's a wind in my face, I switch to spinning gear because it's difficult to control backlashes with a light lure on a conventional reel.

Fishing lines have changed completely in my lifetime. I remember one of my jobs with my father was to wash and dry his linen fishing line. I would wind it up on a big spool, then spray it with fresh water and leave the spool out in the yard. My basic approach, though, was to start at the house, run the line out to the end of the meadow and hook it around a tree limb and walk back. I found this to be the best way to dry 200 yards of linen line. This was a chore that had to be done after every fishing trip.

Before the war the only real salt water casting lure on the Vineyard was the lead jig. The Cape Codders seemed a little bit ahead of us here. Some Cape Codders had taken muskie lures and used them for stripers or bluefish. But basically, the jig was it. And of course now there's a multitude of things you can use and adapt to the size of the fish. For instance, it would've been impossible fifty years ago when stripers were concentrating on sand eels to approximate that bait, except to go after the bass with flyfishing equipment. So there's no question that the gear has made fishing easier.

There are lures that will swim, lures that will shine, and lures that will emit fish scent. There are also reels that will tell you how much line is out. You may have seen the electronic devices that you lower over the side, and they'll tell you what color lure to use and how deep to fish it. In my opinion, this is all nonsense. People seem to be attracted by it, though.

I remember taking a very primitive little depth finder up to a Maine guide. We were trout fishing in a lake way up in northern Maine. We were going around in his canoe flyfishing. I said, "Did you ever see one of these?" It was a very simple little depth-sounder device; you just lowered it over the side and it would tell you how much water. It had a needle that went back and forth. The guide was so fascinated with that device that I don't think he paid any attention to the fishing for the rest of the day. I honestly think that some of this new gimmickry can get in your way. You have to strike a balance all the time.

The charter-boat skippers on Lake Ontario, with their depth recorders and downriggers, have taken a scientific approach to fishing. They look on their depth recorders, they see the baitfish, they see the big fish, they lower the downrigger ball to the right depth, and they catch fish. But that type of fishing doesn't appeal to me. I prefer trying to get a feel of where the fish are, whether it's in the surf, a stream or a lake; if they're not visible, I fish where I think they should be, and the hell with all this other stuff.

My choices for tackle are rather basic. If we consider daytime surf fishing, I would be using a conventional rod, probably eleven feet long and a revolving-spool reel. If I was after bluefish I would certainly start out with a good-size popper—one as close to four ounces as I could get, because I want the distance. I figure I can cover more water. If, after several casts the fish showed up at half that distance or a third that distance, then I might switch to something lighter. But basically with bluefish I start with a surface popper. If they make a swipe at a surface popper, you can see them and you know they're there. You've accomplished that much.

If they don't hit on top, then the next step is to go to something like a darter, working it one or two feet below the surface. And if that doesn't work, then I would go to the final step, if the bottom wasn't rocky, to some kind of metal. A replica of a Ferron, a heavy Kastmaster or a Hopkins might be effective. These work fine if blues are feeding on good-size bait.

Some fishermen say a bluefish will hit anything, and most of the time that's true. But there are occasions when they're picky. It's for that reason, in recent years, I've been putting a teaser fly ahead of the lure, no matter what lure I'm using. I figured if they are concentrating on sand eels, which is what the teaser is intended to resemble, I stand a chance. And I have, off Chappaquiddick, caught quite a few bonito. I thought they were bluefish when I saw them breaking at first. They were caught on the teaser fly.

I don't like to use wire leaders with flies. But, if I'm using a teaser fly on monofilament off a barrel swivel, I run a wire leader down to my plug. Most of the bluefish I've taken, including the big ones, have that fly in the outer part of their mouth, and there's nothing to worry about. But often the bluefish will make a swipe at the fly and hit the leader attached to the plug. If that leader is mono there's a good chance of getting cut off.

For daytime striper fishing the best plugs are the Atom or the

Danny plug swimmer. I use an extremely slow retrieve—just enough to get that tail swishing. That seems to be extremely important. I'm inclined to stay with surface swimming plugs at night, too. And if that doesn't work, I try to carry with me a light rod and use light lures such as the Rapala, Rebel, or Redfin. Again, at night, that teaser fly is a good thing to use—even with the light lures.

I'm not a truly good fisherman. I can be if I can keep myself focused, but I seem to be on other tracks at the same time I'm fishing. Now, there are occasions when I will get extremely excited and very intense and think of nothing but that fish. But more often than not, particularly if there are blank periods while I'm surf fishing, I'll find myself throwing the same lure and using the same retrieve, when I should have changed lures and varied my retrieve.

It's important to realize how my work ties into the outdoors. After you do a column, like the one I write, for so many years, you get into a situation in which every time you're fishing, hunting, running white water, or taking a walk in the woods, you're not just simply enjoying it, but you're thinking, "Where's the lead paragraph? How could I write about his? What am I going to say about it? Is there a picture I ought to take?" So, sometimes I get enmeshed with duty and not with experience.

A great many sensitive, intelligent people are horrified that a member of their species is getting pleasure out of a sport that sometimes results in the death of a creature. But what I tell people is, instead of fighting hunting and fishing, why don't we all join hands and try to save the habitat, stop development and pollution, get a hold of acid rain and make the planet a liveable place for all its creatures, because in the end it's the destruction of habitat that's going to knock them off."

I had a great deal of pleasure introducing my children to fishing. All the kids fish. And I love to introduce my friends to fishing, especially the type that's done on the Vineyard.

Epilogue

Fall brings changes to the Northeast. Those changes create movement. Layers of pigment shift in the leaves of red maples, and winter buds form on white birches. Screeching starlings begin to fill the sky, often blotting out the sun. Eels burrow in the silt-covered bottoms of brackish ponds.

The cooling waters have sent the bonito, bluefish, and much of the baitfish to more southern environs. The bass stay late, stubborn like many fishermen, before realizing they are uncomfortable, and they, too, head for warmer climes. A hard frost will often wilt the remaining summer blooms before the last stripers leave Vineyard waters. Soon only memories of another fishing season will cradle fishermen through the winter.

Al Reinfelder expressed his sentiments on the Vineyard, its fishing, and the last of the stripers in his poem "Farewell Sunday on Martha's Vineyard," which he wrote in 1967 after his first visit to the Island.

> Martha's Vineyard rested quietly in the golden haze of her warmth,
> Her sandy thighs cooling in the wide blue-white wash of the sea.
> The passions of the night had wearied her,
> But her rest was peaceful and she glowed,

EPILOGUE

AL REINFELDER

Like burnished gold in the late morning, easy warming,
Sun of this so fine a Sunday.
A grey dorsal cut the crest of a Katama-bound roller,
My plug reached out to pop and gurgle through the wash,
And the last bass came and went in one lovely rolling
    splash.

Index

A
Alou Eel, 74–75
Amaral, Eddie, 59
Amaral, Gus, 240
Amaral, Steve, 136, 139
Anthiers Bridge, 75, 79, 183
Arruda, Bernie, 27, 29, 48, 165, 187
Arruda, George and Joan, 138–39
Arruda Point, 139

B
Baird, Timmy, 178–80
Baitfishing, 28–29, 104
Ballistic Missile, 207, 209
Beal, John, 6
Beecher, John, 15, 16, 17
Bernard, Francis, 24, 26, 144, 163–75
  awards, 164
  in dangerous situations, 170–71
  early experiences of, 165
  eel-skin plugs, use of, 168–69
  and fishing clubs, 164
  live herring bait, 173–74
  night fishing, 166–67, 174
Bird watching, 34
  highest recorded number, 36
Blaisdell, Pop, 142

Bluefish, best time, on Vineyard, 210–12
Bramhall, Kib, 67–84, 129, 155, 182, 198
  on conservation of bass, 74, 77–78
  early experiences of, 68–70
  on excitement of fishing, 71
  on flyfishing, 80–84
  on night fishing, 67–68
  on secrecy of others, 73, 78–79
  on Sergei de Somov, 72–74
Brauer's Flaptail plugs, 104–5
Brickman, Al, 5
Bridge fishing method, 75, 77
Brooks, Joe, 80, 237
Brown, Wally, 227, 228
Bryant, Danny, 239–41
Bryant, Nelson, 10, 12, 231–47
  approach to fishing, 235–36, 246
  and Danny Bryant, 239–41
  dry spells, 238–39
  early experiences of, 232–34
  efforts for the record, 236–37
  on fishing equipment, 243–46
  journalistic career, 233–35
  lost fish, approach to, 231–32
  North Shore as favorite spot, 241–43

INDEX

on tarpon fishing, 238
Bryant, Steve, 9–21, 97, 167, 221
   eels, use of, 15–16, 18
   fifty-pounder, 17–18
   first fish, 10
   on night fishing, 12
   fog, fishing in, 15–17
   morning-night fishing tale, 13–15
   on switching plugs, 14
   weakfish experience, 19–21
   weights, use of, 18
Burt, Henry, 30
Butterfish, 194

C

Cape Higgon, 170
Cape Poge Pond, 59, 81, 198
Case, Ralph, 195, 196
Chappaquiddick, 81, 206–7
Chilmark Pond, 23, 167
Clark, Harry, 135
Clark, John, 207
Carke, Art, 107
Columbus Day Blitz
   Cooper Gilkes on, 186–88
   and menhaden fishing, 77
   Whit Manter on, 27–31
Connecticut, fishing off, 90–91
Conservation
   of bass, 74, 77–78, 214–215
   and "hungry" fishermen, 74, 77
Cordts, Alan, 15
Coutinho, Dick, 27
Coutinho, Jack, 27, 28, 227
   and Janet Messineo, 218–24, 225

D

David, Donald Ben, 167, 173
Deep Hole, Rhode Island, 55–57
de Somov, Louise, 5, 72
de Somov, Sergei, 24
   bait used, 159–60
   Bramhall on, 72–74
   mysterious nature of, 72
   Schauer on, 109–10
   secrecy of, 109–10
Dietz, Michael, 181
Dogfish Bar, 97, 152, 211
Double-headers, 138
Doyle, Al, 136, 165
Drag marks, erasing, 78
Duarte, David, 111
Duck Blind, 198

E

East Beach, 189, 192
Edgartown Great Pond, 70, 71
Eel Pond, 134
Eels, 15–16, 18
   Hearn's technique, 41–47
   history of eel fishing, 41–42
   Schauer's use of, 107–8
   skin, uses of, 168–69
Evanoff, Vlad, 41
Experimental lures, 58–59

F

Fair, Rob, 19
Farrington, Chisie, 224–25
Finkelstein, David, 133
Fisher, Albert III, 167–68
Fishing logs, 41, 193
Flyfishing, 201
   Bramhall on, 80–84
   Germani on, 60–62
   popularity of, 79–80

G

Gasper, Tony, 70, 143, 165
Gay Head, 12, 51, 99–100, 152
   Landon's experiences at, 96–97
Gentle, Steve, 134, 143
Germani, Roberto, 53–65, 211–12
   bass-spotting technique, 60–61
   experimental lures, 58–59
   first surf-fishing experience, 54
   fishing at Deep Hole, R.I., 55–57
   on flyfishing, 60–62
   on handlining, 63–64
   mystifying-the-bass concept, 61

INDEX

obsession with shore, 53–54, 55, 58, 65
  primitive nature of, 55
Gibbs, Stan, 70
Gilkes, Cooper III, 29, 177–89, 195, 196
  on Columbus Day Blitz, 186–88
  early experiences of, 177–81
  fights with forty-nine pound bass, 183–86
  first fifty-pounder, 179–81
  hesitancy revealing spots, 181–83
  shark experience, 189
Gill netting, 56
Goff's, 181–183
Goldstein, Sherm, 78, 103–4, 125
Grant, Ralph, 70, 133–45, 155–56, 165
  on the Arrudas, 139
  bluefish stories, 144
  on Dick Hathaway, 139–40
  double-header, 138
  early experiences of, 134–35
  on seiners, 144–45
  shark stories, 141–43

H

Handlining, 63–64
Hartley, Henry, 5
Hathaway, Richard, 24, 79, 91, 137, 139–40
  first fish, 140
Hearn, Kevin, 18, 27, 39–51, 167
  on being self-taught, 40–41
  catches fifty-pounder, 50–51
  eels, use of, 41–47
  first fish, 40
  fishing in a crowd, 45–47
  secrecy of, 39–40
  switches to plugs, 48–49
Heave-and-haul technique, 62
Henley, Ted, 79
Herring, use by Indians, 173
Herring Creek, 122, 143
Hobby, Barry, 170

Hokansen, John, 151, 152–53
Homer's Pond, 27, 29
Honig, Don, 115
Hope, Roy, 29
Hornblowers, 222
Houle, Ray, 140–41
Hudson River bass, 91
Hurricane Gloria, 47

J

James Pond, 241, 242
Jansen, Jerry, 147–61
  author of *Successful Surf Fishing*, 157–58, 159
  on Buddy Oliver, 155–57
  early experiences of, 147–48, 150, 160
  early spots, 150–52
  fishing cap of, 147
  Montauk, fishing at, 148–49
  on Morty Ross, 153–54
  on Sergei de Somov, 159–60
  on surf fishing, 160–61
  teaches fishing, 158–59
Jerome, Eddie, 27, 29, 186–88
Jetty fishing, 110, 111–13, 116
Joannidi, Greg, 58

K

Katama, 9, 70, 98
  Navy bunker at, 105
Keniston, Chris, 27, 28
Killer lures, 208
King, George, 181–82
Kreh, Lefty, 80

L

Lamborn, John, 135
Landon, Richard, 87–101
  Connecticut, fishing off, 90–91
  Derby winner and Hank Schauer, 113–15
  encounters with other animals, 99–100
  Gay Head, experiences at, 96–97

INDEX

and Joel Radding, 89–90
learning style of, 89
on Whit Manter, 97–98
wins Derby, 91–96
Laux, Vern, 34
Lima, Charlie, 136
Lima, Manuel, 71
Lobster tail as bait, 159
Lobsterville, 10, 59, 81, 84, 98, 152, 239
Long Beach, 18–19, 27, 51, 165
Luck, 115, 120
Lure color, 199–200
Lyman, Henry, 21, 103

M

Mackerel, 212–13
Makonikey, 40
Manter, Daniel, 97
Manter, Whit, 15, 23–36, 46–47, 97–98, 186, 188
on being self-taught, 25
catches one-hundred-thirty-seven-pound tuna, 34–36
catches two-hundred-twelve-pound shark, 32–33
Columbus Day Blitz, 27–31
as Derby winner, 23, 26–27
favorite spots, 27–30, 31
first fish, 24
Junior Division winner, 24, 26
on live-bait fishing, 28–29
missed events, 27
on night fishing, 25
secrecy of, 97
Marshall, George, 149, 151
Martha's Vineyard Fishing Club, 164
Martha's Vineyard Striped Bass and Bluefish Derby, 5–6
bass dropped from, 225
beginning of, 5
See also individuals for Derby experiences
Maryland Fish Management Plan, 213
Mattakesett Creek Company, 143

Medeiros, Ed, 27, 29, 30, 186–88
Menemsha, 211–12
Menhaden fishing, 77
Messineo, Janet, 217–28
early experiences of, 218–20
forty-nine-pounder on Derby day, 222–24
and Jack Coutinho, 218, 224, 225
on 1985 Derby, 225–26
taxidermy, 227–28
on three-species blitz, 220–21
Metcalf, Ray and Bernadette, 120–31
butterfishing technique, 121
on cycles of fishes available, 122–23
early experiences of, 120–21
health/age factors, 130
lost-fish story, 128–29
and Metcalf's Hole, 123–25
Ray as Derby winner, 125–28
sand-spikes story, 129–30
Metcalf's Hole, 10, 129, 187
origins of, 123–25
Montauk Point, L.I., fishing at, 148–49
Morgan, Bob, 10
Morris, Steve, 31
Morton, Ben, 73
Moshup's Trail, 99
Mussel Bed, 135, 150–51

N

Nauset Beach, 31
Netting bass, 116
Newman, Rick, 19
Night fishing, 12, 25, 61, 67–68, 166–67, 171–72, 174
Nordeen, Ned, 107
North Shore, 12, 39, 50, 83
Nelson Bryant on, 241–43
Norton, Tom, 31, 33, 48
Norton Point bar, formation of, 123

O

Oliver, Buddy, 70, 143, 155

INDEX

P
Pachico, Eric, 30
Palma, Lou, 238–39
Paremely, John, 111–12
Paul's Point, 236
Philbin Beach, 92, 100
Pilot's Landing, 71, 97–98, 125, 152
Pollock Derby, 71
Pond, Bob, 137
Pratt, Bruce, 80

R
Radding, Joel, 89–90, 92, 96, 99
Ray, Andy, 57
Reinfelder, Al, 75
Rhodes, Bucky, 128
R. J. Schaefer Salt Water Fishing Contest, 164
Rodman, O. H. P., 21, 214
Rogers, John, 62
Rose, Manny, 60
Rosko, Milt, 111
Ross, Morty, 153–54
Rum Runners Rock, 136–37

S
Sandy Hook, N.J., Schauer's experiences at, 105–7, 108
Sargent, Dick, 34
Schauer, Hank, 18, 93, 96, 103–18
  catches fifty-pounder, 115–16
  and Dick Landon's Derby winner, 113–15
  early experiences of, 104–5
  eels, use of, 107–8
  and jetty fishing, 111–13, 116
  on netting bass, 116
  Sandy Hook, N.J. experiences, 105–7, 108
  on Sergei de Somov, 109–10
Schultz, Paul, 191–202
  dead-tuna experience, 194–96
  early experiences of, 192–94
  fall fishing spots, 200
  finds tarpon, 196, 198
  fishing diary of, 193
  flyfishing, 201
  yellow Rebels, use of, 199–200
Scrubby Neck, 15, 222
Seal, hooked, 99–100
Sea robins, 70
Secrecy, of fishermen, 73, 78–79, 109–10, 119, 181–83
Seiners, 144–45, 213, 214
Sharks, 16, 141–43, 189
  beached shark, 141–42
  blitz of, 70–71
  catching two-hundred-twelve pounder, 32–33
  caught with swimming plug, 142
  sand sharks, 33
  sea-robin bait, 70–71
Siciliano, Paul, 106
Silva, Roger, 28
Silvia, Arthur, 79, 80, 81, 128
"Smelling the fish," 166
Snowden, Mert, 24
Sosin, Mark, 207
Sperber, Nat, 5
Spofford, Arnold, 203–15
  on bluefishing, 203, 209
  on decline of striped bass, 214–15
  development of lures, 207–10
  early experiences of, 204–5
  mackerel fishing, 212–13
  Senior Division Derby winner, 206
Squibnocket, 12, 19, 50, 51, 79, 135, 150
Squibnocket Bass Club, 159, 160
Stonewall Beach, 44–45, 78, 79, 115, 136, 141
Striped bass
  conservation issue, 214–15
  cycles of abundance, 213–15
  decline of, reasons for, 214
  defecation of, 60–61
  dropped from Derby, 225
  sensory ability of, 198–99

INDEX

Sturgeon, 87
Successful Surf Fishing (Jansen), 157–58, 159
Surf fisherman, heroes, profile of, 25
Sylvester, Jerry, 113, 165

T

Tarpon, 196, 198, 238
Taxidermy
  historical view, 226–27
  methods of, 226–27
  skin mounting, 226–28
Taylor, Tom, 27
Three-species fish blitz, 220
Tisbury Great Pond, 10, 11, 27, 30, 71
  annual opening of, 47
  reading the water, 47–48
Toth, Butch, 106–7
Tuna, 34–36, 194–96
  as prey for whales, 196
  yellowfin caught, 87

U

Urosky, Mort. *See* Ross, Morty

W

Wasque, 9, 63–64, 70, 103, 133, 139
Weakfish, 19–21, 114
  cyclical nature of, 21
  power of, 20, 21
Weights, use of, 18
Weiss, Cathy, 219
West, Bob, 143
West, Percy, 63, 70, 137, 138, 142, 143
West Chop, 40, 41
West Tisbury Fishing Club and Derby, 163
White, Tim, 218, 219, 223, 227
Winter, Arthur, 184–86
Woolner, Frank, 21, 103

Z

Zacks Cliffs, 92, 93, 155, 159–60, 222